Quantitative Methods in Finance using R

Quantitative Methods in Finance using R

John Fry and Matt Burke

Open University Press

Open University Press
McGraw Hill
Unit 4,
Foundation Park
Roxborough Way
Maidenhead
SL6 3UD

email: emea_uk_ireland@mheducation.com
world wide web: www.openup.co.uk

First published 2022

A catalogue record of this book is available from the British Library

Associate Editor: Beth Summers
Editorial Assistant: Hannah Jones
Content Product Manager: Ali Davis

ISBN-13: 9780335251261
ISBN-10: 0335251269
eISBN: 9780335251278

Library of Congress Cataloging-in-Publication Data
CIP data applied for

Typeset by Transforma Pvt. Ltd., Chennai, India

Praise page

"This book will be hugely popular in the field of Finance as it provides a hands on guide to how to address topics facing financial academics, managers and practitioners in an easy to understand, logically laid out and coherent form. The example datasets, graphical analysis, tutorial sessions and use of R software make the book more versatile for use across disciplines. The book will form a solid foundation to support the transition of Finance students into the world of work or further research."

Professor Jane M Binner, Chair of Finance, Department of Finance, University of Birmingham, UK

"The textbook by John Fry and Matt Burke takes a highly hands-on approach in teaching quantitative finance. It introduces fundamental, intermediate, and some advanced statistical concepts and modelling techniques and illustrates them with ample working examples relevant to professional practice in this discipline. The book uses the R programming language as the software tool for practical work, which is a good choice for students without a prior background in programming. The book can be highly recommended to undergraduate and post-graduate students in finance, economics, and business analytics. It will also be of much interest to professionals in related fields, wishing to gain the knowledge in statistical and econometric techniques as well as in practical data analysis."

Viktor Pekar, Lecturer in Business Analytics, Aston University, UK

"Fry and Burke have done a marvellous job in assembling a package for students and lecturers alike to achieve the effective learning and teaching of this important subject. The topics included have been carefully selected and sequenced and the explanations pitched at the right level. Solutions to all exercises have been included which is a real bonus. Furthermore, links to the website offer additional resources for the enthusiastic learner/teacher. In over 20 years of teaching quantitative methods, I have rarely come across a book such as this which meets/exceeds all the expectations of its intended audience so well. I recommend this book very highly indeed!"

Tuan Yu, Lecturer, Kent Business School, Canterbury, UK

"Quantitative Methods in Finance using R equips readers with a practical set of modelling skills readily applicable to financial data. For those new to R (a great addition to any quant CV), commands are easy to follow and replicate.

Detection of, and remedies for, violations of common regression model assumptions are described clearly, and more advanced topics in time series are presented with appropriate technical detail as well as a thorough commentary.

For those seeking to make sense of the data deluge in finance, this text offers readers the chance to navigate the data waves with confidence."

Dr James Abdey, Associate Professorial Lecturer in Statistics,
London School of Economics and Political Science, UK

To my parents Ingrid Fry and Martyn Fry
John
To my parents Elaine and Patrick
Matt

Contents

Throughout this book, you will find references to the Online Learning Centre, which can be found here: **https://www.mheducation.co.uk/professionals/ open-university-press/olc/fry-quantitative-methods-in-finance-r**
   We have made this companion website to reinforce your learning and to enhance your understanding. On this site, you will find datasets, exercises and test questions which provide opportunities for you to practise what you have learnt.

List of figures

List of tables

Preface

This book derives from MSc modules in Quantitative Methods in Finance delivered by the first author at the University of Sheffield and latterly at the University of Bradford. We have also previously used similar materials on courses for final-year undergraduates elsewhere in the UK. The book consists of 13 chapters, covering material for 12 lectures, and tutorial exercises with fully worked solutions. Online materials include datasets and pdf lecture slides written in Beamer. On lecture courses, we have previously excluded material in Chapters 8 and 11 to make a finance-oriented module to fit more conveniently into a 12 week teaching semester in the UK. However, there is some flexibility around this. A less finance-oriented course could reasonably exclude material in Chapters 12–13, for example.

We are pleased to base teaching material around the freely downloadable software R. We have both found R very useful for programming and for mathematical and statistical applications in business and finance in our research. We have also found R a useful tool for teaching. In particular, the freely downloadable nature of R and R packages, together with R's large user community, makes R an ideal package to learn – especially with likely future increases in off-campus teaching in mind. No prior knowledge of the R software is assumed in this book. Additional motivation, and a description of the detailed layout of this book, can be found in the introduction to Chapter 1.

It is a pleasure to acknowledge some of the people who taught us in addition to people that we have taught alongside. John Fry would particularly like to acknowledge David Walshaw, Nick Bingham, John Biggins, Eleanor Stillman, Clive Anderson, Paul Blackwell and Sammy Rashid. At various stages, these people were both excellent teachers and showed me more patience and forbearance than I was entitled to expect. Amongst the people we have taught alongside, John Fry would particularly like to acknowledge Jane Binner, Viktor Pekar, Brian Shea, Ellen Marshall, Richard Jacques and Vasileios Giagos. John Fry would also like to acknowledge the experience gained in joint applied statistical work with Andrew Brint. Matt Burke would like to acknowledge Raphael Markellos and Apostolos Kourtis. My PhD supervisors provided me with the most exciting research opportunities; I frequently found myself being challenged intellectually and in terms of my skill as a researcher. Matt Burke would like to thank his co-author, John Fry, for motivating his own first experiences with R. These would prove foundational for my PhD and developing skills in other open-source programming languages. We would both like to acknowledge additional help and support from Oliver Smart. Finally, we would particularly like to acknowledge the classic text on basic econometrics by Gujarati and Porter (2009) that has heavily influenced our teaching and our choice of topics within this book.

1 Introduction

1.1 Motivation

This book serves as an introduction to the use of quantitative methods in finance using R. This is a topic close to our hearts for a number of different reasons. Perhaps, most importantly, large swathes of finance are inherently quantitative. Software, especially freeware such as R, is becoming increasingly important in finance. This is especially true in academic settings bearing in mind likely future increases in off-campus teaching following the recent coronavirus pandemic. In particular, an MSc course in Quantitative Methods that one of us (John) was asked to teach at the University of Bradford serves as the prime driving force behind the book. This module was particularly intended to motivate the use of quantitative methods in dissertation work. We have also included a number of exercises that stem from BSc dissertation examples and other coursework assignments. Exercises, and full solutions, are included at the end of each chapter. Datasets and lecture slides for each chapter can be found in the online materials.

We have both enjoyed applying quantitative methods to financial data and wanted to communicate this enjoyment to readers of this book. This is inevitably a personal journey and reflects the different paths that we as authors have taken. John started as a failed (theoretical) mathematician and took a rather circuitous path to applied finance. Matt began by teaching finance but learnt quantitative and computational techniques later on as his research career developed. We have thus tried to make the book feel as human as possible and have used our experiences to shape the way in which the materials, exercises and worked examples are presented.

This book seeks to ultimately empower students to undertake their own quantitative analyses in dissertation and project work. It also reflects our own enjoyment of the subject. Moreover, as authors, we are delighted to bring you this book as part of what we like to call the Rotherham School of Economics. John went to Wickersley Comprehensive School and lived at Swallownest. Matt attended St Bernard's School and Thomas Rotherham College. We are proud to be able to use this book to represent our local communities. We hope that this personal perspective will add to the reader's enjoyment of the book.

1.2 Layout of this book

This book derives from MSc modules in Quantitative Methods in Finance delivered by the first author at the University of Sheffield and latterly at the University of Bradford. We have also previously used similar materials on courses for final-year undergraduates in the UK. A lot of the analyses contained in the exercises and worked examples are designed to be suitable for demonstrating possible approaches to data analysis for dissertation and coursework students at both final-year undergraduate and postgraduate level.

The book consists of 13 chapters, covering material for 12 lectures, and tutorial exercises with fully worked solutions. On lecture courses, we have previously excluded material in Chapters 8 and 11 to make a finance-oriented module fit more conveniently into a 12 week teaching semester in the UK. However, there is some flexibility around this. A less finance-oriented course could reasonably exclude material in Chapters 12–13, for example.

Chapter 2 provides an introduction to summary statistics and elementary data presentation. In part, this is intended to convey the importance of good writing and presentation skills in project work and in data analysis more generally. The aim of any quantitative data analysis should be to communicate information rather than tell other people about how clever we are. We seek to motivate location-scale problems in finance. Measures of location or central tendency can often be thought of as representing the rate of return of a financial investment. Measures of dispersion or spread, such as the variance/standard deviation or the inter-quartile range, can often be seen as measures of financial risk. The chapter also seeks to provide an intuitive graphical representation of regression problems.

Chapter 3 discusses basic hypothesis tests. We cover the basic chi-squared test which can often be used to analyse simple count data in project-type work. However, the main thrust of the chapter lies in t-tests and F-tests. These tests have specific relevance in relation to analysing the mean (t-test) and variance (F-test) of different samples. These tests also form part of the core theory underpinning the subject of regression.

Chapter 4 covers operational aspects of regression. Basic mechanical techniques such as plots, R^2, t-tests for the significance of individual parameters and F-tests for the significance of multiple parameters are discussed. The chapter also provides an introduction to multiple regression problems. This is intended to reflect the fact that, in terms of the mathematics and the underlying computation, simple linear regression is just a special case of multiple linear regression.

Chapter 5 discusses the extra sum of squares principle and regression modelling assumptions. The early part of this chapter is intended to encourage a more systematic approach to multiple regression problems. This is taken one step further by a detailed discussion of regression modelling assumptions. We provide a more extensive treatment of this issue compared with other introductory econometric texts. Further, some of this material may be particularly suitable for modules in research methods. Detailed graphical and numerical tests for heteroscedasticity, in violation of the standard regression modelling assumptions, are also discussed.

Chapter 6 discusses autocorrelation as a further instance of when the standard regression modelling assumptions may be violated. This is particularly likely to be a problem when, as is common in many areas of accounting and finance, data such as stock prices is collected over time. Graphical and statistical tests for autocorrelation are discussed. A possible remedy using regression with autocorrelated errors is outlined. Based around our specific research interests in finance, some additional time-series topics are discussed later in Chapters 11–13.

Chapter 7 outlines multicollinearity as another way in which the classical regression modelling assumptions can be violated. Multicollinearity occurs when there is a redundancy or collinearity within the set of explanatory variables that are included in a regression model. Some multicollinearity testing procedures are explained and stepwise regression techniques are suggested as a possible remedy for this problem.

Chapter 8 discusses dummy variable regression models. These are common topics in classical econometric texts and are important conceptually. However, in problems of practical size, these are better treated in R via analysis of variance problems (where all the explanatory variables are categorical) or analysis of covariance problems (where the explanatory variables are a mix of the continuous and the categorical). This can be more efficiently enabled in R using the command **factor**. The chapter also serves to motivate more complex panel data problems in Chapter 10. Exercises at the end of the chapter are derived both from dissertation problems and from an industrial problem discussed in Brint and Fry (2021).

Chapter 9 discusses an alternative deviation from the classical linear regression model where the dependent variable y is categorical in nature. In this case, the regression outcomes are usually best visualized as probabilities. Here, we refer to these as probability regression models although the conventional term used is qualitative-response regression models. We present logit and probit models as practical alternatives to the linear probability model.

Chapter 10 discusses panel data problems using the terminology linear mixed and generalized linear mixed models. Our presentation is derived from two separate industrial problems discussed in Brint and Fry (2021) where the nature of the data collection causes correlations due to repeat measurements from the same unit. Separate examples of how these correlations can occur in dissertation-type problems are discussed in the exercises at the end of this chapter.

Chapter 11 discusses non-financial time-series models. This is an important subject in its own right and one that we cannot do full justice to. The interested reader is referred to fuller treatments in Brockwell and Davis (2016) and Venables and Ripley (2003) and the references therein. Here, our emphasis is on computational ARIMA modelling in R. Viewed in this way, ARIMA models serve as a natural counterpart of the classical linear regression model but for time-series data. Chapter 11 also serves as motivation for the modelling of financial market data in Chapters 12–13 using non-classical time-series models.

Chapter 12 discusses the preliminary modelling for financial time series. Material in this chapter derives from our own interests in finance and covers material on the stylized empirical facts of financial time series (Cont 2001; Cont and Tankov 2004). This subject is often ignored by classic econometric texts. Moreover, conventional techniques may be ill-suited to financial time-series data. However, this subject is important and interesting in its own right and may serve as a natural source of freely downloadable data for student projects and dissertations. It can be relatively simple to conduct appropriate analyses of this data using a combination of graphical and statistical methods. Material in this chapter also provides the invaluable lesson that real-world financial data may be much more complex and much more risky than any mathematical model used to (approximately) describe that data.

The Nobel-prize-winning model of a stock market in Black and Scholes (1973) assumes that prices follow a normally distributed random walk. However, financial market data often violates this assumption in very clearly defined ways. These are often referred to as the stylized empirical facts of financial time series (Cont 2001; Cont and Tankov 2004). For example, for dissertation and project work, it can be of interest to compare how well assets from different classes (e.g. stocks, cryptocurrencies, commodities and national currencies) obey these stylized empirical facts.

Finally, these stylized empirical facts of financial time series serve to motivate the study of more specialized models that can better match aspects of real-world data. As part of this, Chapter 13 presents a simplified analysis of ARCH/-GARCH models in R to account for long-range dependence in volatility. ARCH/-GARCH models correspond to ARMA-type models for a time varying volatility but are often presented as being non-standard. Empirical applications to cryptocurrency markets are discussed and represent a live topic of academic research (Katsiampa 2017).

2 Summary statistics and elementary data presentation

2.1 Motivating quantitative methods

Many of our students often think (wrongly) that they are scared of mathematics. However, in the past, we have had very good student results (97+% pass rates) in large quantitative modules at both undergraduate and postgraduate levels. We would earnestly like to see students continue to do well on such modules.

It is extremely important for students to attempt to use quantitative research methods, e.g. in dissertations. Quantitative methods often demonstrate important wider skills such as independence of thought and receptiveness to new ideas. It is also important to recognize that the purposes of quantitative research methods can be deceptively simple-minded and to think about what you ultimately want quantitative methods to achieve. Usually, the main point is communication rather than a demonstration of intellectual prowess per se.

Reasons to apply quantitative methods include:

1 Data display
2 Measures of location and spread
3 Regression-type approaches
4 Models for categories and groups based on survey-type data
5 Specialist financial time-series models (beware here of important differences between accounting and finance research and general business research)

It turns out that you cannot really adequately do justice to items 3–5 onwards without proper (inferential/hypothesis testing) statistics. The core topics thus discussed in this chapter are:

1 Measures of locations and spread
2 Regression analysis and correlation

2.2 Location and scale

Location and scale are technical statistical terms that deal with two basic questions that are of prime importance.

1 Location.
   This asks, 'What is a typical observation?' Literally, 'Where does a typical observation live?' Examples include the mean, median and mode.
2 Scale
   This asks, 'How spread out is the data?' Examples include variance, standard deviation, inter-quartile range and the range. Students sometimes find it easier to perform the mechanical calculations associated with the standard deviation and the variance rather than thinking about the kind of questions these are really intended to answer.

These basic ideas are illustrated with the following mental picture shown below in Fig. 2.1. The notion of dispersion or spread is an important innovation in statistics, as opposed to pure mathematics, as it emphasizes the likely margin of error that you have around point estimates and 'best guesses'.

In addition to the above, skewness (asymmetry) and kurtosis (propensity for extreme values) are also important – especially for finance (see, e.g., Taleb 2007). Methods involving skewness and kurtosis tend to be more difficult to apply and hence are inherently specialist. Note that skewness and kurtosis will

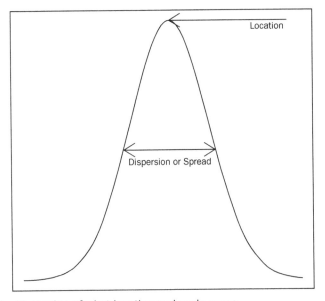

Figure 2.1 Illustration of what location and scale mean

be of only background importance in this introductory book but will often be extremely important in financial problems in the real world!

Common measures of location include the mean, median and mode. The *mean* is the prototypical weighted average. Simply add up all the observations and divide by the number of observations in the sample.

$$\text{Mean} = \bar{x} = \frac{\sum_{i=1}^{n} x_i}{n}$$

Example 2.1

Calculate the mean of these data values $(19, 4, 3, 13, 10)$.

$$\text{Mean} = \bar{x} = \frac{19 + 4 + 3 + 13 + 10}{5 \quad observations} = \frac{49}{5} = 9.8$$

The median is the 'midpoint' of the ordered data. This may often be a better summary of financial data than the mean as it will be less affected by extreme values!

$$\text{Median} = \frac{n+1}{2} \text{ ordered data point}$$

If there is an odd number of observations, then the median is the 'middle' data point. In contrast, if there is an even number of observations

$$\text{Median} = \text{average of the two 'middle' data points}$$

For example, to find the median of $(19, 4, 3, 13, 10)$:

1 *Order the data from smallest to largest:*

$$(3, 4, 10, 13, 19)$$

2 *Median* $= \left(\dfrac{5+1}{2}\right) = 3rd\ data\ point = 10$

For example, to find the median of $(19, 4, 3, 13, 10, 19)$:

1 *Order the data from smallest to largest:*

$$(3, 4, 10, 13, 19, 19)$$

2 *Median* $= \left(\dfrac{6+1}{2}\right) = 3.5th\ data\ point$

$$Median = \frac{3rd\ obs. + 4th\ obs.}{2} = \frac{10 + 13}{2} = 11.5$$

An alternative measure of location is the mode – although this is usually not very useful practically in comparison with the mean and the median.

$$Mode = most\ commonly\ observed\ value$$

Note that the mean and median are often better summaries of practical datasets. Further, the mode may not always exist, unlike the mean and median.

Example 2.2

Estimating location.
Consider the following data:
$(11, 14, 19, 18, 10, 13, 22, 18, 11, 14, 1, 12, 12, 18, 6, 12, 11, 19, 18, 2, 22, 18)$

$$Mode = most\ common\ value = 18$$

Computation in Excel works as follows. Suppose you have data in cells A1 : A10 and wish to calculate the mean.

1. *Click on the insert formula icon f_x*
2. *Choose category Statistical*
3. *Select Average. Press OK*
4. *Enter A1 : A10 in the box titled* **Number 1**

The median and mode can be calculated in exactly the same way as above using the commands MEDIAN and MODE.SNGL. Finally, a useful rule of thumb (although not actually strictly technically correct) is

$$mean > median \approx positively\ skewed$$
$$mean < median \approx negatively\ skewed$$

With the picture in Figure 2.1 in mind, when looking at the question of scale you are trying to measure how spread out a particular dataset is. The most commonly used measure of *spread* or *dispersion* is the standard deviation or the variance

$$v = variance = standard\ deviation^2$$
$$s = standard\ deviation = \sqrt{variance}$$

In practical examples, use of the standard deviation may be preferred, for example, if looking at weekly sales figures measured in units of $£$. The standard deviation will be measured in £ and the variance will be measured in $£^2$, so it may be more convenient to communicate this information using the standard deviation. The formula for the variance and the standard deviation are

$$v = \frac{\sum_{i=1}^{n}(x_i - \bar{x})^2}{n-1} = \frac{\sum_{i=1}^{n}x_i^2 - n\bar{x}^2}{n-1} = s^2$$

$$s = \sqrt{\frac{\sum_{i=1}^{n}(x_i - \bar{x})^2}{n-1}} = \sqrt{\frac{\sum_{i=1}^{n}x_i^2 - n\bar{x}^2}{n-1}} = \sqrt{v}$$

In practice, if calculating these by hand, e.g. in an assignment, the formula to use are best expressed as

$$v = \frac{\sum_{i=1}^{n}x_i^2 - n\bar{x}^2}{n-1}$$

$$s = \sqrt{\frac{\sum_{i=1}^{n}x_i^2 - n\bar{x}^2}{n-1}}$$

Example 2.3

Consider the following data: $(19, 4, 3, 13, 10)$.

$$Mean = \bar{x} = \frac{19 + 4 + 3 + 13 + 10}{5} = \frac{49}{5} = 9.8$$

$$\sum_{i=1}^{n} x_i^2 = 19^2 + 4^2 + 3^2 + 13^2 + 10^2 = 655$$

$$Variance = \frac{\sum_{i=1}^{n}x_i^2 - n\bar{x}^2}{n-1} = \frac{655 - 5(9.8)^2}{4} = 43.7$$

$$Standard\ deviation = \sqrt{variance} = \sqrt{43.7} = 6.611$$

Recall that, when measuring location, the median is the 0.5 point or the half-way mark for the ordered data. We can also define other quartiles (and infinitely many other quantiles). In this way, the median can be thought of as just being the second quartile and the 50% quantile. In particular

$$Lower\ quartile = 0.25\ point\ of\ the\ ordered\ data$$
$$Median = 0.5\ point\ of\ the\ ordered\ data$$
$$Upper\ quartile = 0.75\ point\ of\ the\ ordered\ data$$

The inter-quartile range is the difference between the upper and lower quartiles

$$Inter\text{-}quartile\ range = upper\ quartile - lower\ quartile \qquad (2.1)$$

Equation (2.1) is the key formula to remember. The reasons for this are twofold. Firstly, this provides a measure of dispersion or spread in the data. If some of the data take extreme values, then the inter-quartile range may provide a more useful summary than the variance or standard deviation. There are, thus, some occasions when the inter-quartile range may offer a better description of financial data than the variance or standard deviation. Secondly, calculation of quartiles and quantiles is actually deceptively involved and uses something called pivots. It can be an interesting mathematical challenge in its own right. Many different formulae are given and the standard of business mathematics texts and other statistical study guides can most politely be described as varied. We have seen published textbooks make some very large mistakes on this issue. Usually, calculation by hand of quartiles is not required. It is more important to be able to do this by computer.

The *range* is simply given by the difference between the maximum and minimum values.

$$\text{Range} = \text{maximum value} - \text{minimum value}$$

The range gives a fairly crude measure of the spread of the data. The variance/ standard deviation and the inter-quartile range may give better summaries.

Example 2.4

Calculating dispersion.
Consider the following data:
$(11, 14, 19, 18, 10, 13, 22, 18, 11, 14, 1, 12, 12, 18, 6, 12, 11, 19, 18, 2, 22, 18)$

$$Range = maximum\ value - minimum\ value = 22 - 1 = 21$$

Calculation of these measures of dispersion or spread can proceed in Excel as follows. Suppose you have data in cells A1 : A10 and wish to calculate the variance.

1   *Click on the insert formula icon f_x*
2   *Choose category Statistical*
3   *Select VAR.S. Press OK*
4   *Enter A1 : A10 in the box titled* **Number 1**

The standard deviation can be calculated in exactly the same way as above using the command STDEV.S.
   To calculate the range and inter-quartile range, suppose you have data in cells A1 : A10 and wish to calculate the inter-quartile range.

1   *Click on the insert formula icon f_x*
2   *Choose category Statistical*
3   *Select QUARTILE.EXC. Press OK*
4   *Enter A1 : A10 in the box titled* **Array**

5 *In the box marked* **QUART** *insert the value 3 to calculate the upper quartile.*
6 *Repeat these steps and in the box marked* **QUART** *insert the value 1 to calculate the lower quartile.*
7 *The difference between these two values then gives the inter-quartile range*

The range can be calculated in exactly the same way as above. Inserting 4 into the box marked **QUART** *calculates the maximum value. Inserting 0 into the box marked* **QUART** *calculates the minimum value. The difference between these two values gives the range.*

2.3 Regression-type problems

Mathematics and statistics can be hard but the questions asked are often deceptively simple-minded. For example, if you have two variables X and Y (e.g. $X=$ interest rate, $Y=$ GDP), two obvious questions to ask are:

1 If X increases, what happens to Y?
   – Does it increase?
   – Does it decrease?
   – Does nothing happen?
2 If Y increases, what happens to X?
   – Does it increase?
   – Does it decrease?
   – Does nothing happen?

These basic questions lead to a core area of statistics entitled regression – see Chapters 4–10.

When dealing with regression, it is important to distinguish between correlation and causation. However, loosely speaking, the basic idea is that if two variables X and Y are positively correlated, then, as X increases, Y increases. This basic idea is illustrated in Fig. 2.2. Equivalently, as X decreases then Y increases. This basic idea is illustrated in Fig. 2.3. In contrast, if X and Y are uncorrelated, then a change in X does not affect the value of Y. An idealized illustration of this is shown in Fig. 2.4.

Whilst the basic idea is simple in practical examples, you may have to use your imagination a bit. As we shall see in Chapter 3, real datasets will often show versions of the graphs in Figs 2.2–2.4 but with marked imperfections. The imperfect nature of these graphs then means that statistically rigorous regression methods are needed to fit lines to real datasets. We will also see examples later in the book where the graphs produced are curves rather than straight lines.

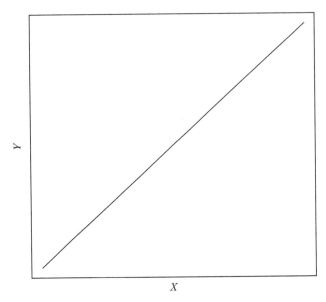

Figure 2.2 Illustration of idealized positive correlation

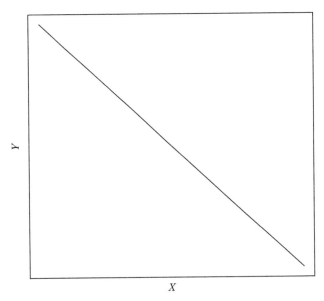

Figure 2.3 Illustration of idealized negative correlation

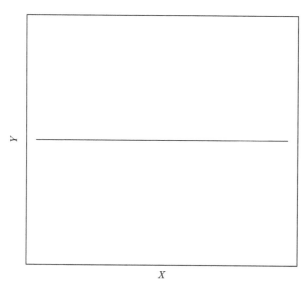

Figure 2.4 Illustration of idealized no correlation

2.4 Data presentation

Building on the graphical methods previously introduced in this section, we discuss different ways of presenting data – typically seen in reports and especially in dissertations. This emphasizes that our fundamental aim is to communicate information simply and effectively and presents an extension to other core professional skills. The following methods are covered:

1 Stem and leaf plots
2 Frequency tables
3 Frequency polygons
4 Histograms

The reasons why such an apparently simple-minded approach is important include the following:

1 Simple ways to communicate and display information
2 General numeracy
3 Attention to detail
4 A simple cross-check of more complex financial or statistical information – e.g. the bit that you might need an MSc, PhD (or more) in order to properly understand

The first type of graph we discuss is a *stem and leaf plot*. Stem and leaf plots provide a simple, alternative way to write down the data.

$$\text{Stem} = \text{left-most digit}$$
$$\text{Leaves} = \text{right-most digit}$$
$$\text{Leaves} \quad \text{should be in size order}$$

The advantages of stem and leaf plots include their simplicity and the fact that they help to give an overview of the sample. Stem and leaf plots give an indication of the spread of the data within each subcategory. They also retain the original values – unlike some other methods, they do not rely on the class midpoint.

Example 2.5

Suppose we have the following data for a set of exam scores:
70, 68, 72, 53, 56, 44, 64, 48, 46, 40, 64, 54, 46, 71, 61, 51, 50, 48, 35, 67, 29, 73, 61, 42, 53.
A stem and leaf plot for this data is shown in Table 2.1.

Example 2.6

Illustration with different data types.
Suppose we have the following data on wages ($ 000s): 51, 51, 48, 45, 45, 45, 44, 43, 42, 42, 41, 38, 37, 36, 35, 33, 33, 33, 32, 27, 23, 20, 18, 18.
A stem and leaf plot for this second dataset is shown in Table 2.2

Another important data-presentation technique is the *frequency table*. These are used to organize data in a systematic way – an important aspect, especially for large problems. Frequency tables may also be used to create further graphs and tables such as frequency polygons and histograms. Frequency tables are not

Table 2.1 Stem and leaf plot for first dataset

Stem	Leaf
2	9
3	5
4	0, 2, 4, 6, 6, 8, 8
5	0, 1, 3, 3, 4, 6
6	1, 1, 4, 4, 7, 8
7	0, 1, 2, 3

Key: 2 | 9 represents 29 marks

Table 2.2 Stem and leaf plot for second dataset

Stem	Leaf
1	8, 8
2	0, 3, 7
3	2, 3, 3, 3, 5, 6, 7, 8
4	1, 2, 2, 3, 4, 5, 5, 5, 8
5	1, 1

Key: 1 | 8 represents $18,000

amazingly exciting, but do touch on important themes such as general numeracy, systematic analysis of data and attention to detail.

> **Example 2.7**
>
> *Suppose that we have the following data on mortgage interest rates: 7.29, 7.23, 7.11, 6.78, 7.47, 6.69, 6.77, 6.57, 6.80, 6.88, 6.98, 7.16, 7.30, 7.24, 7.16, 7.03, 6.90, 7.16, 7.40, 7.05, 7.28, 7.31, 6.87, 7.68, 7.03, 7.17, 6.78, 7.08, 7.12, 7.31, 7.40, 6.35, 6.96, 7.29, 7.16, 6.97, 6.96, 7.02, 7.13, 6.84.*
>
> *This can be rearranged into a frequency table, as shown in Table 2.3.*

Table 2.3 Frequency table for mortgage interest rate data

Interval	Frequency	Class midpoint	Relative frequency	Cumulative frequency
6.30–6.50	1	6.40	0.025	1
6.50–6.70	2	6.60	0.05	3
6.70–6.90	7	6.80	0.175	10
6.90–7.10	10	7.00	0.25	20
7.10–7.30	13	7.20	0.325	33
7.30–7.50	6	7.40	0.15	39
7.50–7.70	1	7.60	0.025	40

The frequency table thus contains five important components:

1 Interval

- A convenient grouping of the observations, usually using numbers ending in 5 or 10
2 Frequency
   - A raw count of the numbers in each category
   - For example, there are seven observations (6.78, 6.77, 6.80, 6.88, 6.87, 6.78, 6.84) in the previous dataset in the category 6.70–6.90. Note that it is easy to make a mistake here if you do not pay close enough attention to detail!
3 Class midpoint

$$\text{Class midpoint} = \frac{\text{upper boundary} + \text{lower boundary}}{2}$$

The class midpoint is often needed for subsequent additional computations. The class midpoint may sometimes also give a useful way of visualizing data in its own right. Remember that communication is the name of the game!
4 Relative frequency

$$\text{Relative frequency} = \frac{\text{class frequency}}{\text{total number}}$$

In the previous dataset, we have seven observations in the category 6.70–6.90, so the relative frequency $= 7/40 = 0.175$. Similarly, there are 13 observations in the category 7.10–7.30, so the relative frequency $= 13/40 = 0.325$. The relative frequency is thus a proportion or probability between 0 and 1 measuring how common each category is. As such, the sum of all the relative frequencies should equal 1.
5 Cumulative frequency. To accumulate means 'to gather'. The cumulative frequency is the running total of all the previous observations.
   (a) For the previous mortgage interest rate example, there is one observation in the first category 6.30–6.50, so the cumulative frequency is 1.
   (b) There are two observations in the second category 6.50–6.70. The cumulative frequency is the previous value (1) + 2 = 3.
   (c) There are seven observations in the third category 6.70–6.90. The cumulative frequency is the previous value (3) + 7 = 10.

As constructed above, a *frequency polygon* is a plot of class midpoint against cumulative frequency. An example is shown below in Fig. 2.5. Frequency polygons can be constructed in Excel as follows. You need a column of midpoint values and a column of cumulative midpoints side by side. The column of class midpoint values needs to be on the left.

1 Highlight the two columns.
2 Insert→Scatter→Scatter with Straight lines.

A *histogram* is essentially a bar chart of the grouped data. In Excel you need a column of category names to the left of a column of observed frequencies.

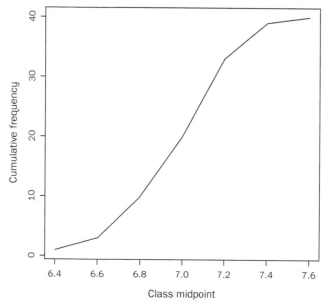

Figure 2.5 Example of a frequency polygon

1 Highlight the two columns.
2 Insert→Bar→2-D Bar.

However, there is an implicit assumption in the above that all the classes are of equal size. If this is not the case, then an adjustment has to be made using the *frequency density*.

$$\text{Frequency density} = \frac{\text{frequency}}{\text{class width}} = \frac{\text{frequency}}{\text{upper bound} - \text{lower bound}}$$

As constructed, the frequency density measures how likely a class is to occur once the differing class widths have been taken into account. Suppose we have the data shown in Table 2.4 on people's ages. We might think that there are clearly more people in the 60–100 category than in the 0–15 category. However, using frequency density rather than the raw frequencies shows that this rather extreme finding is not really true once we adjust for different class widths.

Histograms with unequal class sizes can be constructed in Excel as follows. You need a column of category names to the left of a column of frequency densities.

1 Highlight the two columns.
2 Insert→Bar→2-D Bar.

Table 2.4 Example comparison of frequency and frequency density

Age	Frequency	Class width	Frequency density
0–15	15	15	$\frac{15}{15} = 1$
15–25	28	10	$\frac{28}{10} = 2.8$
25–40	30	15	$\frac{30}{15} = 2$
40–60	42	20	$\frac{42}{20} = 2.1$
60–100	20	40	$\frac{20}{40} = 0.5$

2.5 Tutorial exercises

1 Produce a stem and leaf plot for the following data: 54, 11, 91, 66, 92, 19, 1, 77, 83, 57, 30, 52, 100, 39, 62, 35, 99, 68, 53, 7, 79, 10, 13, 50, 9, 34, 74, 88, 18, 24, 24, 69, 40, 83, 32.

2 What data corresponds to the following stem and leaf plot?

Stem	Leaf
0	1 2 3 8
2	0 7
4	5
6	8
10	5
16	0

Key: 2 | 0 represents 20

3 Construct a frequency polygon for the data in Q2.
4 Construct a frequency table for the data in Q2.
5 In Q4 what is the midpoint of the highest group?
6 In Q4 what is the width of the lowest group?
7 Give the relative and cumulative frequencies of the 3rd class.
8 The cumulative frequency of Class $n-1$ is 10, the relative frequency of Class n is 0.031 and there are 128 observations. What is the cumulative frequency of Class n?
9 The relative and cumulative frequencies for adjacent classes are 0.067, 0.2 and 4, 16 respectively. How big was the sample?

2.6 Solutions

1 **Table 2.5** Stem and leaf plot for Question 1

Stem	Leaf
0	1, 7, 9
1	0, 1, 3, 8, 9
2	4, 4
3	0, 2, 4, 5, 9
4	0
5	0, 2, 3, 4, 7
6	2, 6, 8, 9
7	4, 7, 9
8	3, 3, 8
9	1, 2, 9
10	0

Key: 1 | 0 represents 10

2 1, 2, 3, 8, 20, 27, 45, 68, 105, 160

3

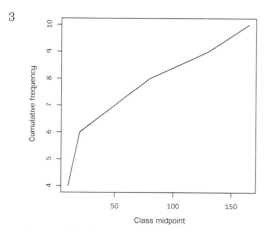

Figure 2.6 Frequency polygon for Question 3

4 **Table 2.6** Frequency table for Question 4

Class	Frequency
0–20	4
20–40	2
40–60	1
60–100	1
100–160	1
160–170	1

5 Midpoint $= 165$
6 Width $= 20$
7 Relative frequency $= 1/10 = 0.1$ Cumulative frequency $= 7$
8 Cumulative frequency $= 128 \times 0.031 + 10 = 14$
9 The information given to you in the question is illustrated in Table 2.7. This shows that the 12 observations in the second category represent 0.2 (or $1/5$) of the original sample. Hence the total number of observations in the sample is $12 \times 5 = 60$.

Table 2.7 Frequency table for Question 9

Relative frequency	Cumulative frequency
0.067	4
0.2	16

3   Basic hypothesis tests

This chapter is important both for the preparation of students' dissertations and for motivating the study of regression.

1   Link to dissertations
   - In 2013, one of our students used related techniques to analyse mergers and acquisitions.
   - In 2013, one of our students used a paired *t*-test to analyse accounting ratios.
   - In 2014, techniques used by our students who got distinctions ranged from time-series econometrics to unpaired *t*-tests.
   - In 2019/20 and 2020/21, many of our students successfully used statistical modelling in EViews/R in their dissertations. There were too many cases to mention them all. Here, and in subsequent chapters, we have thus tried to use real dissertation topics in the exercises and worked examples. This is intended to illustrate the richness of the subject and the idea that everybody should be able to find something interesting that they can apply quantitative research methods to.

2   Link to regression
   - Regression is the prototype model for all applied statistics and econometrics. Regression underpins much of the research in finance, economics and social sciences. The content of this chapter will help you to understand and apply advanced regression techniques

The golden rule with mathematics is not to panic. Many of our students have successfully applied mathematical and statistical methods and achieved high marks in modules and in dissertations. The key thing here is that mathematics and statistics are often simpler than might at first seem to be the case. We also like to remind students that mathematics is designed to make sense of data and to convey useful information about it.

As far as this book is concerned, statistics is primarily geared towards answering simple but useful questions in as systematic a manner as possible.

1   Generic data
   - What is a 'typical' observation
     - What is the mean?

- How spread out is the data?
  - What is the variance?
2 Regression
  - What happens to Y as X increases?
    - Does it increase?
    - Does it decrease?
    - Does nothing happen?

In this chapter, we look at the first question about analysing a generic data set. As shown in Fig. 2.1 in the last chapter, there are two basic values of interest:

1 Location or mean
2 Spread or variance

Statistics is vital for research and enables us to answer these questions systematically. The techniques discussed in this chapter that enable us to answer these questions are:

1 One-sample and two-sample t-tests
2 Chi-squared test and F-test

3.1 One-sample *t*-test

We illustrate this test by means of an example. Suppose we have the data shown in Table 3.1 on consumer confidence in 2007 and 2009. We want to see if the crash of 2008 has had a lasting impact upon consumer confidence. We want to use a formal statistical test – in this case a t-test – to see if there is a detectable difference from what could occur by random chance alone.

When calculating a t-test you need the estimated mean and the standard deviation/estimated standard error (e.s.e.). In our example, the mean difference is

$$\bar{x} = \frac{\sum x_i}{n} = \frac{62 + 64 + 67 + \ldots + 68 + 69}{12} = \frac{868}{12} = 72.33$$

Table 3.1 Example dataset on consumer confidence

Consumer confidence index	J	F	M	A	M	J	J	A	S	O	N	D
2007	86	86	88	90	99	97	97	96	99	97	90	90
2009	24	22	21	21	19	18	17	18	21	23	22	21
Difference	62	64	67	69	80	79	80	78	78	74	68	69

The standard deviation of the differences is

$$s = \sqrt{\frac{\sum x_i^2 - n\bar{x}^2}{n-1}}$$

$$\sum x_i^2 = 62^2 + 64^2 + 67^2 + \dots + 68^2 + 69^2 = 63260$$

$$s = \sqrt{\frac{63260 - 12\left(\frac{868}{12}\right)^2}{11}} = \sqrt{\frac{474.666}{11}} = 6.5689$$

The t-statistic can be constructed as

$$t = \frac{\text{estimate} - \text{hypothesized value}}{\text{e.s.e.}}$$

where e.s.e. = estimated standard error. Since the hypothesized value is usually zero,

$$t = \frac{\text{estimate}}{\text{e.s.e.}}$$

For a one-sample t-test, e.s.e. $= s/\sqrt{n}$, where n = number of observations. For regression problems, the e.s.e. will usually be given to you or will be calculated for you automatically by the computer software but the basic procedure and interpretation remains the same!

A quick note on p-values is needed here. The p refers to probability. A p-value is a measure of how strange the data is in relation to the null hypothesis. **LOW** p-values would cause you to reject the null hypothesis – some high-school maths teachers and lots of students make mistakes here! For a two-sided test (the default option), you need values in the 0.025 column of the t-tables.

On taught courses, it is often sufficient to simply determine whether or not $p < 0.05$. However, there are occasions where this approach can be misleading. More generally, in project work, $p < 0.1$ gives some weak or inconclusive evidence against the null hypothesis. An apparently mechanical procedure can thus still lead to deceptively nuanced interpretations in applied project work.

LOW p-values are significant. There is a slightly strange way of setting up the problem. It is easiest to first assume for the null hypothesis that the parameter (in this case the mean difference, μ) is equal to zero. Then, if you reject the null hypothesis, you would look for where the true value really is. This process is a lot easier than it sounds but may require some practice.

1 **Calculation**
2 **Reference statistical tables or numerical values**
3 **Interpretation**

For our earlier example:

1 Calculation

$$t = \frac{\text{estimate} - \text{hypothesized value}}{\text{e.s.e.}}$$

$$t = \frac{\sqrt{n}(\bar{x} - 0)}{s} = \frac{\sqrt{12}(72.33)}{6.5689} = 38.145$$

2 Reference the t-tables

- For a one-sample t-test, you need a t distribution with $n - 1$ degrees of freedom.
- For a regression t-test, you need a t distribution with $n - p$ degrees of freedom, where p is the number of parameters in the model including the constant term:

$$t_{0.025}(11) = 2.201, |t| = 38.145 > 2.201, \quad \text{therefore} \quad p < 0.05$$

3 Interpretation

- The mean difference is positive ($\bar{x} = 72.33$) and statistically significant $p < 0.05$.
- Consumer confidence was higher in 2007 than in 2009 – i.e. the 2008 crash reduced consumer confidence.

We now discuss how to repeat the above analysis using R. First, think of R, or any software package, as just being a calculator that is too big to fit into your pocket. All software packages have their quirks but they are also fundamentally designed to make sense.

There are two basic ways of reading data into R:

1 Directly via the command line for trivial lecture examples.
2 Read in using the **read.table** command via the command line from a .txt file in notepad saved to your USB.
   - You need to be able to write down the filepath. This is usually quicker and easier if saved to a USB stick.
   - The .txt file that includes the data has to contain equal numbers of evenly spaced columns. This can get a bit fiddly in large problems.

Our recommendation is that you download R for free on to your own PC or laptop. In Windows, download R on to your computer by searching 'R download CRAN' and following the on-screen instructions. To run R, you would then double-click on the R icon on your desktop. This should bring up the command window which on John's laptop gives you something that looks like Fig. 3.1.

The easy way to do the analysis in R (only possible for problems with small sample sizes) is to enter the data directly, either in the command window in R (pressing enter after each line) or by writing in notepad (see below) and copying into R from there.

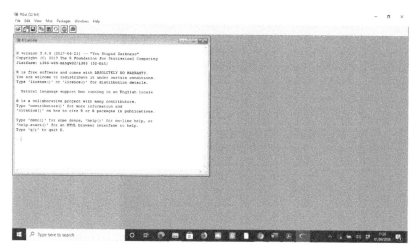

Figure 3.1 Example picture of the R command screen

```
2007score<-c(86, 86, 88, 90, 99, 97, 97, 96, 99, 97, 90, 90)
2009score<-c(24, 22, 21, 21, 19, 18, 17, 18, 21, 23, 22, 21)
difference<-2007score-2009score
t.test(difference)
```

Alternatively, a more practical way with decent-sized datasets is to copy the data into R from a .txt file using the read.table command. This has minimal formatting (the more formatting a program has the more that can go wrong!) but the columns need to line up with each other in order for the read.table command to work. First, you need to access notepad. On our computer you need Windows Accessories→Notepad

Copy the file L2data.txt from the online resources on to your USB stick. On our computer this is drive E but it might be different for yours. If so, you would have to substitute the right letter for the letter E in the code shown below. Read the data in using

```
scores<-read.table("E:/L2data.txt")
score2007<-scores[,1]
score2009<-scores[,2]
```

The previous analysis can then be repeated using

```
difference<-2007score-2009score
t.test(difference)
```

In this case, the results given by R are as follows:

```
data: difference
t = 38.144, df = 11, p-value = 4.861e-13
alternative hypothesis: true mean is not equal to 0
95 percent confidence interval:
68.15960 76.50706
sample estimates:
mean of x
72.33333
```

This inevitably gives a lot of redundant information, although the interpretation is, in fact, relatively simple. We would interpret these results as 'Results give significant evidence ($p < 0.05$) that the mean difference is not equal to zero. The mean difference is positive and significantly different from zero suggesting that consumer confidence was higher in 2007 than in 2009.'

3.2 One-sample variance ratio or χ^2 test

Two central statistical questions surround:

1 the mean
2 the variance.

Interpret these two statistics as:

1 What is my best guess of the value?
2 How far away from the true unknown value am I likely to be?

If the one-sample t-test answers Question 1 above, then the one-sample variance ratio test answers Question 2. This uses a different χ^2 distribution. It is slightly non-standard, and therefore not as natural to use as the one-sample t-test, but it may still be useful for statistical work in dissertations.

Suppose we have the following data on consumer expectations and consumer spending in 2011, as shown in Table 3.2. Suppose, further, that we want to test the null hypothesis that the standard deviation of the difference is equal to 1. (This is important since if the standard deviation is equal to σ, then, with probability around 95%, the consumer spending index should be within $\pm 2\sigma$ of the consumer expectations index.)

The steps involved in the one-sample variance ratio are as follows:

1 Calculate the mean.
2 Calculate the variance.

Table 3.2 Example data on consumer expectations and consumer spending

	J	F	M	A	M	J	J	A	S	O	N	D
Consumer expectation	66	53	62	61	78	72	65	64	61	50	55	51
Consumer spending	72	55	69	65	82	77	72	78	77	75	77	77
Difference	−6	−2	−7	−4	−4	−5	−7	−14	−16	−25	−22	−26

3 Calculate the χ^2 statistic $\dfrac{(n-1)s^2}{\sigma^2}$ and compare against χ^2_{n-1} – the chi-squared distribution with $n-1$ degrees of freedom, where n is the number of observations.

In step 1, the mean $\bar{x}$ and the variance s^2 can be calculated as

$$\bar{x} = \frac{-6 - 2 - 7 - 4 - \dots - 22 - 26}{12} = -\frac{138}{12} = -11.5$$

$$s^2 = \frac{\sum x_i^2 - n\bar{x}^2}{n-1}$$

$$\sum x_i^2 = (-6)^2 + (-2)^2 + (-7)^2 + \dots + (-22)^2 + (-26)^2 = 2432$$

$$s^2 = \frac{\sum x_i^2 - n\bar{x}^2}{n-1} = \frac{2432 - 12(-11.5)^2}{11} = \frac{845}{11} = 76.8182$$

Using these results, the χ^2 statistic can be calculated as

$$\chi^2 = \frac{(n-1)s^2}{\sigma^2} = \frac{11\left(\frac{845}{11}\right)}{1} = 845$$

Then, referencing the statistical tables,

$$\chi^2 = 845 > \chi_1^2(0.025) = 2.201$$
$$p < 0.05.$$

Therefore, we reject the null hypothesis $\sigma = 1$. The χ^2 statistic suggests that the true standard deviation is much larger than this. A better estimate for σ would appear to be $s = \sqrt{845/11} = 8.765$. This, in turn, suggests that, with probability around 0.95, the consumer spending index will be within $2 \times 8.765 = 17.53\%$ of the consumer expectations index.

The solution in R works as follows:

```
difference<-c(-6, -2, -7, -4, -4, -5, -7, -14, -16, -25, -22, -26)
```

1 Calculate the number in the sample
```
n<-length(difference)
```
2 Calculate the chi-squared statistic $\chi^2 = \dfrac{(n-1)s^2}{\sigma^2}$
```
chisquare<-(n-1)*var(difference)/1
```
3 Calculate the p-value
```
1-pchisq(chisquare, n-1)
[1] 0
```
4 Interpretation:
Results give significant evidence ($p = 0.000 < 0.05$) that the variance is not equal to 1.

3.3   Two-sample *t*-test

We want to compare the mean of two independent samples using the following *t*-statistic:

$$t = \frac{\bar{x}_1 - \bar{x}_2}{\sqrt{\frac{s_1^2(n_1-1)+s_2^2(n_2-1)}{n_1+n_2-2}}\sqrt{\frac{1}{n_1}+\frac{1}{n_2}}}$$

where n_1= number in the first sample, n_2= number in the second sample, $\bar{x}_1$= mean of the first sample, $\bar{x}_2$= mean of the second sample, s_1^2= variance of the first sample, s_2^2= variance of the second sample.

Example 3.8

Consider the data shown in Table 3.3. This gives wage data on 10 advertising professionals and 13 accountants. We want to see if there is any evidence for differences in average pay.

Table 3.3   Wage data for advertising professionals and accountants

Advertising professionals	36, 40, 46, 54, 57, 58, 59, 60, 62, 63
Accountants	37, 37, 42, 44, 46, 48, 54, 56, 59, 60, 60, 64, 64

The calculations for the first sample use n_1= number of advertising professionals = 10. The mean $\bar{x}_1$ and variance s_1^2 are

$$\bar{x}_1 = \frac{36 + 40 + 46 + \dots + 62 + 63}{10} = \frac{535}{10} = 53.5$$

$$s_1^2 = \frac{\sum x_{1,i}^2 - n\bar{x}_1^2}{n_1 - 1}$$

$$\sum x_{1,i}^2 = 36^2 + 40^2 + 46^2 + \dots + 62^2 + 63^2 = 29435$$

$$s_1^2 = \frac{29435 - 10(53.5)^2}{9} = 90.2778$$

The calculations for the second sample use n_2 = number of accountants = 13. The mean $\bar{x}_2$ and variance s_2^2 are

$$\bar{x}_2 = \frac{37 + 37 + 42 + \dots + 64 + 64}{13} = \frac{671}{13} = 51.6154$$

$$s_2^2 = \frac{\sum x_{2,i}^2 - n\bar{x}_2^2}{n_2 - 1}$$

$$\sum x_{2,i}^2 = 37^2 + 37^2 + 42^2 + \dots + 64^2 + 64^2 = 35783$$

$$s_2^2 = \frac{35783 - 13(51.6154)^2}{12} = 95.7547$$

The by-hand calculation then works as follows:

1 *Calculating the t-statistic*

$$t = \frac{\bar{x}_1 - \bar{x}_2}{\sqrt{\frac{s_1^2(n_1-1) + s_2^2(n_2-1)}{n_1+n_2-2}}\sqrt{\frac{1}{n_1} + \frac{1}{n_2}}}$$

$$= \frac{53.5 - 51.6154}{\sqrt{\frac{90.2778(9) + 95.7547(12)}{21}}\sqrt{\frac{1}{10} + \frac{1}{13}}}$$

$$= \frac{1.8846}{9.6648 \times 0.4206} = 0.464 \ (3 \ d.p.)$$

2 *Referencing the t-tables*
   - *Degrees of freedom* $= n_1 + n_2 - 2 = 10 + 13 - 2 = 21$, $t_{21}(0.025) = 2.08$.
   - *So* $|t| < t_{21}(0.025) = 2.08$, $p > 0.05$.
3 *Interpretation*
   - *There is no evidence ($p > 0.05$) for differences in the average pay amongst advertising professionals and accountants.*
   - *The average pay levels seem to be roughly the same for both professions.*

Standard statistical tests are easy to do in R. In this respect, this two-sample t-test can be conducted as follows:

1 *Read in the data*
   advertisers<-c(36, 40, 46, 54, 57, 58, 59, 60, 62, 63)
   accountants<-c(37, 37, 42, 44, 46, 48, 54, 56, 59, 60, 60, 64, 64)
2 *The basic command is then* t.test *applied to (first variable, second variable)*
   t.test(advertisers, accountants)
   data: advertisers and accountants
   t = 0.46546, df = 19.795, p-value = 0.6467
   alternative hypothesis: true difference in means is not equal to 0

3.4 Two-sample variance ratio or *F*-test

There are two basic problems in statistics:

1 Mean/location. Where does a typical observation lie?
2 Variance/dispersion. How 'spread out' is the data?

To answer this second question, the two-sample *F*-test asks, 'Given two independent samples, is one more spread out than the other?' The two-sample *F*-statistic,

$$F = \frac{s_1^2}{s_2^2}, \text{ should be compared against } F_{n_1-1, n_2-1}$$

where s_1^2 refers to the sample with the larger variance. Applying this test to the data shown in Table 3.3 gives the following results.

1. Calculating the F-statistic, we have that $s_1^2 = 95.7547$, $s_2^2 = 90.2778$

$$F = \frac{95.7547}{90.2778} = 1.061 \ (3 \ \text{d.p.})$$

2. Reference the F-tables. The degrees of freedom are $n_1 - 1 = 13 - 1 = 12$, $n_2 - 1 = 10 - 1 = 9$. From the F-tables, $F_{12,9}(0.05) = 3.07$. This gives

$$F = 1.061 < F_{12,9}(0.05) = 3.07, \ p > 0.05$$

3. Interpretation. No evidence ($p > 0.05$) for differences in the variances of each group. Wage levels for the two groups appear to be equally well spread out.

In R the basic process works as follows.

1. Read in the data
   ```
   advertisers<-c(36, 40, 46, 54, 57, 58, 59, 60, 62, 63)
   accountants<-c(37, 37, 42, 44, 46, 48, 54, 56, 59, 60, 60, 64, 64)
   ```

2. Apply the function var.test
   ```
   var.test(advertisers, accountants)
   F = 0.94279, num df = 9, denom df = 12, p-value = 0.9505
   ```

Therefore, the results give no evidence, $p = 0.9505 > 0.05$, of a difference in the variance of the two groups.

3.4.1 Aside on by-hand calculations using F-tables

When students sit formal written exams, by-hand calculations using F-tables are important. The most important thing in this instance is that you WRITE DOWN the numbers obtained from the F-tables. The person marking your exam will then be able to give you marks for the correct working – even if you subsequently make mistakes. Remember that anyone marking your exam should ultimately be more interested in what you CAN do than what you cannot! Also, make sure that you WRITE DOWN whether $p < 0.05$ or $p > 0.05$ and include a sentence or two in plain English about **interpretation**.

The F-tables used, unfortunately, contain a lot of gaps. Suppose, for example, that you need to find a value for $F_{13,13}(0.05)$. However, you only have $F_{12,13}(0.05) = 2.60$ and $F_{15,13}(0.05) = 2.53$. Since

$$13 = \frac{2}{3}(12) + \frac{1}{3}(15)$$

in this case, you can use

$$F_{13,13}(0.05) = \frac{2}{3}F_{12,13}(0.05) + \frac{1}{3}F_{15,13}(0.05)$$
$$= \frac{2}{3}(2.60) + \frac{1}{3}(2.53) = 2.53 \ (2 \ \text{d.p.})$$

Similarly, suppose that you need to find a value for $F_{19,8}(0.05)$. However, you only have $F_{15,8}(0.05) = 3.22$ and $F_{20,8}(0.05) = 3.15$. Since

$$19 = \frac{4}{5}(20) + \frac{1}{5}(15)$$

in this case, you can use

$$F_{19,8}(0.05) = \frac{4}{5}F_{20,8}(0.05) + \frac{1}{5}F_{15,8}(0.05)$$
$$= \frac{4}{5}(3.15) + \frac{1}{5}(3.22) = 3.16 \ (2 \ \text{d.p.})$$

3.5 χ^2 test for data on observed counts

The chi-squared test is commonly used for count data and is simple and useful. Examples can be found in Cortinhas and Black (2012), Chapter 16.

Example 3.9

Suppose we have the data in Table 3.4 on the status of residential ownership by region and we want to see whether residential status depends on the region. The null hypothesis is that there is no association between residential status and region. The χ^2 test works as follows. You need to calculate the expected number for each category in the table, E_i, and compare with the observed number in each category O_i.

$$E_i = \frac{row \ total \times column \ total}{total \ number \ of \ observations}$$

Table 3.4 Example data on residential ownership by region

Region	Owner occupied	Rented	Total
North West	2180	871	3051
London	1820	1400	3220
South West	1703	614	2317
Total	5703	2885	8588

Use the following χ^2 statistic to calculate a measure of the difference between the observed and expected values. Large values of this χ^2 statistic (difference) then give evidence against the null hypothesis. Thus, this should also be a one-sided test.

$$\chi^2 = \sum \frac{(O_i - E_i)^2}{E_i} \ compare\ with\ \chi^2_{(r-1)(c-1)}$$

where $r = $ number of rows (going across) $= 3$ and $c = $ number of columns (going down) $= 2$. Expected count calculations for this example are shown in Table 3.5.

Table 3.5 Example calculations for the χ^2 test

Owner occupied	Rented	Total
$\dfrac{3051 \times 5703}{8588} = 2026.066$	$\dfrac{3051 \times 2885}{8588} = 1024.934$	3051
$\dfrac{3220 \times 5703}{8588} = 2138.293$	$\dfrac{3220 \times 2885}{8588} = 1081.707$	3220
$\dfrac{2317 \times 5703}{8588} = 1538.641$	$\dfrac{2317 \times 2885}{8588} = 778.359$	2317
5703	2885	8588

Using the expected counts in Table 3.5, the χ^2 statistic can be calculated as follows:

$$\chi^2 = \frac{(O_i - E_i)^2}{E_i}$$

$$\chi^2 = \frac{(2180 - 2026.066)^2}{2026.066} + \frac{(871 - 1024.934)^2}{1024.934}$$

$$+ \frac{(1820 - 2138.293)^2}{2138.293} + \frac{(1400 - 1081.707)^2}{1081.707}$$

$$+ \frac{(1703 - 1538.641)^2}{1538.641} + \frac{(614 - 778.359)^2}{778.359}$$

$$\chi^2 = 11.695 + 23.119$$

$$= 47.379 + 93.658$$

$$= 17.557 + 34.707$$

$$\chi^2 = 228.12\ (2\ d.p.)$$

Continuing,

$$\chi^2 = 228.12 > \chi^2_2(0.05) = 5.99$$

$$p < 0.05$$

Therefore, there is evidence (p < 0.05) that residential status depends on area. The percentages in Table 3.6 below suggest that, in London, fewer homes are owner occupied and more homes are rented.

Table 3.6 Interpretation of the final results of the house-ownership example

Region	Owner occupied	Rented
North West	71.5%	28.5%
London	56.5%	43.5%
South West	73.5%	26.5%

It easy to run standard tests like the chi-squared test in R. This is a simple two-step process.

1 *You need to enter the data as a matrix with the observations in the right order. Here, enter the data first and then specify how the table is laid out. Printing the data just by stating the word* count *shows you how the variable* count *has now been constructed:*
   count<-c(2180, 871, 1820, 1400, 1703, 614)
   count<-matrix(count, ncol=2, byrow=T)
   count
2 *The basic command to run the test is* chisq.test
   chisq.test(count)

This gives the same results as before, albeit presented slightly differently.
   data: count
   X-squared = 228.11, df = 2, p-value < 2.2e-16

3.6 Tutorial exercises

1 A study reported that the average price of petrol in Europe is 1.37 euros. By performing a one-sample t-test in R, determine whether this finding is consistent with the data in Table 3.7. [R commands to read in this data are given below. Please note that you can copy this data from the pdf available online and then from there into notepad.]. Repeat these calculations by hand.
   R commands to read in the data:
   petrol<-c(1.36, 1.37, 1.32, 1.33, 1.40, 1.33, 1.35, 1.33, 1.33, 1.35, 1.32, 1.28, 1.36, 1.29, 1.40, 1.31, 1.35, 1.31, 1.27, 1.40, 1.34, 1.31, 1.31, 1.28, 1.29)
2 A company wants to know whether the variance of its overtime payments is equal to £25. Using R, perform a one-sided variance ratio test for the data shown below. Repeat these computations by hand. The R commands to read these in are

Table 3.7 Petrol data for Question 1

1.36
1.37
1.32
1.33
1.40
1.33
1.35
1.33
1.33
1.35
1.32
1.28
1.36
1.29
1.40
1.31
1.35
1.31
1.27
1.40
1.34
1.31
1.31
1.28
1.29

payments<-c(57, 56, 52, 44, 46, 53, 44, 44, 48, 51, 55, 48, 63, 53, 51, 50)

3 A study has recently been conducted to test whether or not there is a difference in the price of coffee in Hannover in Germany and in Toulouse in France. Using R, perform a two-sample variance ratio test to determine whether or not prices across the two cities seem equally variable. Repeat

Table 3.8 Coffee prices data for Question 3

57
56
52
44
46
53
44
44
48
51
55
48
63
53
51
50

these computations by hand. The data is listed below. The R commands to enter this data are

hannover<-c(2.55, 2.36, 2.43, 2.67, 2.54, 2.43, 2.50, 2.54, 2.38, 2.61, 2.80, 2.49, 2.43, 2.61, 2.57, 2.36, 2.56, 2.71, 2.50, 2.64, 2.27)
toulouse<-c(2.25, 2.40, 2.39, 2.30, 2.33, 2.40, 2.49, 2.29, 2.23, 2.41, 2.48, 2.29, 2.39, 2.59, 2.53, 2.26, 2.38, 2.45)

4 For the data in Question 3, perform a two-sample t-test in R to see if there is a difference in average coffee price between Hannover and Toulouse. What conclusion do you reach?

5 *Confidence intervals and hypothesis tests.* A 95% confidence interval for μ can be constructed by evaluating the range

$$\bar{x} \pm t_{n-1}(0.025)\text{e.s.e.} \tag{3.1}$$

where e.s.e. denotes the estimated standard error. If the 95% confidence interval does not include μ_0, then using a t-test we would reject the null hypothesis that $\mu = \mu_0$ at the 5% level since $t := \dfrac{\mu_0 - \bar{x}}{\text{e.s.e.}}$ satisfies

Table 3.9 Coffee prices data for Question 3

Hannover	Toulouse
2.55	2.25
2.36	2.40
2.43	2.39
2.67	2.30
2.54	2.33
2.43	2.40
2.50	2.49
2.54	2.29
2.38	2.23
2.61	2.41
2.80	2.48
2.49	2.29
2.43	2.39
2.61	2.59
2.57	2.53
2.36	2.26
2.56	2.38
2.71	2.45
2.50	
2.64	
2.27	

$|t| > t_{n-1}(0.025)$. Because μ_0 does not lie inside the 95% confidence interval given by Eq. (3.1), we know that

$$\mu_0 < \bar{x} - t_{n-1}(0.025)\text{e.s.e. or } \mu_0 > \bar{x} + t_{n-1}(0.025)\text{e.s.e.}$$

In either case, $|t| > t_{n-1}(0.025)$.

(a) If we reject the null hypothesis $\mu = \mu_0$ at the 5% level, show that the 95% confidence interval does not include μ_0.

(b) What are the implications for hypothesis testing?

3.7   Solutions

1   In R, once you have read the data in, use t.test(petrol, mu=1.37) to test the null hypothesis that rather than being zero the mean is equal to 1.37. Results obtained are shown below.
data: petrol
t = -5.1829, df = 24, p-value = 2.617e-05
alternative hypothesis: true mean is not equal to 1.37
95 percent confidence interval:
1.316309 1.346891
sample estimates:
mean of x
1.3316
Interpretation. There is no evidence ($p = 0.000 < 0.05$) that the mean is equal to 1.37. The sample mean appears to be less than this and closer to 1.33 in the sample collected.

2   First, you need to read in the data using the given commands. In R, we need to calculate the chi-squared statistic

$$\chi^2 = \frac{(n-1)s^2}{\sigma^2}$$

where n is the number in the sample, s^2 is the sample variance and σ^2 is the value of the variance under the null hypothesis. This is slightly fiddly to do in R as this is a slightly non-standard test. In R, use
var(payments)
n1<-length(payments)
chisquared<-(n1-1)*var(payments)/25
1-pchisq(chisquared, n1-1)
This gives a calculated p-value of 0.3286712.
Interpretation: There is no evidence ($p = 0.3287$) that the variance of the sample is different from the hypothesized value of 25. Variability in the data would not appear to be a cause for concern.

3   After inputting the data, the required commands are as follows:
n1<-length(hannover)
n2<-length(toulouse)
s12<-var(hannover)
s22<-var(toulouse)
F<-s12/s22
To calculate the value of F, just type
F
This gives a value of 1.621529 > 1, so calculate the p-value as
2*(1-pf(F, n1-1, n2-1)).
This gives a p-value of 0.3181966 > 0.05 so there is no statistically significant evidence of a difference.

Interpretation: There is no evidence ($p = 0.2999 > 0.05$) to suggest a difference in variance in the coffee prices for Toulouse and Hannover. Prices in both cities seem to be equally variable.

4 In R simply use t.test(hannover, toulouse). This gives
   Welch Two Sample t-test
   data: hannover and toulouse
   t = 3.8022, df = 36.751, p-value = 0.0005232
   alternative hypothesis: true difference in means is not equal to 0
   Interpretation: There is some evidence ($p = 0.0006$) that average prices in the two cities are different. Descriptive statistics give the mean coffee price as 2.381111 in Toulouse and 2.521429 in Hannover. This suggests that there is statistical evidence that average coffee prices are higher in Hannover.

5 If we reject the null hypothesis using the t-test, then

$$\frac{|\mu_0 - \bar{s}|}{\text{e.s.e.}} > t_{n-1}(0.025); \ |\mu_0 - \bar{s}| > t_{n-1}(0.025)\text{e.s.e.}$$

So either $\mu_0 < \bar{x} - t_{n-1}(0.025)\text{e.s.e.}$ or $\mu_0 > \bar{x} + t_{n-1}(0.025)\text{e.s.e.}$ Either way, the confidence interval produced does not include μ_0.

The implications for hypothesis testing are:
(a) Construct the confidence interval.
(b) If μ_0 lies inside the confidence interval, retain the null hypothesis $\mu = \mu_0$.
(c) If μ_0 lies outside the confidence interval, reject the null hypothesis $\mu = \mu_0$.

4 An introduction to regression

Regression is extremely important. The subject underpins nearly all applied statistics and also econometrics and financial econometrics. Rigorous statistical techniques are often an integral part of MSc dissertations. (High-level) financial research is inherently quantitative. This is not to deny that finance is inherently subjective. Finance concerns much more than just applied mathematics. However, even calculating subjective benchmarks is quantitative and high-level research in the social sciences is increasingly quantitative in nature.

Maths is not easy but is often easier than it first looks and sometimes the questions asked are deceptively simple. The basic question in regression is what happens to Y as X increases?

1 Does it increase?
2 Does it decrease?
3 Does nothing happen?

In this way, and with a view towards Figs 2.2–2.4, regression can be seen as a more advanced version of high-school maths. However, you do need to remember that a real data set will be more imperfect than this even though the same basic ideas will continue to apply throughout. An example of an imperfect (albeit still useful) regression relationship is shown in Fig. 4.1.

Regression problems can look a lot harder than they really are. The basic question remains, 'What happens to Y as X increases?' There is also a need to beware of jargon. Gujarati and Porter (2009) make an artificial distinction between a two-variable regression and a multiple regression model. Despite this apparent difference, the mathematical methodology and the regression-fitting commands in R for both models are essentially the same.

Some authors use different terminology and notation for essentially the same thing. Remember that maths is usually a lot simpler than you first imagine. For example, Gujarati and Porter (2009) variously refer to a two-variable regression model

$$Y_i = \beta_1 + \beta_2 X_{2,i} + u_i$$

a three-variable regression model

$$Y_i = \beta_1 + \beta_2 X_{2,i} + \beta_3 X_{3,i} + u_i$$

and a multiple regression model

$$Y_i = \beta_1 + \beta_2 X_{2,i} + \beta_3 X_{3,i} + \dots + \beta_p X_{p,i} + u_i$$

In terms of mathematical methodology and R commands etc., all these are special cases of the multiple linear regression model and a lot simpler than may at first seem to be the case.

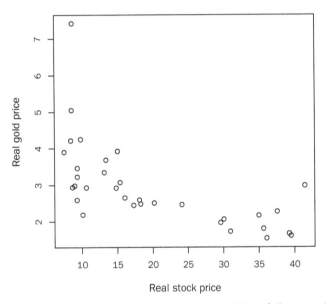

Figure 4.1 Scatter plot showing an imperfect (albeit still useful) regression relationship

4.1 Plotting variables

Suppose that we are interested in the relationship between real (inflation-adjusted) stock prices and gold prices. We want to plot the two variables together. This enables us to cross-check the results of a formal statistical analysis. Although this sounds simple, it is very important in real project work. Remember that we then do the statistical analysis so that we are not restricted to simply looking at the graph and guessing.

In this financial context, there is some suggestion that as the stock price falls there is a flight to quality and people buy gold, and the increased demand may, in turn, increase gold prices. The reverse may also be true – people leave gold to play the market when the stock price rises. The suggestion in both cases is that (inflation-adjusted) stock prices and gold prices may be negatively correlated. These observations are consistent with a plot of the data in Fig. 4.1 although, as stated before, the regression relationship is not perfect.

To examine this data in R, the data is in the file L3egldata.txt available online. Save it to your USB stick and then read in the data using the read.table command

datal<-read.table("E:L3egldata.txt")

The dataset contains two columns containing the real gold price (left column) and the real stock price (right column). Thus, in R, assign variables linking the real gold price to the first column and the real stock price to the second column. (Note that this has to match the name datal given in the above sequence of commands.)

realgoldprice<-datal[,1]
realstockprice<-datal[,2]

The basic plotting command in R is plot. But you have to specify:

1 Axes titles
2 Plotting style (line or dots; dots are often simpler so is the default option)
3 Scaling (using the commands xlim=c(lower, upper), ylim=c(lower, upper))

Whenever you use graphics in R, it is usually best to stick with the simplest default options and then change these only if you need to. The basic command in R is plot. The plot command is applied to the X-variable first and then the Y-variable. For our simple example:

plot(realstockprice, realgoldprice, xlab="Real Stock Price", ylab="Real Gold Price")

These commands then produce the graph shown in Fig. 4.1. This suggests that the two variables are indeed negatively correlated. However, we still need to cross-check this with the results of a formal statistical regression analysis.

4.2 R^2

It is often important to demonstrate an ability to understand and interpret the output of a computer-generated model. R^2 is often one of the quickest and easiest things to make sense of. When running a regression, R calculates R^2 values automatically. The R^2 statistic gives you the proportion of the variability in the data explained by the regression model – the higher the better! However, there is an important caveat. R^2 automatically increases as additional X variables are added to a regression model. An adjusted R^2 statistic can be constructed that tries to take account of this. However, this statistic does not appear to be widely used.

Some quick facts about R^2 are in order:

1 R^2 lies between 0 and 1.
2 $R^2 = 0$ model explains nothing.
3 $R^2 = 1$ model explains everything.
4 Generally, the higher the value of R^2 the better the model.
5 Textbook examples often have high R^2 values, e.g. 0.7 or higher, which may be slightly artificial on occasion.

There is no hard and fast rule about the interpretation of R^2. Usually, an R^2 value of say 0.3 or higher is enough to say that there is a non-trivial amount of variation in the data explained by the model. In our example, there is an R^2 value of 0.395325 showing us that the stock price clearly affects the price of gold. However, it is clear that other factors also affect the price of gold.

Consider the following analysis of variance (ANOVA) table for a generic regression model shown in Table 4.1. We will return to the ANOVA later in Chapter 8. The ANOVA table shows that

$$R^2 = 1 - \frac{SSE}{SST}$$

The R^2 statistic can be constructed as follows.

$$R^2 = \frac{\text{variation explained by the model}}{\text{total variation in the data}}$$
$$= \frac{SSR}{SST} = \frac{SST - SSE}{SST}$$
$$= 1 - \frac{SSE}{SST}$$

When running regression in R, the basic command is lm for linear model. You specify the Y variable and then the X variable with a $\sim$ sign between the X

Table 4.1 Outline analysis of variance (ANOVA) table

Source	df	S.S.	M.S.	F
Regression	$p - 1$	SSR	$MSR = \dfrac{SSR}{p - 1}$	$F = \dfrac{MSR}{MSE}$
Error	$n - p$	SSE	$MSE = \dfrac{SSE}{n - p}$	
Total	$n - 1$	SST	$MST = \dfrac{SST}{n - 1}$	

and Y variables (mathematically this means 'related to'). You also need a + sign between the different X variables on the right-hand side of this symbol.

The best way to run regressions in R is to:

1 Run the regression analysis and store the results.
2 Get R to summarize the results for you in a second command.

For our simple example,
a.lm<-lm(realgoldprice~realstockprice)
summary(a.lm)

Running the regression in R produces a wealth of results – we only need a small portion of the results actually generated. The interesting and useful bits of the results produced are:

1 **R-squared** 0.395325
2 **t-Statistic** for the variable **REALSTOCKPRICE** -4.502
3 **F-statistic** 20.27

The rest of the chapter discusses what these t and F statistics really mean.

4.3 *t*-test

The basic question is always what happens to Y as X increases?

1 Does it increase?
2 Does it decrease?
3 Does nothing happen?

So, is our situation Fig. 2.2 or Fig. 2.4? Some mathematics and equations are inevitable although the underlying ideas are really very simple as per the references to the simple graphs above. Consider the two-variable linear regression model

$$Y_i = \beta_1 + \beta_2 X_i + u_i$$

We want to see whether X affects Y. It is a slightly strange way of thinking, but it turns out that the easiest way to do this is by testing the hypotheses

$$H_0: \quad \beta_2 = 0$$
$$H_1: \quad \beta_2 \neq 0$$

Results produced by R for the real gold price and real stock price example are shown in Table 4.2. You usually fit a constant term so the first row of this table is not really informative. The second row of the table (and downwards if using

Table 4.2 Abridged regression output produced by R

Variable	Coefficient	Std error	t-value	Pr(>|t|)
(Intercept)	4.21285	0.32351	13.022	4.14e-14***
realstockprice	−0.06409	0.01424	−4.502	8.90e-05***

a larger model) is the informative part of the table where the main action is. The asterisks denote statistical significance. Note that although 8.90e-05 may look weird it just means 8.90×10^{-5}.

Construction and interpretation of the t-test follows the example in the previous chapter, but this time with $n - p$ degrees of freedom

$$t = \frac{\text{estimate} - \text{hypothesized value}}{\text{e.s.e.}}$$

Because it is extremely common to test the hypothesis $\beta_2 = 0$, the usual form of the t-statistic becomes

$$t = \frac{\text{estimate} - 0}{\text{e.s.e.}}$$

The t-statistic computed in R can be constructed as

$$t = \frac{\text{estimate} - 0}{\text{e.s.e.}}$$
$$= \frac{-0.064086}{0.014235} = -4.502 \text{ (3 d.p.)}$$

R calculates the p-value to be 8.90×10^{-5}. We cannot calculate the exact p-value by hand but we can produce a bound for the p-value using tables. This increased accuracy hints at how worthwhile computers are! The by-hand calculation to reconstruct the R computations is as follows:

$$n = \text{number of data points} = 33$$
$$p = \text{number of variables in the model} = 2$$
$$df = n - p = 33 - 2 = 31$$
$$t_{31}(0.025) = 2.040$$
$$|t| = 4.502 > t_{31}(0.025) = 2.040, \text{ therefore } p < 0.05$$

The interpretation is that there is some evidence ($p < 0.05$) that stock prices affect gold prices. As the coefficient is negative (and statistically significant), as stock prices increase, gold prices decrease, and vice versa.

4.4 *F*-test

We want some way of systematically testing the overall fit of the model. It is possible to perform a sequence of *t*-tests in order to do this, although, for statistical reasons, this is not really desirable due to multiple testing. The *F*-test performed automatically by R is only one possibility amongst many and may only have limited value in itself. We will see in the next chapter that *F*-tests and the extra sum of squares principle can be applied much more generally.

The *F*-test produced automatically by R tests the overall fit of the model. Effectively, it asks, 'Does at least one of the *X*-variables in the model have a statistically significant effect on *Y*?' In terms of formal hypothesis testing for the multiple linear regression model

$$Y_i = \beta_1 + \beta_2 X_{2,i} + \beta_3 X_{3,i} + \ldots + \beta_p X_{p,i} + u_i$$

this becomes

$$H_0: \quad \beta_2 = \beta_3 = \ldots = \beta_p = 0$$
$$H_1: \quad \text{At least one of the } \beta \text{ is non-zero}$$

In terms of the formal hypothesis testing for the two-variable regression model

$$Y_i = \beta_1 + \beta_2 X_{2,i} + u_i$$

this becomes

$$H_0: \quad \beta_2 = 0$$
$$H_1: \quad \beta_2 \neq 0$$

The output produced by R states
F-statistic: 20.27 on 1 and 31 DF, p-value: 8.904e-05

This would be best interpreted as 'We have strong evidence ($p = 0.000$) that the real stock price affects the real gold price'. We will see in the next example that the interpretation of the *F*-statistic changes slightly when we have more than one *X*-variable in the regression model (in addition to the constant term).

To show where the numbers produced by R come from, the by-hand calculation of this *F*-test runs as follows. In general, for the multiple linear regression model

$$Y_i = \beta_1 + \beta_2 X_{2,i} + \beta_3 X_{3,i} + \ldots + \beta_p X_{p,i} + u_i$$

we want to test the hypothesis

$$H_0: \quad \beta_2 = \beta_3 = \ldots = \beta_p = 0$$
$$H_1: \quad \text{At least one of the } \beta \text{ is non-zero}$$

Construct the F-statistic as

$$F = \frac{\frac{\text{difference in SS}}{\text{difference in d.f.}}}{\frac{\text{residual SS (big model)}}{\text{residual d.f.}}} = \frac{\frac{(R^2)TSS}{p-1}}{\frac{(1-R^2)TSS}{n-p}}$$

$$F = \frac{\frac{R^2}{p-1}}{\frac{1-R^2}{n-p}} \sim F_{p-1,n-p}$$

The R output states **Multiple R-squared: 0.3953**. So construct the F-statistic as

$$F = \frac{\frac{R^2}{p-1}}{\frac{1-R^2}{n-p}} = \frac{(n-p)R^2}{(p-1)(1-R^2)} = \frac{31(0.395325)}{1(0.604675)} = 20.267 \text{ (3 d.p.)}$$

This needs to be compared with the value for $F_{1,31}$. From tables, $F_{1,30} = 4.17$, $F_{1,40} = 4.08$

$$31 = 0.9(30) + 0.1(40)$$
$$F_{1,31} = 0.9F_{1,30} + 0.1F_{1,40}$$
$$F_{1,31} = 0.9(4.17) + 0.1(4.08) = 4.161$$
$$F = 20.267 > F_{1,31} = 4.161$$
$$p < 0.05$$

So there is evidence ($p < 0.05$) that the real stock price affects the real gold price.

4.5 Additional multiple regression example

To show how to best interpret the results from a multiple linear regression model, we use an example from the classical Longley dataset. Our overall aim is to explain the number of employed people in the US in terms of:

1 X_2, GNP
2 X_3, the number of unemployed
3 X_4, the unemployment rate
4 X_5, the 'non-institutionalized' population over the age of 14
5 X_6, the yearly trend.

The data is in the file longley.txt
```
longley<-read.table("E:longley.txt")
x2<-longley[,1]
x3<-longley[,2]
```

```
x4<-longley[,3]
x5<-longley[,4]
x6<-longley[,5]
y<-longley[,6]
```

Fit the model in the usual way using
```
a.lm<-lm(y~x2+x3+x4+x5+x6)
summary(a.lm)
```

R will produce a lot of irrelevant information. The obvious things to look at are:

1 The R^2 statistic.
2 The individual T-statistics.
3 The F-statistic to assess overall fit.

1 The R^2 statistic. R states **Multiple R-squared: 0.9955**

R^2 is very high which suggests that we might have quite a good model. $R^2 = 0.9955$, which means that the model explains around 99.6% of the variability in the data. Whilst this R^2 value is very high, there is a chance that this is potentially too high to be true (see later).

2 The individual t-statistics. As a first step, it is natural to look at the variables for which $p < 0.05$. In project work, for example dissertations, sometimes the interpretation might be different and a p-value satisfying $0.1 < p < 0.05$ might give weak evidence of an effect. We need to analyse the results carefully. Results given by R suggest that not all of the variables are statistically significant.

Coefficients:
```
Estimate Std error t-value Pr(>|t|)
(Intercept) -3.450e+03 8.282e+02 -4.165 0.001932 **
x2 -3.196e-02 2.420e-02 -1.321 0.216073
x3 -1.972e-02 3.861e-03 -5.108 0.000459 ***
x4 -1.020e-02 1.908e-03 -5.345 0.000326 ***
x5 -7.754e-02 1.616e-01 -0.480 0.641607
x6 1.814e+00 4.253e-01 4.266 0.001648 **
```

The literal interpretation of these results would be as follows:
(a) t-statistics show that not all the variables are statistically significant.
(b) Since the convention is to usually include a constant term in the model, the t-statistic for the constant term is not usually very informative.
(c) p-values suggest that the variables X_2 and X_5 are not statistically significant ($p > 0.05$). The sign is irrelevant. There is no formal statistical evidence of an effect.

    (d) The coefficient of X_3 is negative and statistically significant ($p < 0.05$). As the number of unemployed people increases, the number of employed people decreases.

    (e) The coefficient of X_4 is negative and statistically significant ($p < 0.05$). As the unemployment rate increases, the number employed decreases.

    (f) The coefficient of X_6 is positive and statistically significant ($p < 0.05$). As X_6 is the time trend, this suggests that the number employed is generally increasing every year over the period in question.

3 The F-statistic to assess overall fit. According to R,

F-statistic: 438.8 on 5 and 10 DF, p-value: 2.242e-11

This presents evidence ($p = 2.242 \times 10^{-11} < 0.05$) that at least one of the X-variables in the study affects Y. However, for example, do we need to include both the unemployment rate and the number of unemployed people in the same model?

4.6 Tutorial exercises

1 *Additional practice with R.* We have the following data linking the price of an equity to the Gross National Product over a period of 24 months.

Enter this data using the read.table command (the data is available in the file L3tutorialdata.txt in the online resources). The R code we used to do this was

```
tutorialdata<-read.table("E:L3tutorialdata.txt")
month<-tutorialdata[,1]
equity<-tutorialdata[,2]
GNP<-tutorialdata[,3]
```

Alternatively, in this simple example, use the following:

```
month<-seq(1:24)
equity<-c(49, 90, 87, 82, 66, 74, 48, 51, 92, 47, 48, 55, 32, 87, 63, 69,
85, 73, 101, 87, 88, 37, 52, 48)
GNP<-c(5, 9, 9, 8, 7, 8, 4, 6, 9, 4, 5, 5, 3, 8, 6, 7, 9, 7, 10, 8, 9, 3, 6, 5)
```

We will begin with a descriptive statistical analysis. We can produce individual histograms of equity and GNP or plot them side by side using the following code:

```
hist(equity, xlab="Equity Price")
hist(GNP, xlab"GNP")
par(mfrow=c(1, 2))
hist(equity, xlab="Equity Price")
hist(GNP, xlab="GNP")
```

The graphical options can then be returned back to normal using the command par(mfrow=c(1, 1))

Table 4.3 Dataset for tutorial exercise

Month	Equity price	GNP
1	49	5
2	90	9
3	87	9
4	82	8
5	66	7
6	74	8
7	48	4
8	51	6
9	92	9
10	47	4
11	48	5
12	55	5
13	32	3
14	87	8
15	63	6
16	69	7
17	85	9
18	73	7
19	101	10
20	87	8
21	88	9
22	37	3
23	52	6
24	48	5

Probably more useful then the histogram is a simple dot plot of the data. This is often used to motivate a formal regression analysis or to cross-check the results of a regression analysis. In this case, simply use: plot(GNP, equity, xlab="GNP", ylab="Equity Price"). Results in Fig. 4.5 suggest that it is natural to consider fitting a regression model for the equity price against the GNP.

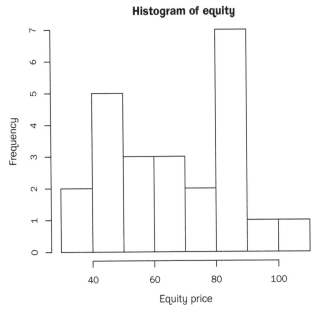

Figure 4.2 Histogram for equity price

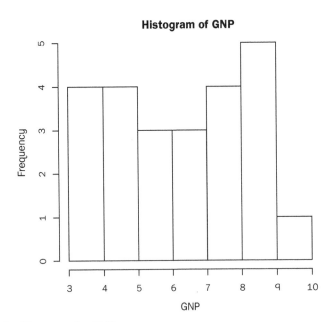

Figure 4.3 Histogram for GNP

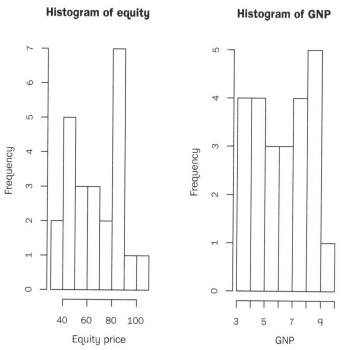

Figure 4.4 Histogram for equity price and GNP placed side by side using the par(mfrow=c(I, 2)) command

We can calculate the correlation between the GNP and equity price using cor(GNP, equity) and run a formal test using cor.test(GNP, equity).
cor(GNP, equity)
[1] 0.9716778
cor.test(GNP, equity)
Pearson's product-moment correlation
data: GNP and equity
t = 19.286, df = 22, p-value = 2.843e-15
alternative hypothesis: true correlation is not equal to 0

The cor function simply calculates the correlation whilst the more advanced cor.test function runs an additional formal statistical test. For any examples you are likely to see, we would suggest that it is probably more meaningful to run a regression model test. As before, this involves two steps. Firstly, run and save the regression model. Secondly, get R to summarize the results:
a.lm<-lm(equity~GNP)
summary(a.lm)
Call: lm(formula = equity ~ GNP)
Coefficients:
Estimate Std error t-value Pr(>|t|)
(Intercept) 4.9102 3.3727 1.456 0.16

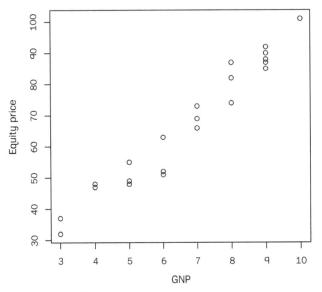

Figure 4.5 Dot plot of GNP and equity price

Table 4.4 Car stopping distances data for Question 2

Speed, x (mph)	Stopping distance, y (metres)
20	12
30	23
40	36
50	53
60	73
70	96

GNP 9.3322 0.4839 19.286 2.84e-15 ***
--- Signif. codes: 0 '***' 0.001 '**' 0.01 '*' 0.05 '.' 0.1 ' ' 1

The interpretation, in this instance, would be that the coefficient of GNP is both positive and statistically significant ($p = 2.84 \times 10^{-15} < 0.05$). Therefore, as GNP increases, the equity price increases.

2 The data in Table 4.4 links the stopping distance (in metres) of a car y to the speed of a car x (speed measured in mph).
   (a) Enter this data into R and list the commands used.
   (b) A useful model for this data would be

$$y = \alpha x + \beta x^2 \tag{4.1}$$

where the α term in Eq. (4.1) is related to the reaction time of the driver and the β term in (4.1) is a quadratic term linked to the physics of stopping and the so-called 'uvast' equations. Fit the regression model suggested by Eq. (4.1) omitting the intercept term.

(c) Using the model fitted in part (b), estimate the stopping distance for speeds of 10, 80, 90 and 100 mph.

(d) For the estimates in part (c), use R to construct a 95% prediction interval for each of these four speeds: 10, 80, 90 and 100 mph. What is the interpretation of the prediction intervals in this case?

(e) How is the process of choosing a regression model in this case different from other regression examples that you might see in accounting and finance?

3 *Politics.* The following regression model is to be fitted to estimate the percentage of parliamentary seats won by party X as a function of the share of the vote of two parties X and Y:

$$f(x, y) = \alpha_0 + \alpha_1 x + \alpha_2 y + \beta_1 x^2 + \beta_2 xy + \beta_3 y^2 \tag{4.2}$$

(a) Fry and Burke (2020) suggest the following constraints shown in Eq. (4.3) below. Explain where these constraints come from.

$$f(0, y) = 0 \text{ and } f(1, 0) = 1 \tag{4.3}$$

(b) Explain why these constraints may represent an over-simplification in relation to UK parliamentary elections.

(c) Use the constraints in Eq. (4.3) to suggest a simplified way of fitting the regression equation shown in Eq. (4.2).

4 *Event study.* Following on from a related analysis in Alam et al. (2020), it is of interest to try to pinpoint the effect of the coronavirus pandemic on stock prices. The data in the file **eventstudy.txt** lists values of the market index (FTSE 100), the transportation index and food sector index. We want to see whether the national lockdown issued on 23 March 2020 had a detectable impact upon prices.

(a) Enter this data into R using the following commands:
```
eventstudy<-read.table("E:eventstudy.txt")
market<-eventstudy[,4]
transportation<-eventstudy[,5]
food<-eventstudy[,6]
```

(b) Put the data into chronological order using the command **rev**.

(c) Calculate the log-returns (first differences of the log-price) for the market index, the transportation sector index and the food sector index.

(d) Using data up to and including the date of the lockdown, fit the following regression models.

$$\text{transportation returns} = \beta_0 + \beta_1 \text{market returns}$$
$$\text{food returns} = \gamma_0 + \gamma_1 \text{market returns} \tag{4.4}$$

(e) Using market returns data after 23 March, calculate the forecast errors for each of the regression models fitted in part (d).

(f) Using a *t*-test, test the null hypothesis that the mean of the forecast errors computed in part (e) is equal to zero.

5 *General-purpose regression for dissertation-type problems*. The data in the file **genreg.txt** relates three separate measures of performance (stock market log-returns, return on assets, return on equity) to two variables describing the capital structure (short term debt to total assets; debt to equity ratio) for large firms listed on the FTSE 100.

(a) Using the following commands, enter this data into R.

```
genreg<-read.table("E:genreg.txt")
stockreturn<-genreg[,1]
roa<-genreg[,2]
roe<-genreg[,3]
shorttermdebt<-genreg[,4]
debttoequity<-genreg[,5]
```

(b) Explain why it might be of interest to use three separate measures of performance here.

(c) Fit the model

$$\begin{aligned}\text{performance} = \beta_1 + \beta_2\text{short term debt to total assets} \\ + \beta_3\text{debt to equity ratio} \end{aligned} \tag{4.5}$$

From the regression models in Eq. (4.5), is there any evidence that capital structure affects a firm's performance?

(d) Give examples of further robustness checks that could easily be employed with this type of analysis.

4.7 Solutions

1 n/a

2 The estimated values are shown in the first column of the solution to part (d) below.

(a) ```
x<-c(20, 30, 40, 50, 60, 70)
y<-c(12, 23, 36, 53, 73, 96)
```

(b)  ```
x2<-x2*x2
a.lm<-lm(y~x+x2-1)
summary(a.lm)
```
Coefficients:
Estimate Std error t-value Pr(>|t|)
x 0.2912565 0.0092164 31.60 5.98e-06 ***
x2 0.0154170 0.0001589 97.01 6.77e-08 ***

(c) ```
newdata<-data.frame(x=c(10, 80, 90, 100),
x2=c(10*10, 80*80, 90*90, 100*100))
predict(a.lm, newdata, interval="predict")
```
```

```
fit lwr upr
1 4.454268 3.705926 5.202611
2 121.969512 120.765579 123.173446
3 151.091028 149.477961 152.704094
4 183.295949 181.151822 185.440077
```
The future observation will lie in the constructed prediction interval with probability 0.95.

(d) Any sensible interpretation should suffice here. You are unlikely to come across many regression models where an intercept term is not appropriate or where there is such a strong theoretical underpinning for a regression model. The dataset in this question is also unusually small and unusually simple.

3 (a) The first constraint suggests that, in the extreme case, the party receives no votes so they will simultaneously win no seats. The second constraint suggests that, in the extreme case, the party receives 100% of the share of the vote so they should win all the contested seats.

(b) The major UK parties do not currently contest seats in Northern Ireland, suggesting an alternative upper limit in Eq. (4.3).

(c) After imposing the constraints in Eq. (4.3), it follows that Eq. (4.2) reduces to

$$f(x, y) = x^2 + \alpha_1(x - x^2) + \beta_2 xy \qquad (4.6)$$

Equation (4.6) can thus be fitted as a regression model with an offset term in x^2 (which imposes the constraint that the coefficient of x^2 is equal to one) and no intercept term.

4 (a) n/a

(b) Via the command **rev** put into chronological order using
```
market<-rev(market)
transportation<-rev(transportation)
food<-rev(food)
```

(c) Since all three vectors should be of the same length, the logreturns, in this instance, can be calculated using
```
length(market)
[1] 131
marketreturns<-log(market[-1])-log(market[-131])
transportationreturns<-log(transportation[-1])
-log(transportation[-131])
foodreturns<-log(food[-1])-log(food[-131])
```

(d) To exclude the post-lockdown data, we have to exclude the last nine observations. Fit the regression models using
```
length(foodreturns)
[1] 130
transport.lm<-lm(transportationreturns[1:121]~
marketreturns[1:121])
food.lm<-lm(foodreturns[1:121]~marketreturns[1:121])
```

(e) Using the above definitions, the forecast errors can be computed in R using

```
transporterror<-transportationreturns[122:130]
-transport.lm$coef[1]
-transport.lm$coef[2]*marketreturns[122:130]
fooderror<-foodreturns[122:130]-food.lm$coef[1]
-food.lm$coef[2]*marketreturns[122:130]
```

(f) Using t.test(transporterror) and t.test(fooderror) gives no evidence ($p = 0.761$ and $p = 0.3616$, respectively) of a detectable effect of the national lockdown on stock prices over the next fortnight.

5 (a) n/a.

(b) Set up in this way, the problem provides a natural comparison between one financial-based measure of performance versus two accounting-based measures of performance. In project work, look for opportunities to make comparisons like this to give you more to analyse and more to ultimately write about.

(c) Firstly, starting with a financial measure, we find no evidence of a relationship between capital structure and firm performance.

```
finl.lm<-lm(stockreturn~shorttermdebt+debttoequity)
summary(finl.lm)
Coefficients:
Estimate Std error t-value Pr(>|t|)
(Intercept) -0.065550 0.073127 -0.896 0.375
shorttermdebt 1.149935 1.240575 0.927 0.359
debttoequity -0.009084 0.013628 -0.667 0.508
```

Secondly, with an accounting measure, return on assets, we find some evidence of a relationship between capital structure and firm performance. This suggests that as the short term debt to total assets increases, the return on assets increases.

```
accl.lm<-lm(roa~shorttermdebt+debttoequity)
summary(accl.lm)
Coefficients:
Estimate Std error t-value Pr(>|t|)
(Intercept) 0.066754 0.020322 3.285 0.00193 **
shorttermdebt 0.714614 0.344758 2.073 0.04370 *
debttoequity -0.003858 0.003787 -1.019 0.31356
```

We seek to verify these findings by looking at another accounting-based measure of firm performance – namely, the return on equity. In this case, results give no evidence of a relationship between capital structure and firm performance.

acc2.lm<-lm(roe~shorttermdebt+debttoequity)
summary(acc2.lm)
Coefficients:
Estimate Std error t-value Pr(>ltl)
(Intercept) 0.192934 0.055887 3.452 0.00119 **
shorttermdebt 1.024488 0.948105 1.081 0.28540
debttoequity -0.008012 0.010415 -0.769 0.44559

(d) Further robustness checks that could be easily employed in dissertations include using data from different years and/or comparing
different-sized firms, e.g. larger FTSE 100 listed firms versus smaller
FTSE 250 listed firms.

5 Regression I: ESS and modelling assumptions

5.1 The extra sum of squares principle

In the last chapter, we saw that R automatically produces an F-statistic to test the overall level of fit. In formal terms, we are comparing the following models:

Model 0

$$Y_i = \beta_1 + u_i$$

Model 1

$$Y_i = \beta_1 + \beta_2 X_{2,i} + \beta_3 X_{3,i} + \dots + \beta_p X_{p,i} + u_i$$

This basic idea can be greatly expanded upon. There are two main statistical tests that are encountered in early regression problems:

1 t-**test**
   This tests the significance of individual parameters.
2 F-**test**
   This tests the joint significance of multiple parameters.

We can expand the scenario above to a more general setting with different nested models. That is, we test the following:

Model 0

$$Y_i = \beta_1 + \beta_2 X_{2,i} + \dots + \beta_{p-m} X_{p-m,i} + u_i$$

Model 1

$$Y_i = \beta_1 + \beta_2 X_{2,i} + \dots + \beta_{p-m} X_{p-m,i} + \beta_{p-m+1} X_{p-m+1,i} + \dots + \beta_p X_{p,i} + u_i$$

The overall aim is to test whether the extra variation in the data that Model 1 explains – the extra sum of squares – is statistically significant. These models are known as nested since if $\beta_{p-m+1} = \ldots = \beta_p$, then the two models are the same. Model 0 thus 'sits inside' Model 1. Using the extra sum of squares principle, comparing Model 0 with Model 1 is equivalent to testing the m **linear** restrictions

$$\beta_{p-m+1} = \beta_{p-m+2} = \ldots = \beta_p = 0 \tag{5.1}$$

In terms of formal mathematics (Bingham and Fry 2010, Chapter 6), it is possible to show that you can use the same approach to test more general **linear constraints**. There is potentially some difficult mathematics involving Lagrange multipliers, but the underlying ideas remain relatively simple. Equation (5.1) gives the simplest linear restriction, but other hypotheses may be possible, e.g.

$$\text{Model 0}: \quad Y_i = \beta_1 + \beta_2 X_{2,i} + \beta_2 X_{3,i} + u_i$$
$$\text{Model 1}: \quad Y_i = \beta_1 + \beta_2 X_{2,i} + \beta_3 X_{3,i} + u_i$$

Whilst this would be a non-standard alternative specification, the same basic testing procedure would apply in each case. The basic question remains 'Is the extra sum of squares or variation in the data explained by the larger (unconstrained) model statistically significant?' The most intuitive construction of the F-statistic is as follows:

$$F = \frac{\frac{\text{difference in residual SS}}{\text{difference in residual df}}}{\frac{\text{residual SS (larger model)}}{\text{residual df (larger model)}}}$$

$$F = \frac{\frac{\text{difference in residual SS}}{m}}{\frac{\text{residual SS (larger model)}}{n-p}} \tag{5.2}$$

As discussed in the previous chapter, the F-statistic can in turn be written in terms of the R^2 statistic. This then leads to further simplification of the formula in Eq. (5.2):

$$F = \frac{\frac{\text{difference in residual SS}}{m}}{\frac{\text{residual SS (larger model)}}{n-p}}$$

$$F = \frac{\frac{TSS(R_1^2 - R_0^2)}{m}}{\frac{TSS(1 - R_1^2)}{n-p}} = \frac{\frac{R_1^2 - R_0^2}{m}}{\frac{1 - R_1^2}{n-p}} \sim F_{m,n-p} \tag{5.3}$$

This can equivalently be written in words as

$$F = \frac{\frac{\text{difference in } R^2}{m}}{\frac{1 - R^2(\text{larger model})}{n-p}}. \tag{5.4}$$

Equations (5.3) and (5.4) are equivalent, although Eq. (5.4) may be the easier way to do this. Using these formula, the F-test for overall significance (considered in the previous chapter and computed by default in R) can be constructed as follows. In this case:

Model 0

$$Y_i = \beta_1 + u_i$$

Model 1

$$Y_i = \beta_1 + \beta_2 X_{2,i} + \beta_3 X_{3,i} + \dots + \beta_p X_{p,i} + u_i$$

$$F = \frac{\frac{\text{difference in residual SS}}{m}}{\frac{\text{residual SS (larger model)}}{n-p}} = \frac{\frac{TSS(R^2-0)}{p-1}}{\frac{TSS(1-R^2)}{n-p}} = \frac{\frac{R^2}{p-1}}{\frac{1-R^2}{n-p}} \sim F_{p-1,n-p}$$

This gives the same formula as given in the previous chapter but shows that this fits into a much more general way of thinking – the extra sum of squares principle.

5.2   F-tests and mathematical formulae

In terms of nested models, the F-test is set up so that Model 0 has m constraints or, equivalently, m fewer parameters to estimate. Model 1 is larger and has no parameter constraints. The obvious easy case to consider is

Model 0: $Y_i = \beta_1 + \beta_2 X_{2,i} + \dots + \beta_{p-m} X_{p-m,i} + u_i$
Model 1: $Y_i = \beta_1 + \beta_2 X_{2,i} + \dots + \beta_{p-m} X_{p-m,i} + \dots + \beta_p X_{p,i} + u_i$

However, more complicated examples exist, e.g.

Model 0: $Y_i = \beta_1 + \beta_2 X_{2,i} + \beta_2 X_{3,i} + u_i$
Model 1: $Y_i = \beta_1 + \beta_2 X_{2,i} + \beta_3 X_{3,i} + u_i$

In this second equation, we then have $m = 1$ constraint. The same mathematical and statistical approach applies in each case – however superficially different these two comparisons may at first appear.

5.3 Examples

We will illustrate the F-test and the extra sum of squares principle with two examples:

1 F-test for joint significance
2 F-test in polynomial regression

5.3.1 *F*-test in multiple regression

To show you how to interpret the results from a multiple linear regression model, we will use an example from the classical Longley dataset. Our overall aim is to explain the number of employed people in the US in terms of:

1 X_2, GNP
2 X_3, the number of unemployed
3 X_4, the unemployment rate
4 X_5, the 'non-institutionalized' population over the age of 14
5 X_6, the yearly trend.

Based on the results of the last chapter, want to see whether BOTH X_2 and X_5 can be excluded from the model. The data is in the file **longley.txt** and can be read into R as follows:

```
longley<-read.table("E:longley.txt")
x2<-longley[,1]
x3<-longley[,2]
x4<-longley[,3]
x5<-longley[,4]
x6<-longley[,5]
y<-longley[,6]
```

Once the data has been entered into R, fit the full unconstrained model using

```
a.lm<-lm(y~x2+x3+x4+x5+x6)
```

Then fit the constrained model simply by not including x_2 and x_5 in the above and using a different name for the constructed regression model.

```
b.lm<-lm(y~x3+x4+x6)
```

The F-test using the extra sum of squares principle can then be performed using the command **anova**:

```
anova(a.lm, b.lm, test="F")
```

The results produced by R are shown below:

```
anova(a.lm, b.lm, test="F")
Model 1: y ~ x2 + x3 + x4 + x5 + x6
Model 2: y ~ x3 + x4 + x6
Res.Df RSS Df Sum of Sq F Pr(>F)
1 10 0.83935
2 12 1.32336 -2 -0.48401 2.8833 0.1026
```

Since the result is non-significant ($p = 0.1026 > 0.05$) this gives statistical evidence that X_2 and X_5 can be excluded from the model. Using summary(a.lm) and summary(b.lm) tells you that, in each case, the R^2 values are 0.9955 and 0.9928. Similarly, the residual degrees of freedom are 10 and 12, respectively. The F-statistic can hence be reconstructed as

$$F = \frac{\frac{\text{difference in } R^2}{m}}{\frac{1-R^2(\text{larger model})}{n-p}} = \frac{\frac{0.9955-0.9928}{2}}{\frac{1-0.9955}{10}}$$

$$F = \frac{0.00135}{0.00045} = 3$$

Note that, in this case, heavy rounding errors mean that this deviates substantially from the 'exact' value of 2.8833 calculated by R above. However, this is how the F-test can be constructed from first principles.

5.3.2 F-test in polynomial regression

Data sourced from a popular newspaper (shown in Table 5.1) gives the percentage of divorces caused by adultery as a function per year of marriage. The original analysis claimed that the risk of divorce peaks at year 2 and then decreases thereafter. But is this conclusion misleading? Healthy scepticism is perhaps one of the most important professional skills in the era of Big Data? In response to the original analysis, we wanted to test whether a quadratic model offers a better fit than a straight-line model to this data. This example is also interesting as it shows that a non-linear model in X can still be treated as a linear regression model because it remains linear in the regression coefficients β. This is because the quadratic regression model can be simply written as

$$y_i = \beta_1 + \beta_2 x_i + \beta_3 x_i^2 + u_i$$

Table 5.1 Data on divorces caused by adultery

Year	1	2	3	4	5	6	7
%	3.51	9.50	8.91	9.35	8.18	6.43	5.31
Year	8	9	10	15	20	25	30
%	5.07	3.65	3.80	2.83	1.51	1.27	0.49

Analysis in R proceeds as follows. To enter the data into R use
year<-c(1, 2, 3, 4, 5, 6,7, 8, 9, 10, 15, 20, 25, 30)
percent<-c(3.51, 9.5, 8.91, 9.35, 8.18, 6.43, 5.31, 5.07, 3.65, 3.8, 2.83, 1.51, 1.27, 0.49)
Then introduce a squared term for year.

```
yearsq<-year∧2
```
We can begin by plotting the data in R.
```
plot(year, percent, xlab="Year", ylab="% divorces due to adultery")
```

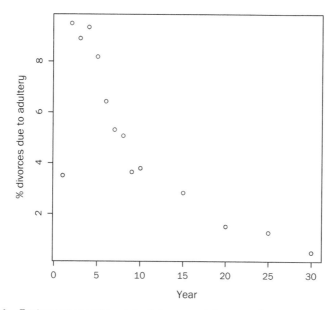

Figure 5.1 Exploratory scatter plot of divorces data example

The results are shown in Fig. 5.1. There is a suggestion that the divorce rate is unusually low in the first year and then decreases steadily over time.

In R, we can fit a linear regression model followed by a quadratic regression model. Results for the quadratic regression model give no evidence ($p = 0.3943 > 0.05$) that the quadratic term is needed in the model. The suggestion is that the original analysis in the newspaper is probably mistaken.
```
a.lm<-lm(percent~year)
b.lm<-lm(percent~year+yearsq)
summary(b.lm)
```

```
Coefficients:
Estimate Std error t-value Pr(>|t|)
(Intercept) 8.751048 1.258038 6.956 2.4e-05 ***
year -0.482252 0.235701 -2.046 0.0654 .
yearsq 0.006794 0.007663 0.887 0.3943
```

We can also test for model improvement using an F-test. We should get the same answer as in the previous t-test. Indeed, results obtained below give no evidence ($p = 0.3943 > 0.05$) that the quadratic term is needed in the model.

anova(a.lm, b.lm, test="F")
anova(a.glm, b.glm, test="F")
Model 1: percent ~ year
Model 2: percent ~ year + yearsq
Resid. Df Resid. Dev Df Deviance F Pr(>F)
1 12 42.375
2 11 39.549 1 2.826 0.786 0.3943

We can summarize the final linear model fitted using summary(a.lm). The results obtained are shown below. The interpretation of these results is as follows. The coefficient of the year is negative and statistically significant ($p = 0.000442 < 0.05$.) As the number of years of marriage increases, the percentage of divorces caused by adultery decreases. There is some suggestion that the newspaper data is misleading. It is probably safer to say that the divorce rate caused by adultery generally decreases over time but is unusually low in the first year.

Estimate Std error t-value Pr(>|t|)
(Intercept) 7.88575 0.78667 10.024 3.49e-07 ***
year -0.27993 0.05846 -4.788 0.000442 ***

5.4 Regression modelling assumptions

The classical linear regression model is

$$Y_i = \beta_1 + \beta_2 X_{2,i} + \beta_3 X_{3,i} + \ldots + \beta_p X_{p,i} + u_i \qquad (5.5)$$

Assumptions

1 The model is linear in the parameters β.
2 The X variables are independent of the error term.
3 The disturbance has zero mean: $E[u_i] = 0$.
4 There is homoscedasticity or constant residual variance: $\text{Var}(u_i) = \sigma^2$.
5 The u_i are normally distributed.
6 The disturbances are uncorrelated.
7 $n > p$.
8 There is no exact linear relationship between any pair of X variables.
9 There is no specification bias – the model is correctly specified.

This is not quite the same list as used in Gujarati and Porter (2009). This is symptomatic of wider problems with econometric textbooks in that they are sometimes not very clear about the modelling assumptions made and tend to emphasize applications. Whilst understandable, this may lead to significant problems when undertaking more advanced research beyond the scope of this book.

Responses to failures in regression modelling assumptions include the following.

1 This should be easy to see from the specification of the model.
2 This may be violated in some time-series problems – this is largely outside the scope of this book but is discussed to some extent in Chapter 6 and Chapter 11.
3 The fitted residuals will automatically have a zero mean.
4 See later in this chapter.
5 This may be remedied to some extent by trying to model log y instead of y.
6 See Chapter 6.
7 $n < p$ occurs, e.g. in certain specialized bioinformatics and computer science problems, but this is outside the scope of this book.
8 See Chapter 7.
9 This is outside the scope of the course – but it may be solved to some extent if the models used are derived from an underlying theory or literature review.

For the remainder of this chapter, we will discuss heteroscedasticity. For the classical linear regression model shown in Eq. (5.5), it is assumed that, for each observation

$$\text{Var}(u_i) = \sigma^2 \text{ for all } i \tag{5.6}$$

Equation (5.6), therefore, defines homoscedasticity. If Eq. (5.6) does not apply for all i then instead we have heteroscedasticity. Now the basic techniques of applied statistics are largely mechanical in nature:

1 R^2
2 F-statistic
3 t-tests

These alone may be enough to pass an exam – particularly if your lecturer is benevolent or not very cunning! However, it is important to realize that it is often more difficult to use such statistical methods well in applied project work. Statistics requires critical thinking as well as mechanical calculations – and most of the calculations are done by computer these days! As part of this, heteroscedasticity is one very commonly encountered problem.

It is important to realize that the underlying mathematics of the classical linear regression model assumes that we have homoscedasticity as shown in Eq. (5.6). If this assumption does not hold, then the maths does not work! If we have heteroscedasticity and not homoscedasticity, then confidence intervals, hypothesis tests, F-tests etc. all break down and are liable to produce untrustworthy results. For instance, the parameter estimates obtained by ordinary least squares (OLS) remain unbiased but are no longer optimal. In order to detect heteroscedasticity there are the following formal tests:

1 Goldfeld–Quant test
2 White's test for heteroscedasticity

However, it is often more important to just perform graphical checks which can be simpler and more robust. You can show mathematically (Bingham and Fry 2010, Chapter 3) that if a model is correctly specified, then the residuals and the fitted values should be independent. You can judge heteroscedasticity by plotting residuals against fitted values or squared residuals against fitted values. Alhough this is often overlooked, plotting squared residuals may also give a better indication about how the residual variance changes.

5.5 Graphical detection of heteroscedasticity

Regression residuals can be analysed in R as follows. In the previous chapter, we fitted the following regression model.
a.lm<-lm(realgoldprice~realstockprice)
summary(a.lm)
Having run these commands, we can then use the named regression model to obtain a residual series as follows.
residuals<-a.lm$resid
We can then use, e.g. hist(residuals) or ts.plot(residuals) to obtain, e.g. a histogram or a time-series plot of the residuals, as appropriate. The fitted values from a regression model can similarly be obtained using
fitted<-a.lm$fitted

Graphical tests of residuals are less precise than some of the mathematical techniques we have discussed in previous chapters. There are more interesting things in life and in mathematics and statistics, but graphical tests of residuals are deceptively important in applied project work. Because the area is so widely studied, there are a number of commonly encountered patterns that it is often important to look out for. These graphs are not necessarily very easy to interpret (this is discussed at length in the excellent book on applied regression by Draper and Smith (1998)). However, these graphs are easy to produce using modern software and so are perhaps over-discussed.

Draper and Smith (1998) outline a number of patterns that are commonly encountered. In these special cases, we can transform the data to avoid the problem of heteroscedasticity.

1 No systematic pattern suggesting no heteroscedasticity – this is the ideal scenario that we want to happen as this corresponds to the constant variance or homoscedasticity assumption of the classical linear model
2 Funnelling out of residuals
3 Funnelling in of residuals
4 Linear – error variance proportional to $\hat{Y}_i$
5 Quadratic – error variance proportional to $\hat{Y}_i^2$
6 Quadratic – error variance proportional to $\hat{Y}_i^{\frac{1}{2}}$

Examples of approximate funnelling in and funnelling out of residuals are shown in Figs 5.2–5.3.

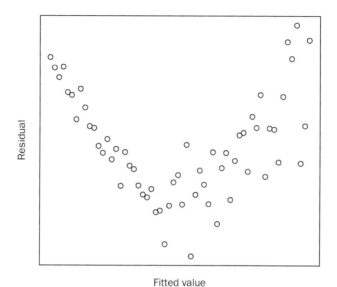

Figure 5.2   Graph showing approximate funnelling out of residuals

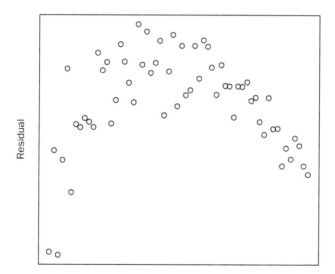

Figure 5.3   Graph showing approximate funnelling in of residuals

In the imperfect cases 2–6 identified by Draper and Smith (1998), there are the following suggested remedies.

1 n/a
2 Fit a model for log y or $\sqrt{y}$. In general terms, fitting a model for log y may often help to reduce problems with heteroscedasticity.
3 Fit a model for y^2.
4 Fit a model for $\sqrt{y}$.
5 Fit a model for log y.
6 Fit a model for log y.

It is also possible that heteroscedasticity may be associated with some of the X-variables. Usually, as one of the X-variables increases, the residual variance increases. To investigate this, plot the residuals or squared residuals against X instead of the fitted values in the above. Gujarati and Porter (2009) discuss the following two cases of heteroscedasticity.

1 The error variance is proportional to X_i^2

$$E[u_i^2] \approx \sigma^2 X_i^2$$

2 The error variance is proportional to X_i

$$E[u_i^2] \approx \sigma^2 X_i$$

In each case, divide through by the square root of the offending X-term to obtain an error variable with a constant variance.

1 Error variance proportional to X_i^2. Start with the model

$$Y_i = \beta_1 + \beta_2 X_{2,i} + u_i$$

Divide through by X_i

$$\frac{Y_i}{X_i} = \frac{\beta_1}{X_i} + \beta_2 + \frac{u_i}{X_i} \tag{5.7}$$

Estimate Eq. (5.7) by the usual OLS regression approach.
2 Error variance proportional to X_i. Start with the model

$$Y_i = \beta_1 + \beta_2 X_{2,i} + u_i$$

Divide through by $\sqrt{X_i}$

$$\frac{Y_i}{\sqrt{X_i}} = \frac{\beta_1}{\sqrt{X_i}} + \beta_2 \sqrt{X_i} + \frac{u_i}{\sqrt{X_i}} \tag{5.8}$$

Estimate Eq. (5.8) by the usual OLS regression approach.

In rare circumstances, we may encounter heteroscedasticity and **know** the exact form of the heteroscedasticity that occurs. The only example of this that we have seen is using a weighted least squares approach to estimate a generalized linear model. Since generalized linear models can now be fitted using specialist modern software, there is no need to use an approximate approach based on weighted least squares. Consequently, weighted least squares arguably has limited importance for modern applied statistics. However, weighted least squares may still have foundational importance in terms of getting people to think carefully about what the right mean and variance functions might be.

5.6 Numerical testing of heteroscedasticity

Numerical tests for heteroscedasticity include:

1 Goldfeld–Quandt test
2 White's general heteroscedasticity test

As we saw above, often the heteroscedastic variance σ_i^2 increases as one of the X-variables increases. One commonly encountered case that is useful in applications is

$$\text{Var}(u_i) = \sigma^2 X_i^2 \tag{5.9}$$

Equation (5.9) is the hypothesis tested by the Goldfeld–Quandt test

$$H_0 : \quad \text{Var}(u_i) = \sigma^2$$
$$H_1 : \quad \text{Var}(u_i) = \sigma^2 X_i^2$$

As discussed in Chapter 11 of Gujarati and Porter (2009), the basic procedure behind the Goldfeld–Quandt test is as follows.

1 Order or rank the observations according to the values of the X_i from smallest to largest.
2 Omit the central c observations and divide the sample into two groups of size $\dfrac{n-c}{2}$.
3 Fit separate OLS regressions to each segment.
4 Form the statistic

$$\lambda = \frac{\frac{RSS_2}{df}}{\frac{RSS_1}{df}} = \frac{RSS_2}{RSS_1}$$

where RSS_1 = residual SS for the first segment and RSS_2 = residual SS for the second segment. Under the null hypothesis of homoscedasticity,

$$\lambda = \frac{RSS_2}{RSS_1} \sim F_{\frac{n-c-2p}{2}, \frac{n-c-2p}{2}}$$

Pragmatic empirical experience suggests that, for $n = 30$, take $c = 4$, and if $n = 60$, take $c = 10$.

An alternative to the above is White's general heteroscedasticity test (see Gujarati and Porter (2009), Chapter 11). Suppose we want to fit the regression model

$$Y_i = \beta_1 + \beta_2 X_{2,i} + \beta_3 X_{3,i} + u_i \tag{5.10}$$

1. Estimate Eq. (5.10) and obtain the residuals $\hat{u}_i$.
2. Fit the auxiliary regression

$$u_i^2 = \alpha_1 + \alpha_2 X_{2,i} + \alpha_3 X_{3,i} + \alpha_4 X_{2,i}^2 + \alpha_5 X_{3,i}^2 + \alpha_6 X_{2,i} X_{3,i} + v_i \tag{5.11}$$

Note that the form of Eq. (5.11) comes from

$$\left(1 + X_{2,i} + X_{3,i}\right)^2$$

3. Compare the R^2 value for the auxiliary regression (5.10) using

$$nR^2 \sim \chi^2_{\text{residual d.f. from Eq. (5.10)}} \tag{5.12}$$

4. If the value for Eq. (5.12) is significant, then we have evidence for heteroscedasticity.

What happens if we find evidence for heteroscedasticity? Statistics in practical project work is not easy and there are not necessarily any 'right' answers. If evidence is found for heteroscedasticity, the easiest thing to do is use White's formula for heteroscedasticity-consistent variance and estimated standard errors (see below). This typically results in larger estimated standard errors than the OLS estimates and so gives a more robust approach to assessing statistical significance than OLS.

5.7 Heteroscedasticity-consistent standard errors

Identification of heteroscedasticity is perhaps most appropriately remedied by using standard errors which are robust to heteroscedasticity, or just **robust standard errors**. In cases where there is no heteroscedasticity, robust standard errors will be the same as OLS standard errors. As a result, robust standard errors can often be regarded as the only appropriate standard errors to report. One caveat is that this methodology relies on a large sample.

To carry out this calculation in R, install and load the lmtest and sandwich packages. These packages enable you to specify the variance–covariance matrix and the specific matrix which enables you to generate the robust standard errors, respectively.

```
install.packages("lmtest")
install.packages("sandwich")
library(lmtest)
library(sandwich)
```

To generate heteroscedasticity-consistent standard errors use the command
coeftest(model, vcov = vcovHC(model, type = "HC0"))

In the above, the term model refers to a lm object. Further, we specify type = "HC0" which determines the appropriate matrix to generate robust standard errors.

5.8 Tutorial exercises

1 *Multiple regression.* Using the example in Chapter 4, apply the extra sum of squares principle to see if the model without x_5 will suffice. That is, test the model

$$y = \beta_1 + \beta_2 X_2 + \beta_3 X_3 + \beta_4 X_4 + \beta_6 X_6 + u_t$$

against the unconstrained model

$$y = \beta_1 + \beta_2 X_2 + \beta_3 X_3 + \beta_4 X_4 + \beta_5 X_5 + \beta_6 X_6 + u_t$$

Repeat the R calculations by hand.

2 The data in the table below show the number of full-time equivalent hospital staff members (y) against the number of beds x.

(a) Enter the data into R using the following commands.
beds<-c(23, 29, 29, 35, 42, 46, 50, 54, 64, 66, 76, 78)
ftes<-c(69, 95, 102, 118, 126, 125, 138, 178, 156, 184, 176, 225)

(b) Fit a regression model for y against x.

(c) Using graphical tests, determine whether there is there any evidence for heteroscedasticity for the regression model fitted in part (b).

(d) Interpreting the residual plot in part (c) as evidence of funnelling in of residuals, fit a regression model for y^2.

(e) Suppose that the residual variance increases with the value of x. A model that reproduces this effect can be constructed using

$$y = \beta_1 + \beta_2 x + x u_t \tag{5.13}$$

Table 5.2 Dataset for Question 2

Hospital	Number of beds	FTE
	x	y
1	23	69
2	29	95
3	29	102
4	35	118
5	42	126
6	46	125
7	50	138
8	54	178
9	64	156
10	66	184
11	76	176
12	78	225

Show how the model in Eq. (5.13) can be fitted using OLS regression and fit this model in R.

(f) Construct an estimate and a 95% prediction interval for a future observation with 50 beds for each of the regression models constructed in parts (b), (d) and (e). Do similar models lead to similar estimates in this case?

3 Using the data below, investigate the impact of average student expenditure (x) against test score outcomes (y).
(a) Load the data into R from the **textScore.txt** file.
(b) Plot the average student expenditure against the average test score.
(c) Fit a regression model of the form

$$testscr_i = b_0 + b_1 * expnstu_i + u_i$$

and label the model **test.model**
(d) Provide a summary of the regression model and an economic interpretation of the primary result.
(e) Perform a graphical test for heteroscedasticity on the model **test.model**
(f) Using the **lmtest** package, conduct the Breusch–Pagan test against heteroscedasticity.

4 Using the data in the previous question, fit a regression model using the robust standard errors procedure outlined in Chapter 5.7.

5 (a) Load the data contained within gdpLifeExpectancy.txt into your R console.

(b) Develop a regression model which explains the impact of GDP per capita on life expectancy.

(c) Using the tests in this chapter, determine whether the data is heteroscedastic.

(d) Compare the OLS standard errors with the robust standard errors.

(e) What do the regression results suggest about the impact of GDP per capita on life expectancy?

5.9 Solutions

1 Enter the data into R using
longley<-read.table("E:longley.txt")
x2<-longley[,1]
x3<-longley[,2]
x4<-longley[,3]
x5<-longley[,4]
x6<-longley[,5]
y<-longley[,6]
Fit the models and perform the extra sum of squares test using
full.lm<-lm(y~x2+x3+x4+x5+x6)
constrained.lm<-lm(y~x2+x3+x4+x6)
anova(full.lm, constrained.lm, test="F")
Res.Df RSS Df Sum of Sq F Pr(>F)
1 10 0.83935
2 11 0.85868 -1 -0.019332 0.2303 0.6416

The results thus present no evidence ($p = 0.6416 > 0.05$) that the full unconstrained model is needed in order to explain this data. This F-statistic calculation can be constructed as follows. Using summary(full.lm) and summary(constrained.lm), we can see that the R^2 value of the full model is 0.9955 with 10 residual degrees of freedom and the R^2 value of the constrained model is 0.9954 with 11 residual degrees of freedom. The F-statistic can thus be constructed as

$$F = \frac{\Delta R^2}{\Delta \text{ in residual d.f.}} \times \frac{\text{residual d.f. (larger model)}}{1 - R^2 \text{ (larger model)}}$$
$$= \frac{0.0001}{1} \times \frac{10}{1 - 0.9955} = \frac{0.001}{0.0045} = 0.222$$

The calculation serves as a salutary example of just how large a seemingly innocuous rounding error can be in practical calculations.

2 (b) The regression model can be fitted using
a.lm<-lm(ftes~beds)
summary(a.lm)
Coefficients:
Estimate Std error t-value Pr(>Itl)
(Intercept) 30.9125 13.2542 2.332 0.0419 *
beds 2.2315 0.2526 8.835 4.89e-06 ***

Signif. codes: 0 '***' 0.001 '**' 0.01 '*' 0.05 '.' 0.1 ' ' I
Residual standard error: 15.65 on 10 degrees of freedom
Multiple R-squared: 0.8864, Adjusted R-squared: 0.8751
F-statistic: 78.05 on 1 and 10 DF, p-value: 4.886e-06

(c) The residual plot can be created using
plot(a.lm$fitted, a.lm$resid, xlab="Fitted values", ylab"Residuals")

The graph produced is shown in Fig. 5.4.

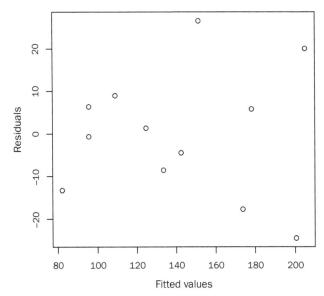

Figure 5.4 Plot of residuals against fitted values. There is some suggestion of funnelling in of residuals although the effect remains unclear in the light of the small sample size

(d) The regression can be fitted using
```
y2<-ftes^2
b.lm<-lm(y2~beds)
summary(b.lm)
```
Coefficients:
Estimate Std error t-value Pr(>|t|)
(Intercept) -10072.2 4643.9 -2.169 0.0553 .
beds 643.6 88.5 7.272 2.69e-05 ***

Signif. codes: 0 '***' 0.001 '**' 0.01 '*' 0.05 '.' 0.1 ' ' I
Residual standard error: 5483 on 10 degrees of freedom
Multiple R-squared: 0.841, Adjusted R-squared: 0.8251
F-statistic: 52.89 on 1 and 10 DF, p-value: 2.687e-05

(e) In this case, by dividing through by x gives

$$y = \beta_1 + \beta_x + xu_t; \; y/x = \frac{\beta_1}{x} + \beta_2 + u_t$$

Fit this model in R as follows:
```
y3<-ftes/beds
xinv<-1/beds
c.lm<-lm(y3~xinv)
summary(c.lm)
```
Coefficients:
Estimate Std error t-value Pr(>|t|)
(Intercept) 2.3936 0.2368 10.109 1.44e-06 ***
xinv 23.5641 9.3604 2.517 0.0305 *

Signif. codes: 0 '***' 0.001 '**' 0.01 '*' 0.05 '.' 0.1 ' ' I
Residual standard error: 0.3046 on 10 degrees of freedom
Multiple R-squared: 0.3879, Adjusted R-squared: 0.3267
F-statistic: 6.337 on 1 and 10 DF, p-value: 0.03052

(f) For the first example with a regression of y against x, the prediction interval can be obtained using R as follows:
```
newdata1=data.frame(beds=50)
predict(a.lm, newdata1, interval="predict")
```
fit lwr upr
1 142.4877 106.1936 178.7817
For the second example with a regression of y^2 against x, the prediction interval can be obtained using R as follows:

```
newdata2=data.frame(beds=50)
predict(b.lm, newdata2, interval"predict")
fit lwr upr
1 22107.06 9390.611 34823.5
sqrt(22107.06)
[1] 148.6844
sqrt(9390.611)
[1] 96.90516
sqrt(34823.5)
[1] 186.6106
```

For the third example with a regression of y/x against $1/x$, the prediction interval can be obtained using R as follows:

```
newdata3=data.frame(xinv=1/50)
predict(c.lm, newdata3, interval="predict")
fit lwr upr
1 2.864845 2.15466 3.57503
> 2.864845*50
[1] 143.2422
> 2.15466*50
[1] 107.733
> 3.57503*50
[1] 178.7515
```

The interpretation is a little unclear. Usually, similar models should all lead to roughly similar conclusions if they have been chosen sensibly. The data set is really too small to draw any firm conclusions about heteroscedasticity. Since the first and third models give very similar answers, it is tempting to think that these estimates are probably the most sensible ones to use.

3 (a) Load the data into R from the **textScore.txt** file.
dfl <- read.table(textScore.txt)

(b) Plot the average student expenditure against the average test score.
plot(dfl$expnstu, dfl$testscr)

(c) Fit a regression model of the form
$testscr_i = b_0 + b_1 * expnstu_i + u_i$
and label the model **test.model**
test.model <- lm(testscr ~ expnstu, data = dfl)

(d) summary(test.model)
Coefficients:
Estimate Std error t-value Pr(>|t|)
(Intercept) 6.318e+02 9.000e+00 70.205 <2e-16 ***
expnstu 3.964e-03 1.681e-03 2.358 0.019 *

Signif. codes: 0 '***' 0.001 '**' 0.01 '*' 0.05 '.' 0.1 ' ' 1
Residual standard error: 18.39 on 298 degrees of freedom
Multiple R-squared: 0.01831, Adjusted R-squared: 0.01502
F-statistic: 5.559 on 1 and 298 DF, p-value: 0.01903

The primary economic interpretation is that there is a mean increase in test scores of 0.0039 for every $1 spent on students. However, it may also be the case that there are a substantial amount of other factors that may determine test scores.

(e) Perform a graphical test for heteroscedasticity on the model **test.model**.

There are multiple ways to perform this test. As in the solutions to Question 2 above, we can carry out the following:

plot(test.model$fitted, test.model$resid, xlab="Fitted values", ylab="Residuals")

Alternatively, you can simply type

plot(test.model)

This will produce a range of diagnostic plots, which are not limited to the plot we are looking for.

(f) Using the **lmtest** package, conduct the Breusch–Pagan test against heteroscedasticity.

Once you have loaded the **lmtest** package, you will be able to use the following command:

bptest(test.model)

studentized Breusch-Pagan test

data: test.model

BP = 0.25485, df = 1, p-value = 0.6137

These results indicate that heteroscedasticity is not present as we have failed to produce enough statistical evidence to reject the null hypothesis of homoscedasticity. Whilst our residuals do not appear to be distributed uniformly, they do not deviate enough to produce sufficient statistical evidence of heteroscedasticity.

4   Using the data in the previous question, fit a regression model using the robust standard errors procedure outlined in Section 5.7.

We can just reuse the syntax in Section 5.7 here and replace the linear model object with our model.

coeftest(test.model, vcov = vcovHC(test.model, type = "HC0"))

t test of coefficients:

Estimate Std error t-value Pr(>|t|)

(Intercept) 6.3183e+02 8.6989e+00 72.6340 < 2e-16 ***

expnstu 3.9640e-03 1.6327e-03 2.4279 0.01578 *

Signif. codes: 0 '***' 0.001 '**' 0.01 '*' 0.05 '.' 0.1 ' ' 1

Here, we can note a small correction in the p-value for the **expnstu** coefficient. However, this is not enough to change the primary interpretation of the regression.

5 (a) Load the data contained within gdpLifeExpectancy.txt into your R console.

dfl <- read.table("gdpLifeExpectancy.txt")

(b) Develop a regression model which explains the impact of GDP per capita on life expectancy.

The following syntax is appropriate in this scenario.

gdp.model <- lm(lifeExpectancy ~ gdpPerCapita, data=dfl)
summary(gdp.model)
Call: lm(formula = lifeExpectancy ~ gdpPerCapita, data = dfl)
Coefficients:
Estimate Std error t-value Pr(>ltl)
(Intercept) 6.751e+01 5.846e-01 115.48 <2e-16 ***
gdpPerCapita 2.493e-04 2.089e-05 11.93 <2e-16 ***

Signif. codes: 0 '***' 0.001 '**' 0.01 '*' 0.05 '.' 0.1 ' ' 1
Multiple R-squared: 0.4417, Adjusted R-squared: 0.4386
F-statistic: 142.4 on 1 and 180 DF, p-value: < 2.2e-16

(c) Remember that we have a range of tests available including both graphical methods and numerical.

A graphical test may look like the following:
plot(gdp.model$fitted, gdp.model$resid, xlab="Fitted values, ylab="Residuals")

Alternatively, an appropriate numerical test can be conducted using bptest():
bptest(gdp.model)
studentized Breusch-Pagan test
data: gdp.model
BP = 0.73987, df = 1, p-value = 0.3897

(d) The estimates, t-statistics and p-values for the OLS estimation should resemble the following:
Estimate Std error t-value Pr(>ltl)
(Intercept) 6.751e+01 5.846e-01 115.48 <2e-16 ***
gdpPerCapita 2.493e-04 2.089e-05 11.93 <2e-16 ***

Signif. codes: 0 '***' 0.001 '**' 0.01 '*' 0.05 '.' 0.1 ' ' 1

Our results using robust standard errors are:
Estimate Std error t-value Pr(>ltl)
(Intercept) 6.7514e+01 7.1247e-01 94.7595 < 2.2e-16 ***
gdpPerCapita 2.4933e-04 3.1278e-05 7.9711 1.747e-13 ***

Signif. codes: 0 '***' 0.001 '**' 0.01 '*' 0.05 '.' 0.1 ' ' 1

There is some correction here, as we can see that the statistical significance of our finding is slightly overstated. However, this correction does not alter the primary interpretation of the result.

(e) These results strongly support the idea that wealthier countries have greater longevity outcomes for individuals. These results are highly significant and explain a high proportion of the variance in life expectancy.

6 Regression II: Violations of assumptions – autocorrelation

6.1 The nature of autocorrelation

Auto means 'self' so, by extension, autocorrelation means 'correlated with one-self'. The classical multiple linear regression model shown in Eq. (5.5) assumes that

$$\text{Cor}(u_i, u_j) = 0 \ (i \neq j) \tag{6.1}$$

However, if we have autocorrelation,

$$\text{Cor}(u_i, u_j) \neq 0 \text{ for some } i \neq j$$

If the modelling assumptions break down, we may not be able to trust computer-generated statistical output. Autocorrelation occurs whenever you have correlation between observations that have been in ordered in time or space. Observations or measurements taken close together, typically, take similar values. Autocorrelation, is usually associated with time-series data. This is especially relevant for datasets in accounting, finance and economics etc. if the data have been recorded over time – e.g. daily, weekly, monthly, quarterly or yearly prices.

The classical multiple linear regression model assumes no autocorrelation between the disturbances u_i, as shown in Eq. (6.1). This model thus assumes that errors are not influenced by errors corresponding to other observations. For example, for the data on real gold and real stock prices, naive application of the classical linear regression model would assume that errors pertaining to observations for, say, 2000 and 2001 would be independent. Clearly, this is a big assumption and gives a clear indication of how autocorrelation can be caused by economic and financial data being collected over time.

If the assumptions underpinning the classical linear regression model are wrong, then you cannot take computer-generated statistical output at face value. Ignoring autocorrelation may:

1 Under-estimate σ^2.
2 Over-estimate R^2.
3 Invalidate the usual t-tests and F-tests and may give rise to misleading conclusions about statistical significance.
4 Generally lead to over-confidence on the part of the analyst.

If autocorrelated errors are a problem with regression, then it is probably best to fit a regression model with autocorrelated errors using the command arima (see below).

6.2   Causes of autocorrelation

The causes of autocorrelation include:

1 Inertia
2 Non-stationarity
3 Model mis-specification
4 Cobweb phenomenon
5 Data limitation and manipulation

1 *Inertia.* This is an extremely common problem in financial and economic time series caused by observations being recorded over time. Economic time series tend to exhibit cyclical behaviour. Examples include GNP, price indices, production figures, employment statistics etc. Since these series tend to be quite slow moving, the effect of inertia is that successive observations can be highly correlated.
2 *Non-stationarity.* This is an extremely common problem in financial and economic time series caused by observations being recorded over time. If X and Y are non-stationary, it is possible that the error term will also be non-stationary. The error term may then also exhibit autocorrelation.
3 *Model mis-specification.* A model specification error occurs if important variables that should be included in the model are excluded or if the model is formed using the wrong function. In either case, the set-up of the model is incorrect or 'mis-specified'. Specification errors mean that it is important to consider financial/economic theory and/or other relevant academic literature – mathematics is only part of the story. Specification errors mean that residuals from an incorrectly fitted model may exhibit a systematic pattern, rather than a purely random pattern, and so may be autocorrelated as a result. A commonly encountered example is a failure to account for the lagged effects of economic variables.

4 *Cobweb phenomena.* These are commonly encountered with agricultural commodities. Economic agents such as farmers commonly base decisions on the prevailing price from last year when deciding how many goods to supply to the market. For example, the amount of crops farmers supply to the market at time t might have the form

$$\text{Supply}_t = \beta_1 + \beta_2 P_{t-1} + u_t \tag{6.2}$$

The disturbances u_t in Eq. (6.2) are therefore unlikely to be completely random and patternless because they represent the actions of intelligent economic agents (i.e. farmers, in this case). For example, high prices one year might lead to an over-supply and low prices in the subsequent year. The net result may be autocorrelated error terms. This reflects economic themes of wider importance – i.e. financial and economic variables always represent the collective investment decisions of many different people and so will often be inherently more complicated than the mathematical and statistical tools used to describe them!

5 *Data limitation and manipulation.* Quarterly data may smooth out some of the wild fluctuations typically seen in monthly sales figures. Low frequency census and economic survey data may be interpolated. Such data transformations may be inevitable and unavoidable. In social sciences, unlike physical sciences, data quality may be variable and may induce systematic patterns and autocorrelation into the disturbances u_i of a regression model. There is not necessarily a clear solution to this problem but this issue of data quality remains an important consideration throughout.

6.3 Graphical tests for autocorrelation

There are two basic approaches for detecting autocorrelation in the residuals of a regression model.

1 *Graphical methods.* These are simpler but may be more robust and more informative in applied project work.
2 Statistical tests:
   - Runs test
   - Durbin–Watson test

In applied project work, graphical and statistical methods may serve as a useful cross-check of each other! In terms of graphical tests for autocorrelation, there are the following two main possibilities to consider:

1 *Time-series plot of residuals.* Plot the residuals over time and visually check to see whether any evidence of a systematic pattern exists
2 *Autocorrelation plot.* It is natural to think that u_t and u_{t-1} may be correlated. To see if this is the case, plot $\hat{u}_t$ against $\hat{u}_{t-1}$.

We illustrate these tests with an application to the gold price and stock price example considered previously. The data is in the file L3egldata.txt available in the online resources. Save it to your USB stick then read in the data using the read.table command:

datal<-read.table("E:L3egldata.txt")

The dataset contains two columns containing the real gold price (left-hand column) and the real stock price (right-hand column). In R, assign variables linking the real gold price to the first column and the real stock price to the second column. (Note that this has to exactly match the name datal given in the above sequence of commands.)

realgoldprice<-datal[,1]
realstockprice<-datal[,2]

Producing the time-series plot of residuals in R is essentially a two-step process:

1 Fit the regression model.
2 Produce a time-series plot of the residuals produced.

1 Fit the regression model.
   a.lm<-lm(realgoldprice~realstockprice)
2 Produce a time-series plot of the residuals produced.
   resid0l<-a.lm$resid
   plot(resid0l)
   length(resid0l)
   [1] 33
   lines(seq(1:33), rep(0, 33))

The time-series plot produced is shown in Fig. 6.1 and suggests some evidence for autocorrelation since there are successive runs of residuals on either side of the line. If the model is correctly specified, then it should be a 50:50 coin toss as to whether or not each residual is positive or negative.

Autocorrelation means correlated with itself so it is natural to expect that adjacent residuals may be correlated with each other. One way to test for this is to plot the lag 0 residuals, $\hat{u}_t$, against the lag 1 residuals, $\hat{u}_{t-1}$. Since it is a higher-level programming language, this is actually easier to do in R than in some alternative software. In order to conduct the autocorrelation plot of residuals in R, use

length(resid0l)
33
Lag 0

– Lose one observation here – actually the first observation.
   residl0<-resid0l[2:33]

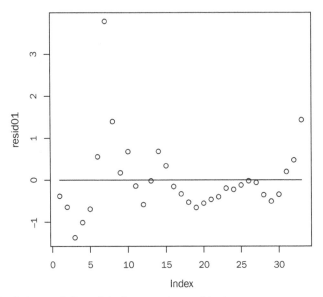

Figure 6.1 Autocorrelation plot of regression residuals

Lag 1

– Lose one observation here – actually the last observation.
  residll<-resid0l[l:32]

– Then you just have to use the basic plot command
  plot(residll, residl2)

The autocorrelation plot produced by R is shown in Fig. 6.2 and suggests clear evidence of positive autocorrelation.

6.4 Statistical tests for autocorrelation

In this book, we consider two main statistical tests for autocorrelation:

1 *Runs test*. Under the classical multiple linear regression model, residuals are equally likely to be positive or negative.
2 *Durbin–Watson test*. This tests whether the regression residuals are AR(1).

The runs test is conceptually simple but not very powerful. Define

$$R = \text{number of runs}$$
$$E[R] = \frac{2N_1N_2}{N} + 1$$

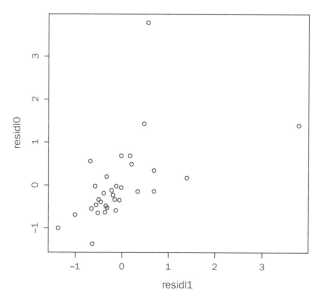

Figure 6.2 Autocorrelation plot of regression residuals

$$\sigma_R^2 = \frac{2N_1N_2(2N_1N_2 - N)}{N^2(N - 1)}$$

where N = total number of observations, N_1 = number of positive residuals, N_2 = number of negative residuals. Then you perform a t-test using the bottom row of your t-tables (in case this sounds incredibly complicated, this is just an approximation based on using the normal distribution).

$$t = \frac{R - E[R]}{\sigma_R}$$

In the gold market example, the residuals have the following signs
$(-,-,-,-,-)(+,+,+,+,+,+)(-,-,-)(+,+)(-,-,-,-,-,-,-,-,-,-,-,-,-,-,-)(+,+,+)$
This gives us $R = 6$ runs or 6 different subsequences of residuals that each share the same sign. Form the t-statistic ($N_1 = 10$ positive residuals, $N_2 = 23$ negative residuals, $N = 33$).

$$|t| = \frac{R - E[R]}{\sigma_R} = \frac{|6 - 14.9394|}{\sqrt{5.6365}} = 3.765 \text{ (3 d.p.)}$$

From tables, $t_\infty(0.025) = 1.96$, and

$$t = 3.765 > t_\infty(0.025) = 196$$
$$p < 0.05$$

so there is evidence from the runs test ($p < 0.05$) that there is autocorrelation in the residuals.

Running a runs test in R requires the following three steps:

1   Produce a character vector in R that determines whether the residuals are positive or negative using the command factor
    resatidsign<-I*(residOI>0)
    residsign<-I*(residOI>0)
    residsign<-factor(residsign)
2   Load the tseries package in R (see below).
3   Apply the function runs.test
    runs.test(residsign)

This presents evidence (Standard Normal = -3.7653, p-value = 0.0001663 <0.05) that the residuals are autocorrelated.

If you want to run a runs test in R, you have to download the R package tseries – which stands for time series. In R, to upload packages use

Packages—→load packages—→tseries—→OK

In R, to see what packages are available for loading use
Packages—→Load packages
If the package is not there, you might have to download the required package from CRAN. To do this use

Packages—→Install package(s) ...—→Choose a CRAN mirror

It is better to choose the UK (London or Bristol) or wherever you are in the world. You should then be able to see a long list of packages that are available for download. On John's work computer, standard packages load fine. On your personal computer, you should be able to update the list of packages via the R repository CRAN. This maintenance of packages and the active online R community are probably the best things about R and the best reasons for using it. However, it may not be possible to update packages directly if you are working on a PC on a university network. You can get round this by saving the package code to a USB stick and then using the option

Packages—→Install package(s) from local files ...

You may find that loading R packages is fiddly the first time that you try it but it should become much easier after that.

A second statistical test for autocorrelation is the Durbin–Watson test. This test asks what proportion of the residual sums of squares can be explained by the correlation between successive residuals. This question is important because the residual sum of squares means information that cannot be explained by the model. The Durbin–Watson test is important historically and is widely used, although we have some reservations about how practical it is to use it in large-sample problems.

The Durbin–Watson d-statistic is defined as the the sum of squared differences in successive residuals relative to the residual sum of squares

$$d = \frac{\text{squared distance between successive residuals}}{\text{residual sum of squares}}$$

$$= \frac{\sum_{t=2}^{n} \left(\hat{u}_t - \hat{u}_{t-1} \right)^2}{\sum_{t=2}^{n} \hat{u}_t^2}$$

The assumptions underpinning the Durbin–Watson test, as discussed in Chapter 12 of Gujarati and Porter (2009), are:

1 The regression model includes the intercept term.
2 The X variables are non-stochastic.
3 The disturbances are autocorrelated with order one

$$u_t = \rho u_{t-1} + \epsilon_t$$

4 The error term u_t is normally distributed.
5 The regression model does not include lagged values of the dependent variable, such as Y_{t-1} etc. on the right-hand side.
6 There are no missing observations in the data.

The interpretation of the Durbin–Watson test according to published statistical tables is shown in Table 6.1.

The Durbin–Watson test can be conducted in R as follows. You need to load the R package **lmtest** which stands for linear model (regression tests). Once this is loaded, run the Durbin–Watson test by applying the function **dwtest** to a named linear regression model. For this example,
dwtest(a.lm)
DW = 0.90424, p-value = 0.0001215
alternative hypothesis: true autocorrelation is greater than 0

Table 6.1 Interpretation of the Durbin–Watson statistical tables

Null hypothesis	Decision	Condition
No positive autocorrelation	No decision	$d_L \leq d \leq d_U$
No positive autocorrelation	Reject	$0 < d < d_L$
No negative autocorrelation	No decision	$4 - d_U \leq d \leq 4 - d_L$
No negative autocorrelation	Reject	$4 - d_L < d < 4$
No autocorrelation (positive or negative)	Do not reject	$d_U < d < 4 - d_U$

6.5 Remedial measures – regression with autocorrelated errors

Standard regression theory and programs assume that the regression residuals are uncorrelated. In Chapter 6.3, we saw graphical evidence that the residuals in the example are correlated. Chapter 6.4 presents formal statistical evidence that residuals in the example are correlated. It is important, here, that the graphical and statistical evidence serve as a cross-check of each other. We also 'know' from the wider context that, since gold and stock prices are collected over time, some autocorrelation is likely to be present. This is a practical problem with a practical solution being to fit a regression model with an autoregressive error term as presented below.

The basic R command to run a regression with autocorrelated errors is arima, which can be used to combine regression with an element of time series. The way this works is as follows:

arima(y-variable, xreg=X-variables, order=$c(p, d, q)$)

In the **xreg** part, specify the regression formula to be used in the model. In the **order** section, specify the ARIMA(p, d, q) component of the model. Often, we would only really need **order=c(1, 0, 0)** to specify an autoregressive model of order one. So, for our earlier example, use
arima(realgoldprice, xreg=realstockprice, order=c(1, 0, 0))

The output produced by R is as follows (which, unfortunately, means that you have to compute the t-statistics yourself).
Coefficients:
ar1 intercept realstockprice
0.5578 3.9406 -0.0487
s.e. 0.1545 0.5675 0.0247
In R, using length(goldprice) tells us that there are 33 observations so that we have $33 - 3$ estimated parameters = 30 residual degrees of freedom. Calculate the t-statistics and then the p-values using
coeff<-c(0.5578, 3.9406, -0.0487)
ese<-c(0.1545, 0.5675, 0.0247)
t<-abs(coeff)/ese
t
[1] 3.610356 6.943789 1.971660
2*(1-pt(t, 30))
[1] 1.100235e-03 1.032974e-07 5.793185e-02

These results can be interpreted as follows. From the t-statistics, there is evidence of autocorrelation in the residuals ($p = 0.001$). Note that, here, autocorrelation reflects the fact that it is harder to establish a genuine link between real gold prices and real stock prices than might otherwise be thought. The literal interpretation of these results would be that there is weak evidence of a relationship between the real stock price and the real gold price ($p = 0.0579$).

- Often, it is easier to continue to investigate whether or not $p < 0.05$ or $p > 0.05$.
- Being in the corridor of uncertainty of $0.05 < p < 0.1$ reflects that the interpretation may be more nuanced in harder examples.
- Issues over such nuanced interpretations have been important in the MSc dissertations that we have supervised in the past.

6.6 Tutorial exercises

1 Table 6.2 gives data on the estimates of the levels of recoverable UK oil and gas over a 21-year period. It is of interest to see how the oil-reserve data may be used to predict the gas data.
  (a) Read the data in to R using the commands
    oil<-c(8.597, 8.572, 8.649, 8.688, 8.879, 8.971, 8.680, 8.349, 8.140, 7.613, 7.355, 7.417, 7.171, 6.847, 6.662, 6.560, 6.465, 6.452, 6.252, 5.881, 5.882)
    gas<-c(1770, 1780, 1805, 1865, 1915, 1910, 1915, 1960, 1980, 1795, 1750, 1630, 1535, 1329, 1241, 1169, 1006, 967, 940, 907, 840)
  (b) Fit an OLS regression of the estimated gas reserves (y) against the estimated oil reserves (x).
  (c) Following the previous examples, conduct graphical tests for autocorrelation in the residuals for the regression model fitted in part (b).
  (d) Use the runs test to test for autocorrelation in the residuals for the regression model fitted in part (b).
  (e) Use the Durbin–Watson test to test for autocorrelation in the residuals for the regression model fitted in part (b).
  (f) Fit a regression model with AR(1) errors to this data
  (g) Does the result in part (f) give any statistical evidence of autocorrelation in the residuals?
  (h) What do the results in part (f) suggest would be a better regression line for this data?
2 Suggest a cause for autocorrelation in each of the following five cases.
  (a) Soft commodity prices
  (b) Official statistical data
  (c) Inflation
  (d) Cryptocurrency data
  (e) Relationship between popular vote share and electoral outcomes
3 Load the data contained within **BrexitBookies.txt** into your R console. This data shows the probability of the UK remaining in the EU in column 1 and the probability of leaving in column 2.
  (a) Plot a scatter diagram to show whether the probability of remaining is increasing or decreasing over time.
  (b) Using the lm() function, find out whether the errors in the probability of remaining are autocorrelated. Consider regressing time on the probability of remaining and then conduct a residual plot as per Fig. 6.1.

Table 6.2 Dataset for tutorial exercise

Year	Oil reserves (million tonnes)	Gas reserves (billion cubic metre)
1	8.597	1770
2	8.572	1780
3	8.649	1805
4	8.688	1865
5	8.879	1915
6	8.971	1910
7	8.680	1915
8	8.349	1960
9	8.140	1980
10	7.613	1795
11	7.355	1750
12	7.417	1630
13	7.171	1535
14	6.847	1329
15	6.662	1241
16	6.560	1169
17	6.465	1006
18	6.452	967
19	6.252	940
20	5.881	907
21	5.882	840

    (c) Repeat the analysis above, but this time regress the first difference remain probability and compare the two residual plots.

4 Load the data contained within **petersen.csv** into your R console. This data shows the stock returns for 500 firms over 10 years in annual observations. Column Y shows the stock return for the corresponding firm/year and column X shows the market return for the same period.

    (a) Plot a scatter diagram using the variable names to correspond to the axis on which they should be plotted (i.e. column X on the x-axis).

    (b) Label the x-axis 'Market return' and the y-axis 'Stock return'.

    (c) Provide an interpretation for this plot.

(d) Regress x on y in a linear model and label the model lm.fit.
(e) Using the packages **sandwich** and **lmtest**, estimate the OLS standard errors and Newey–West 5-day corrected standard errors.
5 Compare and discuss the differences between the standard errors reported by the OLS procedure and the Newey–West correction in question 4(e).

6.7 Solutions

1 (a) n/a
  (b) Run the regression using

```
gas.lm<-lm(gas~oil)
summary(gas.lm)
Coefficients:
Estimate Std error t-value Pr(>|t|)
(Intercept) -1165.38 234.93 -4.96 8.68e-05 ***
oil 357.30 30.91 11.56 4.87e-10 ***
```

  (c) To conduct the first plot, use
```
plot(gas.lm$resid)
length(gas.lm$resid)
[1] 21
lines(seq(1:21), rep(0, 21))
```

The plot obtained is shown in Fig. 6.3 and gives some suggestion of auto-correlation with large runs of residuals obtained that have the same sign. In order to plot residuals against lagged residuals, use
```
residl1<-gas.lm$resid[1:20]
residl2<-gas.lm$resid[2:21]
plot(residl1, residl2, xlab="Lag 1 residuals", ylab"Lag 0 residuals")
```

The result shown in Fig. 6.4 also gives evidence in favour of positive autocorrelation in the residuals.
  (d) With the **tseries** package loaded in R, the runs test can be carried out using
```
posres<-1*(gas.lm$resid>0)
posres<-factor(posres)
runs.test(posres)
Standard Normal = -3.7642, p-value = 0.0001671
alternative hypothesis: two.sided
```

Thus, the runs test gives formal statistical evidence of autocorrelation in the residuals.
  (e) With the **lmtest** package loaded in R, the Durbin–Watson test can be run using
```
dwtest(gas.lm)
DW = 0.28616, p-value = 2.381e-09
```

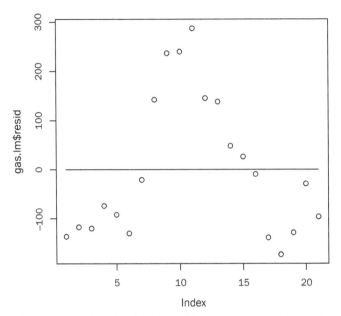

Figure 6.3   Time-series plot of residuals with large runs suggesting autocorrelation

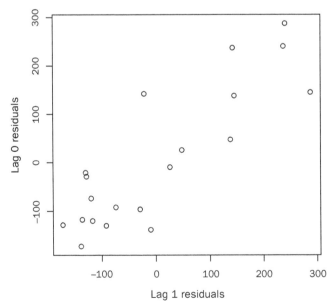

Figure 6.4   Plot of residuals against lagged residuals suggesting positive autocorrelation

alternative hypothesis: true autocorrelation is greater than 0

Thus, the Durbin–Watson test also gives formal statistical evidence of autocorrelation in the residuals.

(f) A regression with autocorrelated errors can be fitted using the arima command:

arima(gas, xreg=oil, order=c(1, 0, 0))
Coefficients:
ar1 intercept oil
0.8978 -646.5226 279.9879
s.e. 0.0989 514.8833 70.8635

(g) Conducting a t-test on the AR(1) parameter above provides another statistical test for autocorrelation in the residuals. There are 21 data points minus three estimated parameters, so 18 residual degrees of freedom. In this case, this computation in R gives

0.8978/0.0989
[1] 9.077856
> 2*(1-pt(9.077856, 18))
[1] 3.873474e-08

Thus, the results give evidence $p = 3.873474 \times 10^{-8} < 0.05$ of autocorrelation in the residuals.

(h) Using the output from part (f), it seems that the best regression line for this data is

$$\text{gas reserves} = -646.5226 + 279.9879 \text{ oil reserves}$$

Part (b) shows that naive use of the ordinary least squares regression without accounting for autocorrelation in the residuals would, instead, estimate this equation as

$$\text{gas reserves} = -1165.38 + 357.30 \text{ oil reserves}$$

2 (a) Cobweb phenomena.
   (b) Data limitation and manipulation.
   (c) Inertia caused by wider economic cycles.
   (d) Model mis-specification. Note that market data is liable to be much more complex than any model used to approximate features of that data.
   (e) Non-stationary. The relationship between vote share and election outcomes is not stable over time and is subject to demographic changes.

3 (a) Plot a scatter diagram using
dfl <- read.table("BrexitBookies.txt")
plot(dfl[,1], type='l')

The graph suggests that the probability of remaining is decreasing over time with substantial fluctuations towards the end.

(b) To get started, we need to create a new variable in **dfl** which represents time.

```
dfl$n <- l:length(dfl$remain)
fit <- lm(remain ~ n, data=dfl)
plot(dfl$n, fit$resid, xlab="Index", ylab="Residual")
```

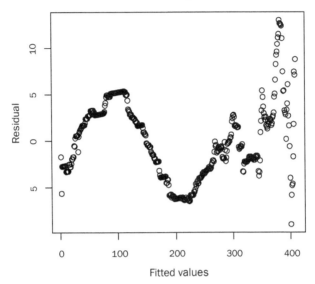

Figure 6.5 Plot of residuals for probability of remaining in the EU

(c) This time, we calculate the first difference and the new time variable:

```
diffRemain <- diff(dfl$remain)
n <- l:length(diffRemain)
```

We then repeat the above by specifying our model again and plotting the values:

```
fit <- lm(diffRemain ~ n)
plot(n, fit$resid, xlab="Index", ylab="Residual")
```

4 Load the data contained within **petersen.csv** into your R console.

(a) Plot a scatter diagram using the variable names to correspond to the axis on which they should be plotted (i.e. column x on the x-axis).

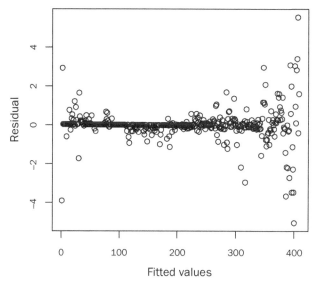

Figure 6.6 Plot of residuals for differenced remain probability

Using the command
dfl <- read.csv("petersen.csv")
plot(dflx, dfly, xlab="Market Returns", ylab="Stock Returns")
will return the graph shown in Fig. 6.7.

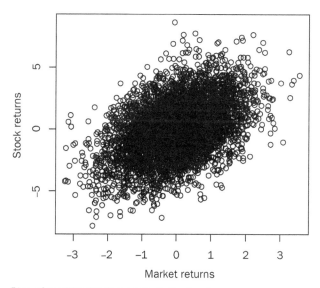

Figure 6.7 Plot of market returns against stock returns

(b) Label the x-axis 'Market return' and the y-axis 'Stock return'.

(c) This plot will be familiar to practitioners who often look up β values for stocks. This graph shows that there is a clear contemporaneous relationship between market returns and stock returns. That is, when the market returns increase, so do stock returns.

(d) Regress x on y in a linear model and label the model lm.fit.

lm.fit <- lm(y ~ x, dfl)

(e) Use the packages sandwich and lmtest to estimate the OLS standard errors and Newey–West 5-day corrected standard errors.

coeftest(lm.fit)

Estimate Std error t-value Pr(>|t|)

(Intercept) 0.029680 0.028359 1.0466 0.2954

x 1.034833 0.028583 36.2041 <2e-16 ***

coeftest(lm.fit, vcov = NeweyWest(lm.fit, lag =5, prewhite = FALSE))

Estimate Std error t-value Pr(>|t|)

(Intercept) 0.029680 0.048614 0.6105 0.5415

x 1.034833 0.039437 26.2402 <2e-16 ***

5 A clear difference between the standard errors reported by the OLS procedure and the Newey–correction is that the standard error for the x coefficient reported by the Newey–West formula is much higher. Accordingly, the t-statistic is lower. Ultimately, this does not affect our interpretation in this case, as the relationship is very strong. However, this outcome reflects the ability of the Newey–West standard errors to control for five periods of autocorrelation and heteroscedasticity, which reasonably lowers our certainty in the results but naturally provides a more robust analysis of the model.

This is an extremely pervasive problem in finance because of the prevalence of panel data. Up until relatively recently, people have been unable to correct for the cross-sectional correlation in the error term and the autocorrelation through time in these asset pricing models. A popular research paper by Mitchell Peterson (Petersen 2009) found that up to 42% of high-ranking research papers in finance ignored this problem.

In short, the Newey–West standard errors correction is widely regarded as the most robust standard errors correction that one can apply in these situations and forms the benchmark for modern asset pricing research.

7 Regression III: Violations of assumptions – multicollinearity

This book is not about difficult mathematics. Rather it is about communication of information and critically evaluating computer-generated output. The basic underlying question is, 'Does your computer output and statistical model really do what you think it does?'

The name itself is revealing! Multicollinearity refers to the situation where there are multiple (linear) relationships between the X-variables. If the X variables are themselves collinear ('inter-related') it is hard to isolate the individual influence on Y.

7.1 Sources of multicollinearity

Multicollinearity occurs where there is either an exact linear relationship or an approximate linear relationship amongst the X-variables. For example, consider the illustrative example dataset in Table 7.1. There is perfect collinearity between X_2 and X_3 since $X_3 = 5X_2$. There is not perfect collinearity between X_2 and X_3 but the linear correlation between the two variables is very high (0.9959). Nonetheless, both instances would qualify as multicollinearity.

There is a rich mathematical theory on least squares estimation. The least squares estimator can be defined as

$$\hat{\beta} = (X^TX)^{-1}X^Ty$$

where X is the data vector. The theory thus implicitly assumes that the matrix $(X^TX)^{-1}$ can be inverted and the effect of individual X variables upon Y can be isolated. However, this may not be the case. Exact linear relationships between the X-variables would mean that the matrix inverse $(X^TX)^{-1}$ does not exist. In practice, multicollinearity and approximate linear relationships between the

Table 7.1   Dataset that illustrates multicollinearity

X_2	X_3	X_3^*
10	50	52
15	75	75
18	90	97
24	120	129
30	150	152

X-variables may mean that $(X^TX)^{-1}$ can be calculated but may be numerically unstable. The conclusion under either scenario is that, mathematically, we may not be able to trust the computer-generated output.

We have encountered multicollinearity in our own applied statistical work – so this is not just a purely theoretical problem. For example, when conducting a statistical analysis of survey data this essentially reduced to a regression problem with a large number of redundant X variables. Hence, multicollinearity became an important consideration.

Allied to the above, you often 'know' in advance when you might experience multicollinearity. Sources of multicollinearity include the following.

1   *Data collection method employed.* This can be a problem if you are sampling over a limited range of values taken by the regressors in the population. The net result is that there may be a limited amount of information in the data compared with the number of terms in the model that you want to estimate.
2   *Constraints on the model or the population.* This is a similar problem that can occur if you are sampling over a limited range of values taken by the regressors in the population. For example, variables such as income and house size may be interrelated – especially if your sample is not very broad.
3   *Model specification.* For example, adding polynomial terms to a model when the range of the X-variables is small may mean that there is a limited amount of information in the data compared with the number of terms in the model that you want to estimate.
4   *An over-determined model.* This may be caused by having many explanatory variables compared with the number of observations or by the sheer number of X variables in large problems. Recall that multicollinearity means that it is often difficult to isolate the effects of individual X variables. The problem often occurs in relation to statistical problems associated with the analysis of survey data.
5   *Common trends.* For example, variables such as consumption, income, wealth, population etc. may be correlated due to a dependence upon general economic trends and cycles. A classic example of this may be raw house prices showing exponential growth over time. However, if you adjust for inflation, a whole host of volatile boom–bust cycles may then become apparent.

7.2 Theoretical consequences of mulicollinearity

Multicollinearity is essentially a sampling phenomenon associated with each particular data set – it is always present to a greater or lesser degree. The theoretical effects are, in some sense, muted – but multicollinearity may remain an important practical problem. In the case of (approximate) multicollinearity, OLS estimators retain the following desirable theoretical properties.

1 Unbiased: under repeated sampling, the average of the sample values will converge to the true underlying population value.
2 Best linear unbiased predictor.

However, the extent to which this retains practical relevance is unclear. Consider the OLS estimator $\hat{\beta}$. If you have exact multicollinearity (so that the matrix $(X^T X)$ is not invertible), parameter estimates have infinite variances and covariances. In practical situations, we only have approximate multicollinearity so, in practice, we can calculate $(X^T X)^{-1}$. Nonetheless, under (approximate) multicollinearity, parameter estimates may:

1 Have large estimated standard errors.
2 Be highly correlated.

Multicollinearity is bad news for two reasons:

1 *Large estimated standard errors.* This indicates a lack of precision associated with parameter estimates. This leads to associated problems such as wider confidence intervals, and large estimated standard errors may have a knock-on effect upon hypothesis tests.
2 *Correlated parameter estimates.* These serve as another potential source of errors and may be suggestive of numerical problems with computational routines.

With respect to point 1 above, it becomes harder to reject incorrect hypotheses. To test the null hypothesis that, say, $\beta_2 = 0$ we use a t-ratio:

$$t = \frac{\hat{\beta}_2}{\text{e.s.e.}(\hat{\beta}_2)} \tag{7.1}$$

However, multicollinearity increases the e.s.e. so that the t-ratio reduces in size and the statistical significance in Eq. (7.1) is reduced.

7.3 Practical consequences of multicollinearity

In practical problems look, for something that 'does not look quite right'. In our own experience, alongside multicollinearity you often see high R^2 values coupled with insignificant t-ratios. This is contradictory.

1 The high R^2 suggests that the model is good and explains a lot of the variation in Y.
2 But if individual t-ratios are non-significant, this suggests that individual X-variables do not affect Y.

Alongside high R^2 values and low t-values there are a range of related effects to look out for:

1 Multicollinearity results in large estimated standard errors.
2 Larger estimated standard errors result in non-significant t-ratios.
3 Larger estimated standard errors also result in wider confidence intervals since the width of the confidence interval increases as the estimated standard error increases:

$$95\,\% \text{ confidence interval} = \hat{\beta}_2 \pm t_{n-p}(0.025)\text{e.s.e.}(\hat{\beta}_2)$$

p = number of estimated parameters including the constant

$$n - p = \text{residual d.f.}$$

Numerical instabilities are the chief problem associated with multicollinearity:

1 Parameter estimates and their associated estimated standard errors become very sensitive to small changes in the data.
2 Regression coefficients may 'take the wrong sign' or otherwise 'look strange'.
3 It may be difficult to assess the individual contributions of explanatory variables to the the regression sum of squares or to the R^2 statistic.
4 Parameter estimates may be highly correlated.

Example 7.10

Consider the following illustrative example. We want to explain expenditure Y in terms of income X_2 and wealth X_3. The data is shown in Table 7.2. (Recall that to detect multicollinearity we might anticipate finding a high R^2 value combined with low t-values.)
This data can be entered into R as follows:

```
y<-c(70, 65, 90, 95, 110, 115, 120, 140, 155, 150)
x2<-c(80, 100, 120, 140, 160, 180, 200, 220, 240, 260)
x3<-c(810, 1009, 1273, 1425, 1633, 1876, 2052, 2201, 2435, 2686)
```

This gives the following values for the three basic R^2, F-statistic and t-statistics.

1 $R^2 = 0.9635$. *The model explains a substantial amount of the variation (96.35% of the variation in the data).*
2 $F = 92.40196$. *From tables, $F_{2,7} = 4.74$, so there is some evidence $(p < 0.05)$ that at least one of income and wealth affect expenditure.*

Table 7.2 Example data set on expenditure, income and wealth

Expenditure Y	Income X_2	Wealth X_3
70	80	810
65	100	1009
90	120	1273
95	140	1425
110	160	1633
115	180	1876
120	200	2052
140	220	2201
155	240	2435
150	260	2686

3   *t-statistics. From tables, $t_7(0.025) = 2.365$. The t-statistics are 1.144 for income and -0.526 for wealth. Neither income nor wealth are individually statistically significant ($p > 0.05$).*

We thus have a few of the tell-tale signs of multicollinearity:

1   *High R^2 values, low t-values.*
2   *The wealth variable has the 'wrong sign' – it is likely that expenditure will increase as wealth increases.*
3   *The variables X_2 and X_3 are very highly correlated.*

The variables income and wealth are so highly correlated that it is impossible to isolate the individual impact of either income or wealth upon consumption. The example thus serves to motivate the question of how to detect multicollinearity in practice.

7.4   Detection of multicollinearity

Whilst detection of multicollinearity is important, it is worthwhile to consider Kmenta's warning. The distinction is not between the presence and the absence of multicollinearity but between its various degrees. Multicollinearity is a function of the sample and not of the population. Multicollinearity is always liable to be present in a given dataset to a greater or lesser degree.

Ways of detecting multicollinearity include the following.

1 *High R^2, low t-values.*
2 *High pairwise correlations between explanatory variables.* If the correlation coefficient of regressors is high, say, greater than 0.8, then this indicates that multicollinearity might be a problem. In this example, the correlation between income and wealth is 0.99896. This is very high suggesting that we might have a problem with multicollinearity. Note, however, that in models involving two or more explanatory variables, pairwise correlation will not provide a fool-proof guide to the presence of multicollinearity.
3 *Examination of partial correlations.* Partial correlations may provide a better measure of multicollinearity than the simple pairwise correlations. For example, with three variables X_2, X_3 and X_4, the partial correlation coefficient $r_{23,4}$ would measure the correlation between X_2 and X_3 independent of X_4.
4 *Subsidiary or auxiliary regression.* Multicollinearity arises because one or more of the X variables are linearly related or approximately linearly related to some combination of the other explanatory variables. You can perform a subsidiary or auxiliary regression of X_2, X_3 etc. against the other explanatory variables. These secondary regressions are then subsidiary or auxiliary to the main regression for Y.
5 *Klein's rule of thumb.* This states that multicollinearity may only be a problem if the R^2 obtained from an auxiliary regression is greater than the overall R^2 obtained by regressing Y against all the X variables. For our earlier example, regressing Y against X_2 and X_3 gives $R^2 = 0.963304$. Regressing X_2 against X_3 gives $R^2 = 0.997926$. Thus, for this example, Klein's rule of thumb suggests that multicollinearity will be a serious problem.

7.5 Remedial measures

When considering remedies to the problem of multicollinearity, one possibility is to simply do nothing. The renowned economist Blanchard describes multicollinearity as being 'God's will' and as not being a problem with ordinary least squares or any other statistical technique. When viewed from this perspective, multicollinearity is essentially a data-deficiency problem and sometimes we have no control over the data we have available for analysis. Note that there is an important distinction here in terms of the quality of the available data in quantitative social science (finance and economics) and scientific experiments in physics and chemistry.

A further remedial measure may be to use prior information about some parameters. Textbooks often give some fairly extreme examples to illustrate this. Incorporating prior information about parameters sensibly would require more advanced Bayesian statistical methods (see, e.g., Gamerman and Lopes 2006).

The simplest approach to multicollinearity is to drop one or more of the collinear variables. So, in the above example we could exclude wealth from the model. Some economists might express concerns over specification bias if variables identified by economic theory are not included in the model. Whilst this may be a valid concern, it does depend, to some extent, on how much trust you want to place upon economic theory. It is sometimes useful to use stepwise regression/similar techniques related to computer science to choose a model – see the worked example in Chapter 7.6. This may provide an 'objective' approach to messy practical problems.

The problem of multicollinearity may be reduced by transforming variables. This may be possible in a variety of ways. For example, if you have time-series data, you might consider forming a new model by taking first differences. This approach may reduce the problem of multicollinearity – see Gujarati and Porter (2009) Chapter 10.

Multicollinearity is a sample feature. It is possible that in another sample involving the same variables the multicollinearity will not be as serious a problem as in the first sample. Sometimes, just acquiring more data – either increasing the sample size or including additional variables – can reduce the severity of the multicollinearity problem.

There may be times when a model chosen for empirical analysis is not carefully thought out. Some important variables may be omitted. The functional form of the model may have been incorrectly chosen. It is also possible that more advanced statistical techniques may be required. Examples include:

1 Factor analysis
2 Principal component analysis
3 Ridge regression

Multicollinearity has arguably received excessive attention in the literature. Micronumerosity refers to the smallness of the sample size. Micronumerosity is thought by some to be equally as important as multicollinearity. There are no 'right' answers and no substitute for common sense and critical thinking.

7.6 Worked example

We now want to illustrate stepwise regression approaches since they represent an 'objective' way of approaching messy problems. Looking at the famous Longley dataset, we want to explain the number of people employed, Y, in terms of the following:

1 X_2 GNP
2 X_3 Number of people unemployed
3 X_4 Number of people in the armed services
4 X_5 Non-institutionalized population over the age of 14
5 X_6 Time in years

Fitting the full model gives high R^2 values and low t-values and suggests that we might have a problem with multicollinearity.

The data is in the file **longley.txt** and can be read in using
```
longley<-read.table("E:longley.txt")
x2<-longley[,1]
x3<-longley[,2]
x4<-longley[,3]
x5<-longley[,4]
x6<-longley[,5]
y<-longley[,6]
```

Stepwise regression follows three basic approaches:

1 *Forward selection.* Start with the basic model $Y_i = \beta_1 + u_i$ and add successive terms until no more terms are statistically significant.
2 *Backward selection.* Start with the full model $Y_i = \beta_1 + \beta_2 X_{2,i} + \ldots + \beta_p X_{p,i} + u_i$ and delete terms until all the variables remaining in the model are statistically significant.
3 *Stepwise selection.* Start with the basic model $Y_i = \beta_1 + u_i$ and add successive terms until no more terms are statistically significant. However, each time a variable enters the model, a backward regression deletion step is performed to check that all variables included in the model remain statistically significant throughout.

In order to run stepwise regressions in R, begin by fitting the full regression model with all the X-variables included:
```
a.lm<-lm(y~x2+x3+x4+x5+x6)
```

You then need to fit the null model with just the intercept term:
```
null.lm<-lm(y~1)
```

Then, there are two basic differences depending on which of the following you are doing.

1 Forward selection or stepwise regression
   – Start with the null model
2 Backward selection
   – Start with the full model

1 Stepwise and forward selection
   ```
   step(null.lm, direction = "both", scope = formula(a.lm))
   step(null.lm, direction = "forward", scope = formula(a.lm))
   ```
2 Backward selection
   ```
   step(a.lm, direction = "backward")
   ```

In this simple example, all three approaches agree and select a model with the variables X_2, X_3, X_4 and X_6 (no X_5 term).

Table 7.3 Data set for tutorial exercise Chapter 7

Year	IMPORTS $ millions	GNP $ billions	CPI 1967=100
1970	39866	992.7	116.3
1971	45579	1077.6	121.3
1972	55797	1185.9	125.3
1973	70499	1326.4	133.1
1974	103811	1434.2	147.7
1975	98185	1549.2	161.2
1976	124228	1718	170.5
1977	151907	1918.3	181.5
1978	176020	2163.9	195.4
1979	212028	2417.8	217.4
1980	249781	2631.7	246.8
1981	265086	2957.8	272.4
1982	247667	3069.3	289.1
1983	261312	3304.8	298.4

Multicollinearity and inter-relationships between the X-variables mean that there is some redundancy and the X_5 variable is not needed in the model. This means that the number employed just depends on the following:

1 X_2 GNP
2 X_3 Number of people unemployed
3 X_4 Number of people in the armed services
4 X_6 Time in years

To re-fit the model with just these variables and interpret the results use
step.lm<-lm(y~x2+x3+x4+x6)
summary(step.lm)

The R results obtained are as follows:

Estimate Std error t-value Pr(>|t|)
(Intercept) -3.599e+03 7.406e+02 -4.859 0.000503 ***
x2 -4.019e-02 1.647e-02 -2.440 0.032833 *
x3 -2.088e-02 2.900e-03 -7.202 1.75e-05 ***
x4 -1.015e-02 1.837e-03 -5.522 0.000180 ***
x6 1.887e+00 3.828e-01 4.931 0.000449 ***

The conventional interpretation of these results would then be as follows. The coefficient of X_2 is negative and statistically significant. As GNP increases, the number of people employed decreases. The coefficient of X_3 is negative and statistically significant. As the number of people unemployed increases, the number of people employed decreases. The coefficient of X_4 is negative and statistically significant. As the number of people in the armed services increases, the number of people employed decreases. The coefficient of X_6 is positive. This suggests that the number of people employed is generally increasing over time.

The paragraph above details all the interpretation elements that would naturally be expected of students in assessments on our modules. However, there is a sense that there may be a little extra needed here for full interpretation of this example. Since, in this example, the interpretations for X_2 and X_4 appear contradictory, the suggestion here is that the effect of these variables is dwarfed by the general increase in employment over time. One might then reasonably ask whether this trend is likely to continue into the future.

7.7 Tutorial exercises

1 The data in the following table gives data on imports, GDP and the Consumer Price Index (CPI) over the period 1970–1983.
   (a) Enter this data into R using

   imports<-c(39866, 45579, 55797, 70499, 103811, 98185, 124228, 151907, 176020, 212028, 249781, 265086, 247667, 261312)
   gnp<-c(992.7, 1077.6, 1185.9, 1326.4, 1434.2, 1549.2, 1718, 1918.3, 2163.9, 2417.8, 2631.7, 2957.8, 3069.3, 3304.8)
   cpi<-c(116.3, 121.3, 125.3, 133.1, 147.7, 161.2, 170.5, 181.5, 195.4, 217.4, 246.8, 272.4, 289.1, 298.4)

   (b) You are asked to consider the model

$$\ln(\text{imports}) = \beta_1 + \beta_2 \ln(\text{GNP}_t) + \beta_3 \ln(\text{CPI}_t) + u_t.$$

   Estimate the parameters of this model using the given data.
   (c) Do you suspect that there is multicollinearity in the data?
   (d) Regress

$$\ln(\text{imports}) = A_1 + A_2 \ln(\text{GNP}_t)$$
$$\ln(\text{imports}) = B_1 + B_2 \ln(\text{CPI}_t)$$
$$\ln(\text{GNP}_t) = C_1 + C_2 \ln(\text{CPI}_t)$$

   Based on these regressions, what can you say about the nature of multicollinearity in this data?

(e) Suppose there is multicollinearity in the data but $\hat{\beta}_2$ and $\hat{\beta}_3$ are individually significant at the 5% level and the overall F-test is significant. If this is the case, should we worry about the collinearity problem?

2 The data in **hotelpriceratings.txt** lists the average customer rating for hotels in terms of the location and price of the hotel.

(a) Enter the data into R using the code
```
hotelpriceratings<-read.table("E:hotelpriceratings.txt")
location<-hotelpriceratings[,1]
price<-hotelpriceratings[,2]
ratings<-hotelpriceratings[,3]
location<-factor(location)
```

(b) Plot rating against price. What possible model does this suggest?

(c) Using the following R code, fit a regression model for hotel rating in terms of price and location allowing for possible interactions between price and location and between price squared and location.
```
pricesq<-price^2
full.lm<-lm(ratings~price*location+pricesq*location)
```

(d) Are there any possible indications of multicollinearity at this stage?

(e) Test for the significance of the interaction term between price squared and location.

(f) Following on from part (e), test for the significance of the quadratic term.

(g) Following on from part (f), test for the significance of the location term.

(h) Based on results in parts (e–g), suggest and interpret a regression model for how the hotel rating depends on price and location.

3 Apply stepwise regression techniques to the data in Table 7.2. What model do each of the three methods choose?

4 The data in the file **footballresults.txt** records results part way through the 2020–2021 English Premier League season. This question details an approximate solution using classical regression models – sometimes known in this context as a linear probability model. A more exact solution using probability regression models is discussed below in Question 5.

(a) Using the command **read.table**, read this data into R and give this data the label footballresults.

(b) Enter the following code into R:
```
hometeam<-footballresults[,1]
awayteam<-footballresults[,4]
homegoals<-footballresults[,2]
awaygoals<-footballresults[,3]
homewin<-I*(homegoals>awaygoals)
awaywin<-I*(homegoals<awaygoals)
```

(c) Letting y = homewin be the dependent variable, test the null hypothesis that the teams involved do not affect the probability of a home win.

(d) Letting y = awaywin be the dependent variable, test the null hypothesis that the teams involved do not affect the probability of a home win.

(e) Estimate the probability of a home win in the following matches:
   Burnley v Man City
   Fulham v Leicester
   Leeds v Everton
   Aston Villa v West Ham
   Liverpool v Brighton

(f) Estimate the probability of an away win in the matches in part (e).

(g) Estimate the probability of a draw in the matches in part (e).

5 The data in the file **footballresults.txt** records results part way through the 2020–2021 English Premier league season.

(a) Using the command **read.table**, read this data into R and give this data the label footballresults.

(b) Enter the following code into R. What is the purpose of the command cbind in this instance?
```
hometeam<-footballresults[,1]
awayteam<-footballresults[,4]
homegoals<-footballresults[,2]
awaygoals<-footballresults[,3]
homewin<-1*(homegoals>awaygoals)
awaywin<-1*(homegoals<awaygoals)
homesuccess<-cbind(homewin, 1-homewin)
awaysuccess<-cbind(awaywin, 1-awaywin)
```

(c) Enter the following commands into R. Then use the command **anova** to test the null hypothesis that the teams involved do not affect the probability of a home win.
```
nullhome<-glm(homesuccess~1, family=binomial)
teamshome<-glm(homesuccess~hometeam+awayteam,
family=binomial)
```

(d) Enter the commands shown below into R. Then use the command **anova** to test the null hypothesis that the teams involved do not affect the probability of an away win.
```
nullaway<-glm(awaysuccess~1, family=binomial)
teamsaway<-glm(awaysuccess~hometeam+awayteam,
family=binomial)
```

(e) Estimate the probability of a home win in the following matches:
   Burnley v Man City
   Fulham v Leicester
   Leeds v Everton
   Aston Villa v West Ham
   Liverpool v Brighton

(f) Estimate the probability of an away win in the matches in part (e).

(g) Using the results in parts (e–f), how would you estimate the probability of a draw in these matches?

7.8 Solutions

1 (a) n/a
  (b) Using the R function **log** for the natural logarithm ln fit the model
       using
       yl<-log(imports)
       x2<-log(gnp)
       x3<-log(cpi)
       a.lm<-lm(yl~x2+x3)
       summary(a.lm)
       Coefficients:
       Estimate Std error t-value Pr(>|t|)
       (Intercept) -2.3109 1.0294 -2.245 0.04631 *
       x2 3.2302 0.7514 4.299 0.00126 **
       x3 -1.9679 0.9204 -2.138 0.05578 .
  (c) One of the signatures of multicollinearity is that variables do not have
       the right sign as anticipated from the underlying economic theory. If
       we were to interpret the above at face value, we would say the follow-
       ing: The coefficient of X_3 is negative and statistically significant. This
       suggests that as log CPI increases, imports decrease. However, CPI is
       usually taken to be a measure of domestic inflation. Increases in CPI
       actually increase the value of imported goods so, counterintuitively,
       this negative coefficient is actually in conflict with economic theory.
       Allied to the above, typing **cor(x2, x3)** into R shows that the correla-
       tion between X_2 and X_3 is 0.9941029. This very high level of correlation
       also indicates possible multicollinearity.
  (d) The auxiliary regressions can be performed using the following R code:
       b.lm<-lm(yl~x2)
       summary(b.lm)
       Coefficients:
       Estimate Std error t-value Pr(>|t|)
       (Intercept) -0.54311 0.69866 -0.777 0.452
       x2 1.63312 0.09281 17.595 6.19e-10 ***
       Residual standard error: 0.1353 on 12 degrees of freedom
       Multiple R-squared: 0.9627, Adjusted R-squared: 0.9596
       F-statistic: 309.6 on 1 and 12 DF, p-value: 6.188e-10
       c.lm<-lm(yl~x3)
       summary(c.lm)
       Coefficients:
       Estimate Std error t-value Pr(>|t|)
       (Intercept) 1.5081 0.8154 1.85 0.0891 .
       x3 1.9656 0.1564 12.56 2.89e-08 ***
       Residual standard error: 0.1861 on 12 degrees of freedom
       Multiple R-squared: 0.9294, Adjusted R-squared: 0.9235
       F-statistic: 157.9 on 1 and 12 DF, p-value: 2.893e-08
       d.lm<-lm(x2~x3)

summary(d.lm)
Coefficients:
Estimate Std error t-value Pr(>|t|)
(Intercept) 1.18229 0.19986 5.915 7.08e-05 ***
x3 1.21776 0.03835 31.756 6.00e-13 ***
--- Signif. codes: 0 '***' 0.001 '**' 0.01 '*' 0.05 '.' 0.1 ' ' 1
Residual standard error: 0.04563 on 12 degrees of freedom
Multiple R-squared: 0.9882, Adjusted R-squared: 0.9873
F-statistic: 1008 on 1 and 12 DF, p-value: 5.995e-13

Note that the high R^2 values (in each case, > 0.8) violate Klein's rule of thumb discussed previously and so give further evidence that multi-collinearity is a problem with this data set.

(e)   The layout of the original question is perhaps a little misleading. Probably the best way to analyse this data is to use the CPI data to correct both imports and GNP for inflation.

Fitting a regression model involving the inflation-adjusted imports and inflation-adjusted GNP then reinforces just how strong the relationship between GNP and imports is.
logrealimports<-y1-x3
logrealgnp<-x2-x3
real.lm<-lm(logrealimports~logrealgnp)
summary(real.lm)
Coefficients:
Estimate Std error t-value Pr(>|t|)
(Intercept) -2.9785 0.9388 -3.173 0.00803 **
logrealgnp 4.1077 0.4053 10.136 3.09e-07 ***
--- Signif. codes: 0 '***' 0.001 '**' 0.01 '*' 0.05 '.' 0.1 ' ' 1
Residual standard error: 0.123 on 12 degrees of freedom
Multiple R-squared: 0.8954, Adjusted R-squared: 0.8867
F-statistic: 102.7 on 1 and 12 DF, p-value: 3.094e-07

Note that, in this case, the adjustment to real values is made using real GNP $= \dfrac{\text{GNP}}{\text{CPI}}$. This means that when taking logs $(\ln(x/y) = \ln(x) - \ln(y))$, we have that

$$\ln(\text{real GNP}) = \ln\left(\frac{\text{GNP}}{\text{CPI}}\right) = \ln(\text{GNP}) - \ln(\text{CPI})$$

2 (a) n/a
   (b) Use plot(price, ratings) to obtain results shown in Fig. 7.1. Results suggest a possible quadratic relationship between ratings and price.

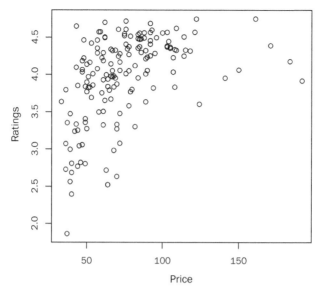

Figure 7.1 Plot of the average hotel rating as a function of price

(c) n/a

(d) Obtain results using summary(full.lm). Non-significant t-ratios give an indication of possible multicollinearity and some redundancy within the full model.

(e) Using an F-test suggests that the interaction term between price squared and location is not needed in the model.
minusone.lm<-lm(ratings~price*location+pricesq)
anova(full.lm, minusone.lm, test="F")
Res.Df RSS Df Sum of Sq F Pr(>F)
1 143 30.772
2 147 32.422 -4 -1.6501 1.917 0.1108

(f) Using an F-test suggests that price squared is needed in the model.
minustwo.lm<-lm(ratings~price*location)
anova(minustwo.lm, minusone.lm, test="F")
Res.Df RSS Df Sum of Sq F Pr(>F)
1 148 37.355
2 147 32.422 1 4.9323 22.363 5.242e-06 ***

(g) Using an F-test suggests that location is not needed in the model.
minusthree.lm<-lm(ratings~price+pricesq)
anova(minusone.lm, minusthree.lm)
Res.Df RSS Df Sum of Sq F Pr(>F)
1 147 32.422
2 155 34.552 -8 -2.1302 1.2072 0.2986

(h) Results suggest that location is not a significant factor and that there is a roughly quadratic relationship between price and rating. This has two alternative theoretical interpretations. Firstly, hotels may choose a price to maximize the rating. Secondly, hotels may fix a desired rating level and choose the highest possible price that is consistent with this objective.

3 Having entered the data, conduct the backward selection using

```
back.lm<-lm(y~x2+x3)
summary(back.lm)
```

Non-significant t-statistics suggest deleting X_3. Continuing to fit the following model suggests fitting the model with just the X_2 term.

```
back2.lm<-lm(y~x2)
summary(back2.lm)
```

For forward and stepwise selection use, e.g.

```
forwardl.lm<-lm(y~x2)
summary(forwardl.lm)
forward2.lm<-lm(y~x3)
summary(forward2.lm)
```

Significant t values suggest X_2 enters the model. In a second forward selection step, the variable X_3 does not enter the model.

```
forward3.lm<-lm(y~x2+x3)
summary(forward3.lm)
```

Note that all three approaches suggest the same regression model with just a single X_2 term.

4 (a) `footballresults<-read.table("E:footballresults.txt")`

(b) n/a

(c) Results from an F-test give conclusive evidence that the probability of a home win does depend on the two teams involved.

```
null.lm<-lm(homewin~l)
full.lm<-lm(homewin~hometeam+awayteam)
anova(full.lm, null.lm)
Res.Df RSS Df Sum of Sq F Pr(>F)
1 170 35.699
2 208 49.139 -38 -13.439 1.6842 0.01347 *
```

(d) Results from an F-test gives weak evidence that the probability of a home win does depend on the two teams involved.

```
nullaway.lm<-lm(awaywin~l)
fullaway.lm<-lm(awaywin~hometeam+awayteam)
anova(fullaway.lm, nullaway.lm)
Res.Df RSS Df Sum of Sq F Pr(>F)
1 170 37.559
2 208 49.828 -38 -12.269 1.4614 0.05444 .
```

(e) The results can be forecast using the R command predict:

```
data<-data.frame(awayteam=c("ManCity", "Leicester", "Everton",
"WestHam", "Brighton"), hometeam=c("Burnley", "Fulham",
"Leeds", "AstonVilla", "Liverpool"))
predict(full.lm, data) 1 2 3 4 5
0.1884178 -0.1682318 0.2025270 0.2937012 0.6730936
```

Hence, estimates for these probabilities are 0.1884178, 0, 0.2025270, 0.2937012 and 0.6730936.

(f) The results can be forecast using the R command **predict**:
predict(fullaway.lm, data) 1 2 3 4 5
0.56310609 0.89833962 0.67555471 0.59961801 -0.01685319
Hence, estimates for these probabilities are 0.56310609, 0.89833962, 0.67555471, 0.59961801 and 0.

(g) Using P(Draw)=1−P(Home win) − P(Away win) the draw probabilities can be calculated as 0.2484761, 0.1016604, 0.1219183 0.1066808 and 0.3269064.

5 (a) footballresults<-read.table("E:footballresults.txt")

(b) The command **cbind** is needed in order to gather the columns of successes and failures. This step is required whenever fitting probability regression models in R.

(c) anova(nullhome, teamshome, test="Chisq")
Analysis of Deviance Table
Model 1: homesuccess ~ 1
Model 2: homesuccess ~ hometeam + awayteam
Resid. Df Resid. Dev Df Deviance Pr(>Chi)
1 208 277.16
2 170 206.69 38 70.472 0.001061 **

Therefore, the results present significant evidence that the outcome of each match depends on the teams involved.

(d) anova(nullaway, teamsaway, test="Chisq")
Analysis of Deviance Table
Model 1: awaysuccess ~ 1
Model 2: awaysuccess ~ hometeam + awayteam
Resid. Df Resid. Dev Df Deviance Pr(>Chi)
1 208 279.97
2 170 220.08 38 59.887 0.01326 *

Therefore, the results present significant evidence that the outcome of each match depends on the teams involved.

(e) The results can be forecast using the R command **predict**:
data<-data.frame(awayteam=c("ManCity", "Leicester", "Everton", "WestHam", "Brighton"), hometeam=c("Burnley", "Fulham", "Leeds", "AstonVilla", "Liverpool"))
exp(predict(teamshome, data))/(1+ exp(predict(teamshome, data)))
1 2 3 4 5
0.13838899 0.01145022 0.19556953 0.25964266 0.79554163

(f) The results can be forecast using the R command **predict**:
data<-data.frame(awayteam=c("ManCity", "Leicester", "Everton", "WestHam", "Brighton"), hometeam=c("Burnley", "Fulham", "Leeds", "AstonVilla", "Liverpool"))

exp(predict(teamsaway, data))/(1+ exp(predict(teamsaway, data)))

1 2 3 4 5

0.58058255 0.89426119 0.68706226 0.64943145 0.04225952

(g) Use P(Draw)=1 − P(Home win) − P(Away win)

8 Dummy variable regression models

8.1 Overview: the nature of dummy variable regression

The subjects of analysis of variance (ANOVA) and analysis of covariance (ANCOVA) present examples of when the terminology used can be confusing and make things look harder than they really are. Quite simply:

1 ANOVA refers to situations where regression models contain purely qualitative X variables.
2 ANCOVA refers to situations where regression models contain a combination of qualitative and quantitative X variables.

It is often convenient to discuss regression models where some of the X variables are qualitative in nature. Amongst the wealth of examples discussed in Gujarati and Porter (2009) are categories such as male/female, black-/white, Catholic/non-Catholic etc. In this case, these variables essentially codify whether the effect is absent $(X = 0)$ or present $(X = 1)$. However, there are numerous examples where the categories involved consist of more than two levels. Examples include seasons of the year (see later in this chapter) or regions in the UK (see Chapter 10).

Dummy variables are often (but not always) associated with the time of the year. Suppose we have data on quarterly fridge sales. A portion of this dataset is shown in Table 8.1.

The data in Table 8.1 hints at two possible approaches:

1 Include $4 - 1 = 3$ dummy variables in addition to the constant term.
2 Include one variable with all four categories listed.

The differences between the two approaches are due to the following:

1 This is how the subject is often taught from first principles.
2 This is the most efficient way of organizing this data in R using the command factor.

Table 8.1 Portion of a dataset on quarterly fridge sales

Fridge sales	Durable goods sales	Q1	Q2	Q3	Q4	Quarter
1317	252.6	1	0	0	0	1
1615	272.4	0	1	0	0	2
1662	270.9	0	0	1	0	3
1295	273.9	0	0	0	1	4

The first approach is often more cumbersome with datasets of any appreciable size. This approach offers another potential shortfall known in econometrics as the dummy variable trap. Suppose you follow the first approach outlined above. If you have four different levels you would need $4 - 1 = 3$ dummy variables in the regression model in addition to the constant term. In general terms, if you have m different levels you would need $m - 1$ dummy variables in the regression model in addition to the constant term. We now show where these numbers come from.

Suppose that you have a qualitative X variable that takes m different levels (e.g. the previous example has $m = 4$ quarters corresponding to the time of the year). Clearly, you need at least $m - 1$ dummy variables plus the intercept term in order to represent each of the m categories that can possibly arise – the m different labels require at least m different ways of encoding the information contained therein. Now, suppose that you include m dummy variables together with the constant term. The regression model now becomes

$$y = \beta_0(1) + \beta_1 D_1 + ... + \beta_m D_m + u \qquad (8.1)$$

where $D_1, D_2, ..., D_m$ denote dummy variables. Now

$$\frac{1}{m} D_1 + ... + \frac{1}{m} D_m = 1$$

This means there is an exact linear relationship between the X-variables on the right-hand side of the regression model in Eq. (8.1). This contradicts the assumptions of the classical linear regression model (see Chapter 5).

8.2 ANOVA models

The full dataset associated with Table 8.1 links the sales of fridges and the sales of durable goods to the time of year. Ignoring, for the moment, data on the sales of durable goods, suppose you want to fit regression and analysis of variance models to link fridge sales to the time of the year. There are two basic ways in which this can be achieved:

1 A regression approach using the command **lm**
2 An analysis of variance (ANOVA) approach using the command **aov**

The data is in the file **ancova.txt**

```
ancova<-read.table("E:ancova.txt")
fridge<-ancova[,1]
durables<-ancova[,2]
q1<-ancova[,3]
q2<-ancova[,4]
q3<-ancova[,5]
q4<-ancova[,6]
quarter<-ancova[,7]
```

Processing dummy variables in R now works as follows. Using the above commands, the variables q1, q2, q3 and q4 take the values 0 and 1. No further data processing is needed for these, although only three of these dummy variables can be included into the regression model if you also include an intercept term. In order to follow the second, more efficient, approach, you need to tell R that the variable **quarter** is a qualitative variable. In R, the command to do this is **factor**:
```
quarter<-factor(quarter)
```
Recall that there are two ways of fitting regression and ANOVA models in R:

1 A regression approach using the command **lm**
2 An analysis of variance approach using the command **aov**

Next, we show that both approaches lead to the same numerical answers in our example. Firstly, using a dummy variable approach (and arbitrarily excluding q1):
```
dummy.lm<-lm(fridge~q2+q3+q4)
summary(dummy.lm)
```

This leads to the following regression output:
```
Coefficients:
Estimate Std error t-value Pr(>|t|)
(Intercept) 1222.12 59.99 20.372 < 2e-16 ***
q2 245.38 84.84 2.892 0.007320 **
q3 347.63 84.84 4.097 0.000323 ***
q4 -62.12 84.84 -0.732 0.470091
```

Next, using the more advanced **factor command**:
```
factor.lm<-lm(fridge~quarter)
summary(factor.lm)
```

This leads to the following regression output and shows that you get the same numerical answers using both approaches:

Coefficients:
Estimate Std error t-value Pr(>|t|)
(Intercept) 1222.12 59.99 20.372 < 2e-16 ***
quarter2 245.38 84.84 2.892 0.007320 **
quarter3 347.63 84.84 4.097 0.000323 ***
quarter4 -62.12 84.84 -0.732 0.470091

Next, we want to repeat the above computations using a formal analysis of variance (ANOVA) model in R. This analysis using ANOVA requires you to make use of the command factor. So there is now no alternative but to use the more advanced factor approach. (As discussed above, this approach is also more convenient for use with datasets of appreciable size.) Using the R syntax in exactly the same way as before leads to the following analysis of variance table:

factor.aov<-aov(fridge~quarter)
summary(factor.aov)
Df Sum Sq Mean Sq F value Pr(>F)
quarter 3 915636 305212 10.6 7.91e-05 ***
Residuals 28 806142 28791

It is now instructive to reconstruct the above F-statistic both computationally in R and also by hand. This then shows you that regression and analysis of variance lead to the same answers despite cosmetic differences in how you interpret model results. In order to reconstruct the F-statistic from scratch, we are testing the null hypothesis that including the four levels of the variable quarter does not improve upon the simple model with just a constant term. In R, define the regression model with just a constant term:

null.lm<-lm(fridge~1)

Then, use the command anova to obtain the same values as above:

anova(factor.lm, null.lm)

The above shows how to computationally verify that regression and ANOVA give the same numerical answers. However, by-hand calculation of the F-statistic is also instructive even though this approach may seem a little old fashioned. We can thus show that the two models give the same answers by repeating the earlier calculations by hand. Using summary(factor.lm), we can see that the R^2 value is 0.5318 and the residual degrees of freedom are given by $n - p = 28$. The change in the degrees of freedom is $4 - 1 = 3$ (equivalent to the number of levels minus 1 and in line with our earlier discussion of the dummy variable trap). The F-statistic can thus be constructed as

$$F = \frac{\frac{\Delta R^2}{\Delta \, \mathrm{d.f.}}}{\frac{1-R^2}{n-p}} = \frac{(0.5318/3)}{(1-0.5318)/28} = \frac{0.1772667}{0.01672143} = 10.60117$$

giving the same answer as above, subject to minor rounding error.

8.3 ANOVA models with two qualitative variables

In a similar way, it is also possible to define ANOVA models with two qualitative X variables. The classical term used is two-way analysis of variance. Really, these models get most interesting with the introduction of interaction terms (as we shall see below). However, it is important to note that you are not constrained to have a limit on the number of X variables. You can also have, for example, three-way ANOVA, four-way ANOVA etc. (although the two-way ANOVA is sufficient to illustrate the general principles). You can also have higher-order interaction terms as the order of the model increases. The only real constraint would be that high-order interaction terms can prove rather difficult to interpret and so are not usually included into regression models.

To illustrate two-way ANOVA, we adopt an example discussed in Gujarati and Porter (2009). Suppose you have the following ANOVA model to investigate average hourly earnings in terms of gender and race

$$Y_i = \beta_1 + \beta_2 D_{2,i} + \beta_3 D_{3,i} + u_i \tag{8.2}$$

where $D_{2,i}$ is 1 if the respondent if female and 0 otherwise, and $D_{3,i}$ is 1 if the respondent is non-white and non-Hispanic and 0 otherwise. The natural question to ask is, 'How would you interpret the results of this model?'

From Eq. (8.2), it follows that, for a male white/Hispanic, the average hourly wage is given by

$$\beta_1 + \beta_2(0) + \beta_3(0) = \beta_1$$

Similarly, for a female white/Hispanic, the average hourly wage is given by

$$\beta_1 + \beta_2(1) + \beta_3(0) = \beta_1 + \beta_2$$

This means that if $\beta_2 < 0$, the suggestion would be that females are generally paid less. In a similar vein, for male non-white and non-Hispanic workers, the average hourly wage is given by

$$\beta_1 + \beta_2(0) + \beta_3(1) = \beta_1 + \beta_3$$

Similarly, for female non-white and non-Hispanic workers, the average hourly wage is given by

$$\beta_1 + \beta_2(1) + \beta_3(1) = \beta_1 + \beta_2 + \beta_3$$

If you compare these values with, for example, the average wage of β_1 for a male who is white or Hispanic, the suggestion is that if $\beta_3 < 0$, then non-white and non-Hispanic workers are generally paid less.

There are at least two ways of fitting two-way ANOVA models in R:

1 lm for linear model
2 aov for analysis of variance

This reflects that ANOVA models can be seen as a special case of linear regression models (Bingham and Fry 2010). In both cases, you need to define the X variables used as qualitative variables or factors. So, for the above wages example, you would use
gender<-factor(gender)
race<-factor(race)

Both approaches use the familiar two-step approach:

1 A computational modelling step that generates no output
2 Use of the command **summary** to explicitly show you the results

Aspects of the R syntax also remain the same for both options. For a regression approach with the lm function use
a.lm<-lm(wage~gender+race)
summary(a.lm)

For an ANOVA approach with the aov function use
a.aov<-aov(wage~gender+race)
summary(a.aov)

8.4 ANOVA models with interactions

Higher-order models are possible but, as before, a two-way model is sufficient to illustrate the general principles. Thus, in this section, we consider a two-way ANOVA model with interactions. In higher-order models, three-way interaction terms and higher are possible. However, in practice, you may be unlikely to see such models as they can quickly become hard to interpret. As before, there are a number of important recurring themes:

1 Models remain part of the general class of linear regression models.
2 The R commands are essentially the same in order to reflect this.
3 Models can, as before, be fitted either using the lm or the aov commands.

The first thing to emphasize is that, loosely speaking, interaction means multiply. Interaction terms thus allow us to account for multiplicative as opposed to purely additive effects within the standard class of general linear regression models. It is easy to see how you can just multiply two quantitative variables X_2 and X_3 to form an additional regressor: $X_4 = X_2 X_3$. For qualitative variables, the effect of the interaction term is to allow for more subtle effects at the intersection of two categories. So, in the context of the gender and race example that we used earlier, we might reasonably ask whether the gender bias encountered is more extreme for non-white and non-Hispanic women.

Now, because interaction means multiply, this has a direct effect on the R commands used.

1   To fit the full second-order model with interactions, use $X_2 * X_3$ in the formula of the regression or ANOVA model.
2   To add a specific interaction term in the formula section of the regression or ANOVA model, use $+X_2 : X_3$.

As an example of a two-way ANOVA with interaction model, recall our previous example exploring how the hourly wage Y depends on gender and race. From first principles, a two-way ANOVA with interactions model can thus be constructed as

$$Y_i = \beta_1 + \beta_2 D_{2,i} + \beta_3 D_{3,i} + \beta_4 (D_{2,i} D_{3,i}) + u_i \qquad (8.3)$$

where $D_{2,i}$ is 1 if the respondent if female and 0 otherwise, and $D_{3,i}$ is 1 if the respondent is non-white and non-Hispanic and 0 otherwise. The basic idea is that if the final term $\beta_4 \neq 0$, then there is evidence of an interaction between gender and race.

The model in Eq. (8.3) can be interpreted as follows. If $\beta_4 = 0$, then Eq. (8.3) reduces to the simple two-way ANOVA model shown in Eq. (8.2). Beyond this, consider a male white/Hispanic worker. The average hourly wage is, in this case, given by

$$\beta_1 + \beta_2(0) + \beta_3(0) + \beta_4(0) = \beta_1$$

Similarly, for a female white/Hispanic worker, the average hourly wage is given by

$$\beta_1 + \beta_2(1) + \beta_3(0) + \beta_4(0) = \beta_1 + \beta_2$$

So, if $\beta_2 < 0$, the suggestion would be that females are generally paid less. We thus get exactly the same results and interpretation as in the previous section. The only difference is if both gender **AND** racial effects are present. Now, if we consider the case of a female non-white and non-Hispanic worker, the average hourly wage is given by

$$\beta_1 + \beta_2(1) + \beta_3(1) + \beta_4(1) = \beta_1 + \beta_2 + \beta_3 + \beta_4$$

So, if $\beta_4 < 0$, this suggests that there is an additional racial effect that women workers are subject to.

There are at least two ways of fitting two-way ANOVA with interaction models in R:

1   lm for linear model
2   aov for analysis of variance

This reflects the fact that ANOVA models can be seen as a special case of linear regression models (Bingham and Fry 2010). In both cases, you need to define the X variables used as qualitative variables or factors. So, for the above wages example, you would use

```
gender<-factor(gender)
race<-factor(race).
```

For a regression approach with the lm function use
```
al.lm<-lm(wage~gender*race)
summary(al.lm)
```
or
```
a2.lm<-lm(wage~gender+race+gender:race)
summary(a2.lm).
```

For an ANOVA approach using aov use
```
al.aov<-aov(wage~gender*race)
summary(al.aov)
```
or
```
a2.aov<-aov(wage~gender+race+gender:race)
summary(a2.aov).
```

8.5 ANCOVA: regression with qualitative AND quantitative dependent variables

Classical linear regression models variously include the following:

1 Regular regression: all X variables quantitative
2 ANOVA: all X variables qualitative

ANCOVA simply combines both of these two extreme cases. Thus, ANCOVA refers to situations where regression models combine **BOTH** qualitative **AND** quantitative X variables.

It is easy to envisage ANCOVA in terms of combining the mathematical and programming elements of previously defined regression models. The main point of ANCOVA from a teaching perspective is that it enables you to envisage regression models with different slopes and different intercept terms to be fitted to different parts of the dataset. This is potentially a very neat and elegant way of condensing quite complex information and complex data. The models constructed are sometimes referred to as segmented regression models as the effect is to potentially fit different regression lines to each segment of the data.

Consider an example with a qualitative variable Q that takes two levels (0 and 1) and a quantitative variable X. In particular, consider the regression model $Y = Q * X$ where $*$ means the interaction term and all main effects terms are present. The model $Y = Q * X$ leads to the regression equation

$$Y = \beta_1 + \beta_2 D_Q + \beta_3 X + \beta_4 D_Q X + u$$

So, if $Q = 0$,

$$Y = \beta_1 + \beta_3 X + u$$

Similarly, if $Q = 1$, the result is a model with different intercepts and different slopes

$$Y = (\beta_1 + \beta_2) + (\beta_3 X + \beta_4) X + u$$

Further, if $Q = 1$ and $\beta_4 = 0$, then the result is a model with a different intercept but the same slope term

$$Y = (\beta_1 + \beta_2) + \beta_4 X + u$$

Thus, as discussed above, this model with the interaction term gives a neat and elegant way of condensing relatively complex information about the fitted regression models.

Example 8.11

As an example of ANCOVA, consider again the data shown in Table 8.1 linking fridge sales (F) to durable goods expenditure (D). It is natural to fit a regression model of the form

$$F = \beta_1 + \beta_2 D + u \tag{8.4}$$

However, suppose we want to fit a regression model of the form shown in Eq. (8.4) in such a way that the values of β_1 and β_2 can potentially change depending on the time of the year. As discussed above, this effect can be achieved by fitting a regression model of the form $Y = Quarter*D$, where Quarter is a categorical variable describing the time of year.

The code to enter the data into R and to define **quarter** *as a factor variable is*

```
ancova<-read.table("E:ancova.txt")
fridge<-ancova[,1]
durables<-ancova[,2]
q1<-ancova[,3]
q2<-ancova[,4]
q3<-ancova[,5]
q4<-ancova[,6]
quarter<-ancova[,7]
quarter<-factor(quarter)
```

First, fit the model with all interaction terms and compare with the simpler model with just the main effects terms present. The non-significant result shown below means that the simpler model without the interaction terms should suffice.

```
ancova.lm<-lm(fridge~quarter*durables)
main.lm<-lm(fridge~durables+quarter)
```

anova(ancova.lm, main.lm)
Analysis of Variance Table
Res.Df RSS Df Sum of Sq F Pr(>F)
1 24 430992
2 27 465085 -3 -34093 0.6328 0.601

Next, fit the simpler model still with no quarterly term in it. Here, in contrast, the significant results shown below mean that the more complex model with the quarterly terms in it is required.
simple.lm<-lm(fridge~durables)
anova(main.lm, simple.lm)
Analysis of Variance Table
Res.Df RSS Df Sum of Sq F Pr(>F)
1 27 465085
2 30 1377145 -3 -912060 17.65 1.523e-06 ***

The regression output for the final model is shown below.

Coefficients:
Estimate Std error t-value Pr(>|t|)
(Intercept) 456.2440 178.2652 2.559 0.016404 *
durables 2.7734 0.6233 4.450 0.000134 ***
quarter2 242.4976 65.6259 3.695 0.000986 ***
quarter3 325.2643 65.8148 4.942 3.56e-05 ***
quarter4 -86.0804 65.8432 -1.307 0.202116

So, as a first segmented linear regression model, the above results suggest that a model with different intercepts but the same slope term is appropriate. In Quarter 1, the appropriate regression line is

$$F = 456.2440 + 2.7734D$$

In Quarter 2, the appropriate regression line is

$$F = 456.2440 + 242.4976 + 2.7734D = 698.7416 + 2.7734D$$

In Quarter 3 the appropriate regression line is

$$F = 456.2440 + 325.2643 + 2.7734D = 781.5083 + 2.7734D$$

In Quarter 4, the appropriate regression line is

$$F = 456.2440 - 86.0804 + 2.7734D = 370.1636 + 2.7734D$$

8.6 Summary

Dummy variable regression models occur when the dependent Y remains a quantitative measurement but some of the X variables are qualitative and denote membership categories rather than numerical measurements. Some of the terminology can be confusing but, essentially, ANOVA models occur when all the X variables are qualitative in nature. In contrast, ANCOVA models occur when the X variables are a mixture of qualitative and quantitative in nature. The same regression theory and programming applies in each case.

Often econometric textbooks give explicit examples of dummy variable construction (see, e.g., Gujarati and Porter 2009). However, this approach is best suited for teaching purposes and is not really appropriate for analysing real datasets. Care has to be taken to avoid the dummy variable trap. A variable with m categories needs $m - 1$ dummy variables associated to it if an intercept term is also fitted. This approach can quickly become cumbersome in problems of appreciable size.

In R, qualitative variables can automatically be incorporated using the command **factor** and this is the most efficient approach to use. In this case, interpretation of the regression output is the same but without the hassle of defining dummy variables. Use of the R command **factor** is useful to demonstrate the importance of abstract thinking in cases when the size of the dataset may make it inconvenient to look at a spreadsheet that shows all the data.

8.7 Tutorial exercises

The first four questions in this section derive from dissertation-type studies of the gender pay gap using data collected from the Office for National Statistics (ONS) website. This has been a favourite subject of some of our past dissertation students. The examples serve to demonstrate that even a relatively simple dataset may require a deceptively complex statistical solution using ANCOVA models. The fifth question comes from an applied industrial problem discussed in Brint and Fry (2021).

1 The data in Table 8.2 estimates the gender pay gap by age and full-time status.
   (a) Enter this data into R.
   (b) Using the mean gender pay gap as the dependent variable, fit a regression model to this data using forward selection.
   (c) What is the interpretation of the final model chosen?
   (d) Repeat the above analysis using the median gender pay gap as the dependent variable.
   (e) What is the purpose of repeating the analysis using the median gender pay gap in part (d)?
2 The data in Table 8.3 shows the evolution of the gender pay gap by full/part-time status over time.

Table 8.2 Data for Question 1. Gender pay gap by age and full-time status

Age	Mid age	Status	Mean gender pay gap	Median gender pay gap
18–21	19.5	FT	0.9	2.5
22–29	25.5	FT	2.1	4
30–39	34.5	FT	1.9	6.5
40–49	44.5	FT	11.4	14.7
50–59	54.5	FT	16.3	19.4
60+	64.5	FT	15.4	17.5
18–21	19.5	PT	0.3	0.9
22–29	25.5	PT	−1.1	1.4
30–39	34.5	PT	−3.5	1.7
40–49	44.5	PT	0	9.6
50–59	54.5	PT	6	19.3
60+	64.5	PT	9.9	20.7

(a) Enter this data into R.
(b) Fit the full main effects model.
(c) Is there any evidence of an interaction between time and status?
(d) Choose the most appropriate model from parts (b–c) and interpret the results.

3 The data in the file AncovaData2.txt records the evolution of the gender pay gap over time for various age groups.
   (a) Enter this data into R using the following code:
   ```
   data2<-read.table("F:AncovaData2.txt")
   year<-data2[,1]
   gpg<-c(data2[,2], data2[,3], data2[,4], data2[,5], data2[,6],
   data2[,7])
   year<-rep(year, 6)
   age<-rep(c("18-21", "22-29", "30-39", "40-49", "50-59", "60+"),
   c(24, 24, 24, 24, 24, 24))
   ```
   (b) Fit a model with main effects terms in year and age to explain the gender pay gap (gpg).
   (c) Is an interaction term needed in this model?
   (d) Choose the most appropriate model from parts (b–c) and interpret the results.

4 The data in the file AncovaData3.txt records the evolution of the gender pay gap over time for low paid, medium paid and high paid workers. It is particularly interesting to see whether the gender pay gap is actually more extreme for higher-paid workers.

Table 8.3 Data for Question 2. Gender pay gap by full/part-time status over time

Status	All	Full-time	Part-time
1997	27.5	17.4	0.6
1998	27.3	17.4	−4.0
1999	26.9	16.4	−2.6
2000	26.7	16.3	−3.5
2001	26.3	16.4	−3.7
2002	26.9	15.5	−0.6
2003	25.1	14.6	−1.3
2004	24.7	14.5	−2.6
2005	22.6	13.0	−3.0
2006	22.2	12.8	−2.2
2007	21.9	12.5	−2.2
2008	22.5	12.6	−3.7
2009	22.0	12.2	−2.5
2010	19.8	10.1	−4.3
2011	20.2	10.5	−5.1
2012	19.6	9.5	−5.5
2013	19.8	10.0	−5.9
2014	19.2	9.6	−5.5
2015	19.3	9.6	−6.8
2016	18.2	9.4	−6.1
2017	18.4	9.1	−5.3
2018	17.8	8.6	−4.9
2019	17.4	9.0	−3.5
2020	15.5	7.4	−2.9

(a) Enter this data into R using the following code:
```
data3<-read.table("F:AncovaData3.txt")
year<-data3[,1]
gpg<-c(data3[,2], data3[,3], data3[,4])
year<-rep(year, 3)
quantile<-rep(c("10%", "median", "90%"), c(24, 24, 24))
```
(b) Fit a model with main effects terms in year and quantile to explain the gender pay gap (gpg).

(c) Is an interaction term needed in this model?

(d) Choose the most appropriate model from parts (b–c) and interpret the results.

5 The data in the file ScoreData.txt consists of online customer satisfaction scores (column 1) for a set of products in column 2 (overview hotels) by the UK region of the reviewer (column 3). Column 4 is an additional variable included to assist manipulation of this dataset in R to exclude cases for which regional data was unavailable. The original aim of the study was to test for possible regional bias.

(a) Enter the data into R using the following commands:
```
scores<-read.table("E:ScoreData.txt")
rating<-scores[,1]
product<-scores[,2]
region<-scores[,3]
regionmissing<-scores[,4]
```

(b) Restrict to full cases with available regional information using the following code:
```
rating<-rating[regionmissing<1]
product<-product[regionmissing<1]
region<-region[regionmissing<1]
```

(c) Use an analysis of variance model to test for regional differences in this customer satisfaction data.

(d) Suggest two possible problems with this analysis.

8.8 Solutions

1 (a) Enter this data into R using
```
midage<-c(19.5, 25.5, 34.5, 44.5, 54.5, 64.5, 19.5, 25.5, 34.5, 44.5,
54.5, 64.5)
status<-c("FT", "FT", "FT", "FT", "FT", "FT", "PT", "PT", "PT",
"PT", "PT", "PT")
meangpg<-c(0.9, 2.1, 1.9, 11.4, 16.3, 15.4, 0.3, -1.1, -3.5, 0, 6, 9.9)
mediangpg<-c(2.5, 4, 6.5, 14.7, 19.4, 17.5, 0.9, 1.4, 1.7, 9.6, 19.3,
20.7)
```

(b) Begin by fitting a model with both main effects terms.
```
a.lm<-lm(meangpg~midage+status)
summary(a.lm)
```
Coefficients:
Estimate Std error t-value Pr(>|t|)
(Intercept) -4.69906 2.67466 -1.757 0.112814
midage 0.31356 0.05786 5.419 0.000422 ***
statusPT -6.06667 1.82357 -3.327 0.008844 **

Both main effects terms are significant. We can now test for the significance of an interaction term.

```
b.lm<-lm(meangpg~midage*status)
anova(a.lm, b.lm)
Res.Df RSS Df Sum of Sq F Pr(>F)
1 9 89.786
2 8 72.219 1 17.567 1.946 0.2005
```
This suggests that the interaction term between age and status is not significant, so the model with both main effects terms is sufficient.

(c) From part (b), the coefficient of age is positive and statistically significant. This suggests that the gender pay gap is more pronounced for older workers. The coefficient of status PT is negative and statistically significant. This suggests that the effect of the gender pay gap is reversed for part-time workers.

(d) Replace **meangpg** with **mediangpg**. As before, there is no evidence of an interaction between age and status.
```
a.lm<-lm(mediangpg~midage+status)
b.lm<-lm(mediangpg~midage*status)
anova(a.lm, b.lm)
Res.Df RSS Df Sum of Sq F Pr(>F)
1 9 72.258
2 8 64.050 1 8.2084 1.0252 0.3409
```
However, in this case, there also seems to be no dependence on full/part-time status. **c.lm<-lm(mediangpg~midage)**
```
anova(a.lm, c.lm)
Res.Df RSS Df Sum of Sq F Pr(>F)
1 9 72.258
2 10 82.342 -1 -10.083 1.2559 0.2914
```
In this case, the best model seems to be a model with a single main effect term for age. The coefficient of age is positive and statistically significant, as before.
```
summary(c.lm)
Coefficients:
Estimate Std error t-value Pr(>|t|)
(Intercept) -8.55440 2.28439 -3.745 0.00382 **
midage 0.45443 0.05257 8.645 5.93e-06 ***
```

(e) This serves as a simple robustness check. The gender pay gap seems chiefly related to age. The effect of full/part-time status is unclear depending on which measure of the gender pay gap is used.

2 (a) Save this data as a .txt file, e.g. AnocovaData1.txt. Then use
```
data1<-read.table("F:AncovaData1.txt")
year<-data1[,1]
all<-data1[,2]
full<-data1[,3]
part<-data1[,4]
year<-rep(year, 3)
gpg<-c(all, full, part)
status<-rep(c("all", "full", "part"), c(24, 24, 24))
```

(b) Fit the main effects model using
a.lm<-lm(gpg~year+status)

(c) Fit the interactions model using
b.lm<-lm(gpg~year*status) Results from an analysis of variance suggests that the model with interactions terms is needed. anova(a.lm, b.lm)
Res.Df RSS Df Sum of Sq F Pr(>F)
1 68 142.768
2 66 67.185 2 75.583 37.125 1.575e-11 ***

(d) Summarize the results using summary(b.lm). This gives
Coefficients:
Estimate Std error t-value Pr(>|t|)
(Intercept) 1039.34058 59.75710 17.393 < 2e-16 ***
year -0.50652 0.02975 -17.025 < 2e-16 ***
statusfull -155.73422 84.50929 -1.843 0.0698 .
statuspart -716.45751 84.50929 -8.478 3.70e-12 ***
year:statusfull 0.07270 0.04208 1.728 0.0887 .
year:statuspart 0.34396 0.04208 8.175 1.29e-11 ***

The coefficient of year is negative and statistically significant ($p < 2\times10^{-16} < 0.05$). This suggests that the gender pay gap is generally decreasing over time. The coefficient of part-time status is negative and statistically significant ($p = 3.70\times10^{-12} < 0.05$). This indicates that the gender pay gap is generally lower for part-time workers. The interaction term for year and part-time status is positive and statistically significant ($p = 1.29\times10^{-11} < 0.05$). This suggests that any advantages female part-time workers have over male workers may be generally decreasing over time.

3 (a) n/a

(b) Fit the main effects model using a.lm<-lm(gpg~year+age)

(c) Fit the model with interactions terms using
b.lm<-lm(gpg~year*age)
ANOVA then suggests that the model with interaction terms is indeed needed.
anova(a.lm, b.lm)
Res.Df RSS Df Sum of Sq F Pr(>F)
1 137 739.17
2 132 419.16 5 320.01 20.155 6.687e-15 ***

(d) Using summary(b.lm), gives
Coefficients:
Estimate Std error t-value Pr(>|t|)
(Intercept) 341.73494 105.54309 3.238 0.00152 **
year -0.16835 0.05255 -3.204 0.00170 **
age22-29 104.91977 149.26047 0.703 0.48334
age30-39 728.41936 149.26047 4.880 3.00e-06 ***

```
age40-49 898.20649 149.26047 6.018 1.64e-08 ***
age50-59 259.91981 149.26047 1.741 0.08395 .
age60+ -383.14535 149.26047 -2.567 0.01137 *
year:age22-29 -0.05339 0.07431 -0.718 0.47375
year:age30-39 -0.36183 0.07431 -4.869 3.15e-06 ***
year:age40-49 -0.44004 0.07431 -5.921 2.61e-08 ***
year:age50-59 -0.12213 0.07431 -1.643 0.10267
year:age60+ 0.19491 0.07431 2.623 0.00975 **
```

These results can be interpreted as follows. The coefficient of year is negative and statistically significant ($p = 0.00170 < 0.05$). This suggests that the gender pay gap is generally decreasing over time. The coefficient of age 30–39 is positive and statistically significant ($p = 3.00 \times 10^{-6}$). The coefficient of age 40–49 is positive and statistically significant ($p = 1.64 \times 10^{-8}$). The implication is that the gender pay gap may be particularly pronounced for those aged 30–39 and for those aged 40–49. The coefficient of age 60+ is negative and statistically significant. This suggests that there is reduced evidence of a gender pay gap in this category. Three significant interaction terms suggest that any particular advantages/disadvantages within these categories are generally decreasing over time.

4 (a) n/a
   (b) To fit the main effects model use a.lm<-lm(gpg~year+quantile)
   (c) To fit the model with interactions terms use
        b.lm<-lm(gpg~year*quantile)
        An ANOVA suggests that interaction terms are needed in the model.
        anova(a.lm, b.lm)
        Res.Df RSS Df Sum of Sq F Pr(>F)
        1 68 101.425
        2 66 41.526 2 59.9 47.602 1.591e-13 ***
   (d) Using summary(b.lm) gives
        Coefficients:
        Estimate Std error t-value Pr(>|t|)
        (Intercept) 8.699e+02 4.698e+01 18.517 < 2e-16 ***
        year -4.292e-01 2.339e-02 -18.350 < 2e-16 ***
        quantile90% -5.458e+02 6.644e+01 -8.215 1.09e-11 ***
        quantilemedian 1.167e+01 6.644e+01 0.176 0.861
        year:quantile90% 2.777e-01 3.308e-02 8.395 5.21e-12 ***
        year:quantilemedian -3.609e-03 3.308e-02 -0.109 0.913

The coefficient of year is negative and statistically significant ($p < 2 \times 10^{-16} < 0.05$). This suggests that the gender pay gap is generally decreasing over time. The coefficient of quantile 90% is negative and statistically significant. This suggests that the gender pay gap may be less for higher-paid workers. However, the year:quantile 90% term is positive and statistically significant ($p = 1.09 \times 10^{-11}$). This suggests that any relative advantages of higher-paid female workers are generally decreasing over time.

5 (a) n/a
   (b) n/a
   (c) The first thing we need to do is to tell R that the variable **product** is a factor variable:

   product<-factor(product)

   The analysis of variance of variance can be conducted using

   aov2<-aov(rating~region+product)
   anova(aov2)
   Df Sum Sq Mean Sq F value Pr(>F)
   region 10 27.8 2.783 2.5463 0.004548 **
   product 45 2819.9 62.665 57.3290 < 2.2e-16 ***
   Residuals 24309 26571.6 1.093

   The results give significant evidence ($p = 0.004548 < 0.05$) of differences between the UK regions.

   (d) The first problem is that the survey data is integer valued rather than continuous. However, treating them as continuous variables ultimately provides the more convenient way of answering the original industrial problem posed. The second, more serious, problem is that the above analysis neglects correlations caused by the sampling structure and the fact that the data as presented consists of repeat measurements from the same hotel. A solution to this problem using linear mixed effects models is presented in Chapter 10.

9 Probability regression models

9.1 Background and overview

The previous linear regression models discussed include dummy variable regression models. In this case, the Y-variable remains a continuous measurement but you may have qualitative or categorical X-variables. In contrast, in this chapter we discuss regression models where the Y-variable is categorical (often best interpreted as a probability of being in one of two categories). Examples might include yes/no, present/absent, Islamic bank/non-Islamic bank, high score/not a high score etc. These probability models are inherently more complex.

Classical regression models are great but run into problems very quickly. For example, simple surveys can generate surprisingly complex data. This complicated data necessitates more complicated statistical models – generalized linear models. However, it is possible to study rather a lot of statistics without covering generalized linear models. Whilst they are a mathematical object, generalized linear models remain interesting and important in practical terms. In applied statistical work, we have previously used generalized linear models to:

1 Model complicated survey data.
2 Model customer satisfaction data in an industrial problem (see Chapter 10).
3 Model the effect of the academic journal on the perceived quality of published research papers (a serious practical problem in academia).
4 Numerically analyse the readability measures of different websites (Burke and Fry 2019).

Our past dissertation students have also successfully used related models.

9.2 Regressing probabilities

Formally speaking, qualitative dependent variable models are regression models in which the Y-variable can be categorized as, e.g. yes/no, present/absent. However, some of the terminology used can be confusing. In our experience,

Table 9.1 Example dataset on the failure of aircraft components

Load (kg)	Tested	Failures
2500	50	10
2700	70	17
2900	100	30
3100	60	21
3300	40	18
3500	85	43
3700	90	54
3900	50	33
4100	80	60
4300	65	51

it is probably best to use the terms **successes** and **failures** to be consistent with R and R coding. In economics and finance, these models are often known as dichotomous/dummy variable regression models. However, we feel that the term probability regression model gives a clearer idea of what you are ultimately trying to do. Consider the following illustrative industrial example for the data shown in Table 9.1. How does the probability that an aircraft component fails depend on the applied load?

The R code to read this data in is as follows:

```
load<-c(2500, 2700, 2900, 3100, 3300, 3500, 3700, 3900, 4100, 4300)
tested<-c(50, 70, 100, 60, 40, 85, 90, 50, 80, 65)
failures<-c(10, 17, 30, 21, 18, 43, 54, 33, 60, 51)
```

You then need to calculate the proportion of successful components:

```
probsuccess<-1-failures/tested
```

Finally, some extra code is needed whenever you fit probability regression models. In this case, you need a column of successes and failures listed side by side. In R, the command you need in order to do this is cbind:

```
successes<-tested-failures
fasteners<-cbind(successes, failures)
```

9.3 The linear probability model

Consider the simple model

$$\text{Probability of success} = \beta_1 + \beta_2 \text{load} + u_i \qquad (9.1)$$

where the u_i in Eq. (9.1) is a normally distributed error term. This model is known as the linear probability model for two reasons:

1 It is understood that the left-hand side of the equation refers to a probability.
2 The model is just a linear regression model such as we have seen in previous chapters.

Looking at Eq. (9.1), it is natural to expect that the component is more likely to fail as the applied load increases. Equivalently, we might anticipate that the success probability is likely to decrease as the applied load increases. This means that it is natural to anticipate finding $\beta_2 < 0$ in Eq. (9.1). The fitted value of the regression model in Eq. (9.1) is to be interpreted as the probability that a component succeeds given the load that is applied. Since this is a probability, we must have that

$$0 \leq \beta_1 + \beta_2 \text{load} + u_i \leq 1 \tag{9.2}$$

However, there is no guarantee that Eq. (9.2) holds unless additional constraints are imposed. In particular, we might anticipate that very low values of the load (respectively, very high values of the load) may result in estimated probabilities being greater than one (respectively, less than zero). We can also show that the linear probability model violates two of the standard regression modelling assumptions:

1 Non-normality of the disturbances
2 Heteroscedasticity

Whilst true, these points are a little artificial and anybody sensible should surely feel uneasy about estimated probabilities potentially being either less than 0 or greater than 1!
    Non-normality of the u_i in Eq. (9.2) can be illustrated as follows. Since probabilities ≥ 0, we must have

$$\beta_1 + \beta_2 \text{load} + u_i \geq 0; \ u_i \geq -\beta_1 - \beta_2 \text{load}$$

Since probabilities are ≤ 1, we must have

$$\beta_1 + \beta_2 \text{load} + u_i \leq 1; \ u_i \leq 1 - \beta_1 - \beta_2 \text{load}$$

The conclusion

$$-\beta_1 - \beta_2 \text{load} \leq u_i \leq 1 - \beta_1 - \beta_2 \text{load} \tag{9.3}$$

shows that u_i can only take certain bounded values and so cannot be normally distributed. From Eq. (9.3), the bounds also depend on the value of the load. The distribution of the u_i, and hence also the variance of the u_i, also depend on the value of the load. Since the variance of the u_i depends on the load, the model is heteroscedastic.

The linear probability model is intuitively appealing since it combines probability estimates with simple linear regression. The model has been misguidedly popularized by classic econometric texts such as Gujarati and Porter (2009). Whilst the linear probability model may give sensible answers in the middle of the sample, extreme X-values are liable to lead to probability estimates that are either less than 0 or greater than 1. To ensure sensible probability estimates that lie between 0 and 1, alternatives such as the logit and probit models should be used.

9.4 Logit and probit models

Linear regression and probability regression models can be compared as follows:

1 Linear regression

$$Y = \beta_0 + \beta_1 X_1 + \ldots + \beta_p X_P \tag{9.4}$$

2 Probability regression

$$f(\text{probability of } Y) = \beta_0 + \beta_1 X_1 + \ldots + \beta_p X_P \tag{9.5}$$

Both of these equations can take either positive or negative values depending on the values of x and β. However, genuine probabilities must lie between 0 and 1. The function $f(\cdot)$ in Eq. (9.5) is known as the **link function**. This function, $f(\cdot)$, literally **links** the regression part of the model to the probability calculation. As shown in Fig. 9.1, the effect is to compress or squash down the fitted regression line so that the estimated probabilities lie between 0 and 1.

In view of the above, our aim is to fix regression to estimate probabilities. Keep the regression bit of the model – don't throw the baby out with the bathwater!

$$\beta_0 + \beta_1 X_1 + \ldots + \beta_p X_P$$

Since the above equation takes values in $(-\infty, \infty)$, we need a link function $f(\cdot)$ to 'squash' the equation so that we get sensible probability estimates:

$$f(p) = \beta_0 + \beta_1 X_1 + \ldots + \beta_p X_P$$

If done in the right way, much of the interpretation stays quite similar to standard regression. For example, if $\beta_i > 0$, as X_i increases, the probability increases. Similarly, if $\beta_i < 0$, as X_i increases, the probability decreases.

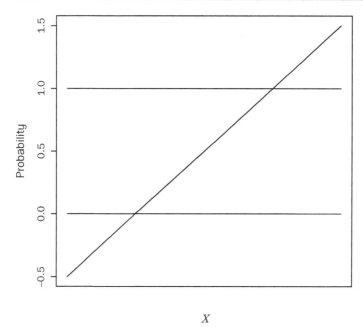

Figure 9.1 Illustration of how fitting unconstrained regression lines violates sensible probability bounds

How do you squash probabilities to lie between 0 and 1 for a logistic regression model? Note that the governing equation is

$$\ln\left(\frac{p_i}{1 - p_i}\right) = \beta_0 + \beta_1 x_i$$

The probability can then be calculated as

$$\frac{p_i}{1 - p_i} = \exp(\beta_0 + \beta_1 x_i)$$
$$p_i = (1 - p_i)\exp(\beta_0 + \beta_1 x_i)$$
$$p_i = \frac{\exp(\beta_0 + \beta_1 x_i)}{1 + \exp(\beta_0 + \beta_1 x_i)}$$

How do you squash probabilities to lie between 0 and 1 for a probit regression model? Note that the governing equation is

$$Z^{-1}(p_i) = \beta_0 + \beta_1 x_i$$

where Z^{-1} denotes the inverse cumulative distribution function (CDF) of a normal distribution. Using the normal distribution tables in the Appendix, the probability can be calculated as

$$p_i = Z(\beta_0 + \beta_1 x_i) \tag{9.6}$$

where $Z(\cdot)$ denotes the normal distribution value from tables. Note that, for values of $x \geq 0$, Eq. (9.6) satisfies

$$Z(-x) = 1 - Z(x) \tag{9.7}$$

In R, the function $Z(\cdot)$ can be calculated using the function **pnorm**.

To fit probability regressions in R, you need to be aware of some background mathematics and the data structure. In terms of the background mathematics, logistic and probit regression are examples of *generalized linear models* (Bingham and Fry 2010). This means that the R command used is **glm** for *generalized linear model*. By contrast, regression models are known as *linear models* (Bingham and Fry 2010). This means that the R command used for regression is **lm** for *linear model*.

In addition to the above, you have to specify the family of distributions used (binomial) to tell R that you are regressing probabilities. You also have to tell R what link function you are using. The default for binomial generalized linear models is the logit. If you do not specify the link function, R will fit a logistic regression model. All these things are essentially bits of R syntax but it is important to be aware that these do have a mathematical and statistical origin and underpinning.

To fit a binomial glm in R, you need the data organized in columns of successes and failures. The R command needed to do this is **cbind**, which has the effect of binding the required columns containing counts of successes and failures together. For our data example in R, use

```
tested<-c(50, 70, 100, 60, 40, 85, 90, 50, 80, 65)
failures<-c(10, 17, 30, 21, 18, 43, 54, 33, 60, 51)
successes<-tested-failures
fasteners<-cbind(successes, failures)
```

The basic set of commands work as follows.

1 Compute the model:
```
a.glm< -glm(fasteners~load, family=binomial)
b.glm< -glm(fasteners~load, family=binomial(link=probit))
```
2 Summarize the results:
```
summary(a.glm)
summary(b.glm)
```

It is important to note that these models can serve as a cross-check of each other in applications. In practical examples, you should expect to have similar models giving you similar interpretations and numerically similar estimates.

9.5 Worked numerical example

Consider the data in Table 9.1.

1 Fit linear probability, logistic and probit models to this data and interpret the results.
2 What value of the load would cause 50% of the components to fail?
3 What is the success probability if loads of 1999 kg and 4891 kg are applied?

Fit the linear probability model using
a.lm<-lm(probsuccess~load)
summary(a.lm)
The logit and probit models can be fitted using
a.glm<-glm(fasteners~load, family=binomial)
summary(a.glm)
b.glm<-glm(fasteners~load, family=binomial(link=probit))
summary(b.glm)

Note that, in all these approaches, the R code follows the same pattern:

1 Tell the computer to do the work.
2 Summarize the results in a separate step.

All statistical software packages produce redundant information. It is natural to imagine that you might be asked to calculate and interpret a t-statistic:

1 Is the variable in question significant?
2 If it is significant, when the variable increases does the probability increase or decrease? (Is the sign of the random variable positive or negative?)

This whole process is liable to actually be a lot easier than it might seem at first. Results for the linear probability model are shown below.
Estimate Std error t-value Pr(>|t|)
(Intercept) 1.692e+00 3.543e-02 47.76 4.08e-11 ***
load -3.460e-04 1.027e-05 -33.68 6.60e-10 ***

Interpret these results as follows:

1 Load has a significant impact on the probability of success $(p < 6.60 \times 10^{-10})$.

2 As load increases the probability of success decreases. A 1 kg increase in the load means that the success probability decreases by around 3.46×10^{-4}. The by-hand calculation of the z- or t-statistic (similar to an exam-type question) would be

$$t = \frac{|\text{estimate}|}{\text{standard error}} = \frac{|-3.460 \times 10^{-4}|}{1.027 \times 10^{-5}} = 33.69036 > 2.0$$

Therefore, $p < 0.05$. Note here, and in the other examples, that the two inequality signs for the t-statistic and the p-value point in opposite directions if you have done this correctly.

Results obtained for the logit model are:
Estimate Std error z-value Pr(>lzl)
(Intercept) 5.3397115 0.5456932 9.785 <2e-16 ***
load -0.0015484 0.0001575 -9.829 <2e-16 ***

Interpret these results as follows:

1 Load has a significant impact upon the probability of success ($p < 2e - 16$).
2 As load increases, the probability of success decreases. The by-hand calculation of the z- or t-statistic (similar to an exam-type question) would be

$$t = \frac{|\text{estimate}|}{\text{standard error}} = \frac{|0.0015484|}{0.0001575} = 9.831111 > 2.0$$

Therefore, $p < 0.05$.

Results obtained for the probit model are as follows:
Coefficients: Estimate Std error z-value Pr(>lzl)
(Intercept) 3.271e+00 3.213e-01 10.18 <2e-16 ***
load -9.488e-04 9.281e-05 -10.22 <2e-16 ***

Interpret these results as follows:

1 Load has a significant impact upon the probability of success ($p < 2e - 16$).
2 As load increases, the probability of success decreases. The by-hand calculation of the t-statistic (similar to an exam-type question) would be

$$t = \frac{|\text{estimate}|}{\text{standard error}} = \frac{|-9.488e - 04|}{9.281e - 05} = 10.22303631 > 2.0$$

Therefore, $p < 0.05$.

The interpretation of the above differs slightly depending on whether you are inside or outside of the exam hall. Inside the exam hall, since the coefficient of load is negative and statistically significant, as load increases the probability

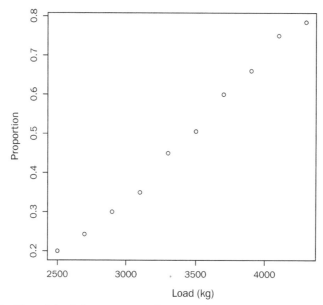

Figure 9.2 Plot of the failure rate as a function of the applied load

of success decreases. Outside of the exam hall look for two different sources of information telling you the same thing ('cross-checks'). It is always worth cross-checking numerical information like this with a graph. Note here that Fig. 9.2 seems to back up the general message of these probability models, i.e. that the probability of failure increases with an increase in the applied load. Note that the logistic and probit models give you similar answers in the example and this may give you an additional numerical cross-check in practical problems.

To provide a graphical check of these analyses, Fig. 9.2 plots the failure rate as a function of the load. In R, use
proportion=failed/tested
plot(load, proportion)

1   For what value of the load is there a 50% failure rate (this implies a 50% success rate)?

For the linear probability model the fitted equation is

$$\text{Success probability} = 1.692 - 3.460 \times 10^{-4} \text{load}$$

Setting this equal to 0.5 gives

$$0.5 = 1.692 - 3.46 \times 10^{-4} \text{load}$$

$$\text{load} = \frac{0.5 - 1.692}{-3.46 \times 10^{-4}} = 3445.087$$

For the logistic regression model, the fitted equation is

$$\ln\left(\frac{p}{1-p}\right) = 5.3397115 - 0.0015484 \times \text{load}$$

Putting in $p = 0.5$ gives

$$0 = 5.3397115 - 0.0015484\text{load}; \ \text{load} = \frac{5.3397115}{0.0015484} = 3448.535 \, \text{kg}$$

For the probit model, the fitted equation is

$$Z^{-1}(p) = 3.271 - 0.0009488 \times \text{load}$$

Now $Z^{-1}(0.5) = 0$, and so putting in $p = 0.5$ gives

$$0 = 3.271 - 0.0009488\text{load}; \ \text{load} = \frac{3.271}{0.0009488} = 3447.513 \, \text{kg}$$

2   What is the success probability if loads of 1999 kg and 4891 kg are applied?

For the linear probability model, we obtain the solutions

$$\text{Probability} = 1.692 - 3.46 \times 10^{-4}(1999) = 1.000346$$

$$\text{Probability} = 1.692 - 3.46 \times 10^{-4}(4891) = -0.000286$$

Do you think these are sensible probability estimates?!

For the logistic regression model, these probabilities can be calculated as

$$\text{Probability} = \frac{\exp(5.3397115 - (0.0015484)(1999))}{1 + \exp(5.3397115 - (0.0015484)(1999))} = 0.9041716$$

$$\text{Probability} = \frac{\exp(5.3397115 - (0.0015484)(4891))}{1 + \exp(5.3397115 - (0.0015484)(4891))} = 0.09678113$$

These are more sensible probability estimates!

For the probit model, the function $Z(\cdot)$ can be computed using the R command **pnorm**. For the probit model these probabilities can be calculated as

$$\begin{aligned} \text{Probability} &= Z(3.271 - 9.488 \times 10^{-4}(1999)) \\ &= Z(1.374349) = 0.9153333 \end{aligned}$$

$$\text{Probability} = Z(3.271 - 9.488 \times 10^{-4}(4891))$$
$$= Z(-1.369581) = 0.08540887$$

These are again more sensible probability estimates and should roughly match the values obtained from the logit model.

In summary, The linear probability model is surprisingly popular but is not really a viable model (so do not use this!) The logit and probit model are more viable ways of regressing and estimating probabilities (so do use these!) In our numerical example, the linear probability model gives reasonable probability estimates in the middle of the sample. The linear probability model is likely to provide poor estimates of probabilities either close to 0 or close to 1. In practical examples, we would usually expect to see similar numerical estimates from viable models (e.g. the logit and probit models described here). This gives a sense of robustness to the results obtained and their interpretation.

9.6 Tutorial exercises

1   In response to consumer concern over the use of chemicals, a large supermarket chain is experimenting with alternative methods of preserving sweetcorn. Instead of spraying the corn with a fungicide to prevent fungal growth during storage, the cobs are exposed to an aerated steam at five different temperatures for three different time periods. After the one month of storage, the number of cobs infected with fungus was recorded. (Although the terminology may sound strange, in this case, instances of fungal infection would be classified as a 'success'.)

(a)   Read the following data into R.
temp<-rep(c(56, 58, 60, 62, 64), 3)
time<-rep(c(10, 20, 30), c(5, 5, 5))
funguscount<-c(15, 20, 15, 4, 5, 17, 17, 12, 3, 3, 15, 9, 8, 1, 0)

(b)   Type the terms temp and time to see how patterned data can be entered into R using the command rep which is short for 'repeat'.

(c)   Set the data up in the appropriate way for a binomial generalized linear model in R.
fungus<-cbind(funguscount, 24-funguscount)

(d)   Fit the following generalized linear model in R and interpret the results.
a.glm<-glm(fungus~temp+time, family=binomial)
summary(a.glm)

(e)   Estimate the probability of infection for a cob treated at 60 degrees for 20 minutes. Use R to find an approximate 95% confidence interval for this probability.

(f)   Estimate the odds ratio of infection with an approximate 95% confidence interval for a cob treated at 62 degrees compared with one treated at 60 degrees.

(g) An alternative model can be specified in which there is an interaction between time and temperature. In this case, the equation for the probability of infection p is

$$\ln\left(\frac{p}{1-p}\right) = \beta_1 + \beta_2\text{temperature} + \beta_3\text{time} + \beta_4\text{temperature} \times \text{time}$$

Using the following R commands, determine whether there is an interaction between time and temperature.
```
b.glm<-glm(fungus~temp+time+temp:time, family=binomial)
summary(b.glm)
```

2 The data in the file **Rugbyresults2.txt** lists historical results for the Six Nations Rugby Union championship. An analysis of this dataset is contained in Fry et al. (2021a).
  (a) Using the command **read.table**, read this data into R and label this data **rugbyresults**.
  (b) Enter the following code into R:
```
hometeam<-rugbyresults[,1]
homescore<-rugbyresults[,2]
awayscore<-rugbyresults[,3]
awayteam<-rugbyresults[,4]
```
  (c) What is the purpose of the following commands?
```
homewin<-1*(homescore>awayscore)
awaywin<-1*(homescore<awayscore)
```
  (d) Copy the following code into R. Explain the use of the command cbind in this instance.
```
homesuccess<-cbind(homewin, 1-homewin)
awaysuccess<-cbind(awaywin, 1-awaywin)
```
  (e) Enter the following commands into R and then use the command **anova** to test the null hypothesis that the teams involved do not affect the probability of a home win.
```
nullhome<-glm(homesuccess~1, family=binomial)
teamshome<-glm(homesuccess~hometeam+awayteam,
family=binomial)
```
  (f) Enter the following commands into R. Following the previous examples use the command anova to test the null hypothesis that the teams involved do not affect the probability of an away win.
```
nullaway<-glm(awaysuccess~1, family=binomial)
teamsaway<-glm(awaysuccess~hometeam+awayteam,
family=binomial)
```
  (g) Using the models constructed in parts (e–f), what is the probability of an England win in the following matches?

England v Scotland
England v Italy

Wales v England
England v France
Ireland v England

(h) Using the models constructed in parts (e–f), what is the probability of an England win in the following matches?

England v Scotland
England v Italy
Wales v England
England v France
Ireland v England

(i) In all the above cases, the estimated probability of a draw is negligible. Why might these estimated draw probabilities be so low compared with other sports such as soccer?

3 The data in Table 9.2 link the probability Y that a sales voucher is redeemed compared with the size of the discount X offered.

(a) Enter the data in Table 9.2 into R and list the commands used.
(b) Fit the regression model $Y_i = \beta_1 + \beta_2 X_i + U_i$.
(c) What is the regression model in part (c) called?
(d) Show that the linear regression model in part (b) cannot satisfy the classical linear regression assumptions listed in Chapter 5.

Table 9.2 Data for question 3

Discount X	Sample size	Number of coupons redeemed	Probability of redemption Y
5	500	100	0.2
7	500	122	0.224
9	500	147	0.294
11	500	176	0.352
13	500	211	0.422
15	500	244	0.488
17	500	277	0.554
19	500	310	0.620
21	500	343	0.686
23	500	372	0.744
25	500	391	0.782

(e) If X is equal to 31.63, estimate the probability that a voucher is redeemed in each case.

(f) Suggest a better model than the model in part (b). Use this model to re-estimate the probability in part (e).

4 *Quasibinomial generalized linear model.* Suppose that a random variable Y satisfies $Y \sim \text{Bin}(3, p)$. In this case,

$$E[Y] = 3p, Var[Y] = 3p(1 - p) \qquad (9.8)$$

(a) In contrast to Eq. (9.8), a quasibinomial model can be constructed that satisfies

$$E[Y] = 3p, Var[Y] = 3p(1 - p)\phi \qquad (9.9)$$

For what values of ϕ in Eq. (9.9) is this distribution either over-dispersed or under-dispersed?

(b) Show that $R := 1 + Y$ satisfies

$$E[R] = 1 + 3p, Var[R] = 3p(1 - p)\phi$$

where the mean and variance of Y are given in Eq. (9.9).

(c) The data in Table 9.3 relates the Research Excellence Framework ratings of submitted journal papers against the journal ranking using the Association of Business Schools journal list (data adapted from Pidd and Broadbent 2015).

Enter the data in Table 9.3 into R using the following R commands to generate patterned data.

```
abs<-rep(c(4, 3, 2, 1, "unrated"), c(239, 554, 97, 18, 67))
abs<-factor(abs)
REF4<-rep(c(4, 3, 2, 1), c(94, 95, 47, 3))
REF3<-rep(c(4, 3, 2, 1), c(80, 296, 150, 28))
```

Table 9.3   REF quality ratings data for Question 4

REF rating	ABS 4*	ABS 3*	ABS 2*	ABS 1*	Unrated
4*	94	80	4	2	3
3*	95	296	29	1	6
2*	47	150	54	9	37
1*	3	28	10	6	21

```
REF2<-rep(c(4, 3, 2, 1), c(4, 29, 54, 10))
REF1<-rep(c(4, 3, 2, 1), c(2, 1, 9, 6))
REFunrated<-rep(c(4, 3, 2, 1), c(3, 6, 37, 21))
REF<-c(REF4, REF3, REF2, REF1, REFunrated)
successes<-REF-1
failures<-3-successes
y<-cbind(successes, failures)
```

(d) Using a logistic quasibinomial model, test for a relationship between y and the abs journal rating. What is the effect of including a -1 term in the formula for the explanatory variables on the right-hand side of the equation?

(e) Using the model output in part (d), calculate the expected rating and the variance for papers published in 4*, 3*, 2*, 1* and unrated journals.

[Hint: You may also find the following R function helpful to convert from estimated binomial probabilities to the mean and expected values given in part (b).]

```
ratefunction<-function(x){
phi<-0.8501518
results<-vector("numeric", 2)
results[1]<-1+3*x
results[2]<-3*x*(1-x)*phi
results}
```

5 The data in the file **creditrating.txt** records a series of sovereign credit ratings and associated government and economic performance indicators.

   (a) Using the command **read.table**, read this data into R and give this data the label creditrating.

   (b) Ensure that you have installed and loaded the following R library using the following commands:
   ```
   install.packages("dplyr")
   library(dplyr)
   ```

   (c) Using the following syntax, filter the creditrating dataframe for investment-grade countries only:
   ```
   creditrating <- dplyr::filter(creditrating, rating>9)
   ```

9.7 Solutions

1 (a) n/a
   (b) n/a
   (c) n/a
   (d) The R results obtained are shown below.

Coefficients:
Estimate Std error z-value Pr(>|z|)
(Intercept) 25.32732 3.05676 8.286 < 2e-16 ***
temp -0.41132 0.05009 -8.212 < 2e-16 ***
time -0.05978 0.01569 -3.809 0.000139 ***
Signif. codes: 0 '***' 0.001 '**' 0.01 '*' 0.05 '.' 0.1 ' ' 1
(Dispersion parameter for binomial family taken to be 1)
Null deviance: 123.474 on 14 degrees of freedom
Residual deviance: 24.361 on 12 degrees of freedom

Interpretation:
The coefficient of temperature is negative and statistically significant. As temperature increases, the probability of fungal infection
decreases. The coefficient of time is negative and statistically significant. As the length of treatment increases, the probability of fungal
infection decreases. These results seem reasonable given the parameters of the experiment.

(e) From the output above, set

$$\ln\left(\frac{p}{1-p}\right) = 25.32732 - 0.41132(60) - 0.05978(20) = -0.54748$$

$$\frac{p}{1-p} = \exp(-0.54748) = 0.57805557$$

$$p = \frac{0.57805557}{1 + 0.57805557} = 0.366449265 = 0.366 \text{ (3 d.p.)}$$

We can now use R to calculate estimated standard errors as follows:
df2<-data.frame(temp=60, time=20)
predict(a.glm, newdata=df2, se.fit=TRUE)
$fit
1
-0.5472981
$se.fit
[1] 0.1281506

From the output above, we have that there are 12 residual degrees of
freedom. Residual degrees of freedom = 15 observations − 3 estimated
parameters (constant, time, temperature) = 12. Let $n - p$ denote the
number of residual degrees of freedom and let $t_{n-p}(0.975)$ denote the
97.5% quantile for a student t-distribution. This means that an approximate confidence interval for the log-odds $\frac{p}{1-p}$ can be calculated as

$$\text{Confidence interval} = \text{estimate} \pm t_{n-p}(0.975)\text{e.s.e.}$$
$$= -0.5472981 \pm (2.178813)(0.1281506)$$
$$= (-0.8265143, -0.2680819) \qquad (9.10)$$

In R, this confidence interval can be calculated as
qt(0.975, 12)
[1] 2.178813
-0.5472981+(2.178813)*(0.1281506)
[1] -0.2680819
-0.5472981-(2.178813)*(0.1281506)
[1] -0.8265143
Using the confidence interval constructed in (9.10), a confidence interval for the underlying probability can be calculated as

$$\text{Confidence interval} = \left(\frac{\exp(-0.8265143)}{1 + \exp(-0.8265143)}, \frac{\exp(-0.2680819)}{1 + \exp(-0.2680819)} \right)$$
$$= (0.3043826, 0.433378)$$

(f) Work first on the log–odds $\ln(p/1 - p)$ scale. The difference in temperature is $62 - 60 = 2$ so, from the estimated equation, the log–odds ratio is

$$2 * \text{temperature coefficient} = 2(-0.41132) = -0.82264$$

The variance is $2^2(0.05009)^2$ so, taking the square root, the associated estimated standard error is $2(0.05009) = 0.10018$. Working as before, the confidence interval for the estimated log–odds ratio is

$$\text{Confidence interval} = -0.82264 \pm t_{12}(0.975)(0.10018)$$
$$= -0.82264 \pm (2.178813)(0.10018)$$
$$= (-1.040913, -0.6043665)$$

The confidence interval for the odds ratio is then obtained by taking the exponential of the log–odds values:

$$\text{Confidence interval} = (\exp(-1.040913), \exp(-0.6043665))$$
$$= (0.3531321, 0.5464205)$$

Interpretation.
The temperature increase seems worthwhile. The confidence interval constructed does not include 1. Increasing the temperature, as suggested, should lead to a reduction in fungal infection by 35.3–54.6%.

(g) Running the commands in R gives the following output:
Coefficients:
Estimate Std error z-value Pr(>|z|)
(Intercept) 17.152454 7.442518 2.305 0.0212 *
temp -0.274065 0.124511 -2.201 0.0277 *
time 0.374153 0.370002 1.011 0.3119
temp:time -0.007314 0.006238 -1.173 0.2410
--- Signif. codes: 0 '***' 0.001 '**' 0.01 '*' 0.05 '.' 0.1 ' ' 1

Interpretation
In R, the interaction term is added using a colon. In this case, we have no evidence from the above ($p = 0.2410$) of an interaction between temperature and time. The simpler model without an interaction term should suffice.

2 (a) Use rugbyresult s<-read.table("E:Rugbyresults2.txt")
  (b) n/a
  (c) The purpose of the commands is to translate logic-based Boolean information into a more convenient numerical form.
  (d) The command cbind is needed to bind together columns of successes and failures. This is something you need to do whenever fitting probability regression models in R.
  (e) The results below give conclusive evidence of a team effect.
     nullhome<-glm(homesuccess~1, family=binomial)
     teamshome<-glm(homesuccess~hometeam+awayteam, family=binomial)
     anova(nullhome, teamshome, test="Chisq")
     Analysis of Deviance Table
     Resid. Df Resid. Dev Df Deviance Pr(>Chi)
     1 74 96.804
     2 64 46.717 10 50.087 2.572e-07 ***
  (f) The results below give conclusive evidence of a team effect.
     nullaway<-glm(awaysuccess~1, family=binomial)
     teamsaway<-glm(awaysuccess~hometeam+awayteam, family=binomial)
     anova(nullaway, teamsaway, test="Chisq")
     Analysis of Deviance Table
     Resid. Df Resid. Dev Df Deviance Pr(>Chi)
     1 74 95.477
     2 64 40.702 10 54.775 3.479e-08 ***
  (g) Firstly, you need to create two data frames corresponding to whether or not England are playing home or away:
     away<-data.frame(hometeam=c("Wales", "Ireland"), awayteam=c("England", "England"))
     home<-data.frame(hometeam=c("England", "England", "England"), awayteam=c("Scotland", "Italy", "France"))

Then the probabilities of an England win in their home matches can be calculated as
```
exp(predict(teamshome, home))/(1+exp(predict(teamshome, home)))
```
1.0000000 0.9777906 0.9753547

Similarly, the probabilities of an England win in their away matches can be calculated using
```
exp(predict(teamsaway, away))/(1+exp(predict(teamsaway, away)))
```
4.579674e-01 5.534259e-09

(h) By symmetry, the probability of an England defeat in their home matches can be calculated using
```
exp(predict(teamsaway, home))/(1+exp(predict(teamsaway, home)))
```
1.904027e-09 2.908802e-02 3.167952e-02

Similarly, the probability of an England defeat in their away matches can be calculated using
```
exp(predict(teamshome, away))/(1+exp(predict(teamshome, away)))
```
0.5777847 0.7908286

(i) The lower probability of a draw may be linked to the higher average scoring rate of Rugby.

3 (a) Use
```
x<-c(5, 7, 9, 11, 13, 15, 17, 19, 21, 23, 25)
samplesize<-rep(500, 11)
redeemed<-c(100, 122, 147, 176, 211, 244, 277, 310, 343, 372, 391)
y<-redeemed/500
```

(b) Use
```
a.lm<-lm(y~x)
summary(a.lm)
Coefficients:
Estimate Std error t-value Pr(>|t|)
(Intercept) 0.0291364 0.0089573 3.253 0.00995 **
x 0.0307000 0.0005502 55.794 9.6e-13 ***
```
Residual standard error: 0.01154 on 9 degrees of freedom. Multiple R-squared: 0.9971. Adjusted R-squared: 0.9968. F-statistic: 3113 on 1 and 9 DF. p-value: 9.604e-13.

(c) Linear probability model

(d) Repeat the argument in Chapter 9 since the Y_i are best interpreted as probabilities $0 \le \beta_1 + \beta_2 X_i + u_i \le 1$; $u_i \le 1 - \beta_1 - \beta_2 X_i$. This shows that the u_i are bounded so cannot be normally distributed. Alternatively, as the distribution of the u_i depends on the value of X_i, this violates homoscedasticity.

(e) The probability can be calculated, in this case, as $0.0291364 + 0.0307 \times 31.63 = 1.000177$.

(f) A better model would be either the logit or probit model. For the logit model calculation use

```
yprob<-cbind(redeemed, 500-redeemed)
a.glm<-glm(yprob~x, family=binomial)
newdata<-data.frame(x=31.63)
predict(a.glm, newdata)
2.208302
```

The probability can then be calculated using

```
exp(2.208302)/(1+exp(2.208302))
0.9009926
```

The probit model calculation gives

```
b.glm<-glm(yprob~x, family=binomial(link=probit))
newdata<-data.frame(x=31.63)
predict(b.glm, newdata)
1.354563
```

The probability can then be calculated using

```
pnorm(1.354563)
0.9122216
```

4 (a) The distribution is under-dispersed (less variable) if $\phi < 1$ and over-dispersed (more variable) if $\phi > 1$. Over-dispersion is more commonly encountered in practice but under-dispersion may occur in specialized areas such as in the analysis of survey data.

(b)

$$
\begin{aligned}
E[R] &= E[1 + Y] = 1 + E[Y] = 1 + 3p \\
\mathrm{Var}[R] &= \mathrm{Var}[1 + Y] = \mathrm{Var}[Y] = \phi 3p(1 - p).
\end{aligned}
$$

(c) n/a

(d) To run the analysis use the following code. Results give evidence of a clear association between journal rankings and research quality rating.

```
a.glm<-glm(y~abs, family=quasibinomial)
summary(a.glm)
Coefficients:
Estimate Std error t-value Pr(>|t|)
(Intercept) -0.7777 0.2702 -2.879 0.00408 **
abs2 0.4800 0.2914 1.647 0.09988 .
abs3 1.1452 0.2740 4.179 3.19e-05 ***
abs4 1.7413 0.2809 6.199 8.41e-10 ***
absunrated -0.1247 0.3059 -0.408 0.68365
```

(e) In order to extract the estimated probabilities, use

```
rle(a.glm$fitted)$values
0.7238494 0.5908544 0.4261168 0.3148148 0.2885572
```

Applying the given function to each of these values in turn shows that the expected values and the variances can be calculated using

```
ratefunction(0.7238494)
[1] 3.1715482 0.5098142
ratefunction(0.5908544)
[1] 2.7725632 0.6165611
ratefunction(0.4261168)
[1] 2.2783504 0.6236916
ratefunction(0.3148148)
[1] 1.9444444 0.5501497
ratefunction(0.2885572)
[1] 1.8656716 0.5235879
```

10 Linear mixed and generalized linear mixed models

10.1 Two industrial problems

10.1.1 Problem 1

In regional monopolies such as the electricity and water industries, customer satisfaction scores form the basis of regulatory fines (Brint and Fry 2021). The whole system is potentially unfair if there is a detectable regional bias, i.e. a regional effect over and above the actual level of service received. To investigate this, we want to try to measure regional bias using data from TripAdvisor. The data recorded are the hotel and the rating (out of 5: the higher the better).

In this chapter, the data is treated as if it is a continuous (numerical) variable. There is a subtlety here in that this may not actually be strictly correct but makes it easier to use and interpret the model. This also shows that important aspects of the subject are not just purely mathematical although they are probably inherently quantitative.

10.1.2 Problem 2

These customer satisfaction scores take the values 1–5:

1 High 4–5
2 Medium 3
3 Low 1–2

We want to investigate whether the probability that a survey respondent gives a high/medium/low score depends on the region of the survey respondent.

10.2 Simplified analysis of Problem 1 using regression

Is there evidence for a regional bias in this data set? To answer this question, we fit the following regression model

$$\text{score}_i = \alpha + \beta \text{region}_i + \text{error}$$

For the moment, we ignore the effect of different hotels (in practice, this would be a simple mistake to make that would give dangerously plausible suggested answers to the question in hand). If the β terms in the regression are significant, then we have statistical evidence of a regional effect. The β terms also help us to quantify the practical effect of any regional bias (Brint and Fry 2021).

When using R, think "R = robot". R will do exactly as commanded; nothing more nothing less. As we have seen in previous chapters, you usually have separate commands:

1 Run the analysis (command=lm)
2 Display the results (command=summary)

The default in R is to fit a constant term, although this is not explicit in the R syntax. This can be suppressed using a -1 term in the sequence of X-variables. You would almost always include a constant term, but occasionally it is easier to present results without this. (This is one of the mistakes we perhaps made in our paper Brint and Fry 2021, so this can be deceptively subtle as it eluded two professional statisticians on this occasion!)

Data in the file **ScoreData**.txt gives the ratings of 24,365 reviewers for a range of different product ('hotels'). It is possible to argue over whether this really is 'Big Data' but our view would be that this is big enough to be non-trivial and informative. Significantly, the data also comes from a genuine industrial application. Some of the data regarding the regional affiliation of the survey respondent is missing and data corresponding to these entries needs to be deleted. The R code to read in the data and then to define the variables one-by-one is as follows:

```
scores<-read.table("G:ScoreData.txt")
rating<-scores[,1]
product<-scores[,2]
region<-scores[,3]
regionmissing<-scores[,4]
```

Next, we need to delete entries for unassigned regions. This is easiest to do in R using its vectorized nature and the subsetting commands as follows:

```
rating<-rating[regionmissing<1]
product<-product[regionmissing<1]
region<-region[regionmissing<1]
```

Then, we need to tell R to put the data in the right form. The data for product and region are labels rather than numerical measurements and R needs to be told this. In R, the command to do this is factor:
product<-factor(product)
region<-factor(region)

As this is a non-trivial problem, it is worthwhile looking at the regional data to see if we might have made a mistake. In R, the command to do this is summary:
summary(region)
EasMid LonEsx NE Yor NorWes Scotlan South SouWes
Wales WesMid
2781 3012 3250 3446 1984 3375 1945
1387 2301

Finally, we can run the regression model as in previous chapters:

1 Run the analysis
   a.lm< −lm(rating~region)
2 Display the results
   summary(a.lm)

The results obtained are as follows.

Coefficients:
Estimate Std error t-value Pr(>|t|)
(Intercept) 3.989932 0.020858 191.288 <2e-16 ***
regionLonEsx -0.064965 0.028927 -2.246 0.0247 *
regionNEYor -0.026855 0.028414 -0.945 0.3446
regionNorWes 0.003394 0.028039 0.121 0.9037
regionScotlan -0.013117 0.032325 -0.406 0.6849
regionSouth 0.031994 0.028170 1.136 0.2561
regionSouWes 0.028577 0.032514 0.879 0.3794
regionWales 0.018720 0.036158 0.518 0.6047
regionWesMid 0.024845 0.030998 0.801 0.4229

The convention would be that it is from the second row of this table onwards that is interesting. This is because we usually fit a constant or underlying average term to the model. This means that, even in the absence of a regional difference, we do not expect the average score to be equal to zero. Taking these results at face value, there is evidence ($p = 0.0247$) that the results for those from the London region are lower than for the other regions. The suggestion would be that electricity and water companies that are based in the London region would be systematically disadvantaged by the current system of regulation and the way in which customer satisfaction scores determine fines.

In this case, the estimated effects of the regional bias can be better presented by re-parameterizing the model. In order to do this, we can suppress the constant term in the fitting of the regression model. In R, this is achieved by including a −1 term into the list of X-variables.

1 Run the analysis
   b.lm< −lm(rating∼region-1)
2 Display the results
   summary(b.lm)

In this case, the results obtained are as follows.

```
Coefficients: Estimate Std error t-value Pr(>ItI)
regionEasMid 3.98993 0.02086 191.3 <2e-16 ***
regionLonEsx 3.92497 0.02004 195.8 <2e-16 ***
regionNEYor 3.96308 0.01929 205.4 <2e-16 ***
regionNorWes 3.99333 0.01874 213.1 <2e-16 ***
regionScotlan 3.97681 0.02469 161.0 <2e-16 ***
regionSouth 4.02193 0.01893 212.4 <2e-16 ***
regionSouWes 4.01851 0.02494 161.1 <2e-16 ***
regionWales 4.00865 0.02954 135.7 <2e-16 ***
regionWesMid 4.01478 0.02293 175.1 <2e-16 ***
```

The numerical projections of the model should be the same under either parameterization. You have to use the first parameterization to test for regional differences. In this, case the significant values indicate that the London scores are lower than the benchmark score for the first East Midlands category. The second parameterization is the easiest way to present the estimated average score. In this case, the significant values indicate that in none of the regions is the average rating equal to zero. The numerical estimates obtained suggest only minor differences in the average scores given by customers from different regions, although this is not formally tested for.

The estimated customer satisfaction scores should be the same under either parameterization. Concentrate for sake of argument on the London region. The second parameterization gives that, in this case the average customer satisfaction score is 3.92497. Under the first parameterization the average customer satisfaction score for the London region would be given by

$$\text{Average score} = \text{intercept} + \text{London adjustment}$$
$$= 3.989932 - 0.064965 = 3.924967$$

10.3 Simplified analysis of Problem 2 with generalized linear models

Commands to read the data into R are as follows:
```
scores< −read.table("E:ScoreData.txt")
ratings< −scores[,1]
rating< −scores[,1]
product< −scores[,2]
region< −scores[,3]
```

```
regionmissing< -scores[,4]
rating< -rating[regionmissing<1]
product< -product[regionmissing<1]
region< -region[regionmissing<1]
```

Next, generate the sequence of high, medium and low values in R using
```
high< -I*(rating>3)
medium< -I*(rating==3)
low< -I*(rating<2)
```

In each case, this generates a sequence of values that take the value 1 if the observation belongs to that category (e.g. high) and 0 otherwise. Strictly speaking, binomial models are formulated for occasions when you have only two categories (e.g. yes/no, successful/unsuccessful, male/female) Our Big Data example with three categories can be modelled using $3 - 1 = 2$ equations. A third equation can be fitted but should be redundant. In practice, it might be still worth fitting this third equation just to check that the rest of our conclusions are still in order.

To fit a binomial glm in R, you need the data organized in columns of successes and failures. The R command needed to do this is cbind which has the effect of binding together columns containing the required counts of successes and failures together. For our data example in R, use
```
yhigh< -cbind(high, I-high)
ylow< -cbind(low, I-low)
ymedium< -cbind(medium, I-medium)
```

To compute the probability of awarding a high score the R, the following commands are needed:

1 Compute the model
   ```
   highl.glm< -glm(yhigh~region, family=binomial)
   high2.glm< -glm(yhigh~region, family=binomial(link=probit))
   ```
2 Summarize the results
   ```
   summary(highl.glm)
   summary(high2.glm)
   ```

Note that these models can serve as a cross-check of each other in applications. You should expect to have similar models giving you similar interpretations and numerically similar estimates.

Results for the logit model are shown below. Results present weak evidence ($p = 0.0539$) that those in the London region may be less likely to give a high score, as the coefficient is statistically significant and negative.

```
Estimate Std error z-value Pr(>|z|)
(Intercept) 1.046081 0.043232 24.197 <2e-16 ***
regionLonEsx -0.114166 0.059219 -1.928 0.0539 .
regionNEYor -0.053799 0.058553 -0.919 0.3582
```

regionNorWes 0.002846 0.058133 0.049 0.9610
regionScotlan -0.039457 0.066637 -0.592 0.5538
regionSouth 0.075978 0.058890 1.290 0.1970
regionSouWes 0.075283 0.068138 1.105 0.2692
regionWales 0.067004 0.075778 0.884 0.3766
regionWesMid 0.018630 0.064408 0.289 0.7724

Results for the probit model are shown below. Results present weak evidence ($p = 0.0538$) that those in the London region may be less likely to give a high score, as the coefficient is statistically significant and negative. Note that this is also the same interpretation as for the logit model.

Estimate Std error z-value Pr(>|z|)
(Intercept) 0.643412 0.025643 25.091 <2e-16 ***
regionLonEsx -0.068089 0.035304 -1.929 0.0538 .
regionNEYor -0.031994 0.034813 -0.919 0.3581
regionNorWes 0.001688 0.034477 0.049 0.9610
regionScotlan -0.023449 0.039614 -0.592 0.5539
regionSouth 0.044895 0.034808 1.290 0.1971
regionSouWes 0.044487 0.040233 1.106 0.2689
regionWales 0.039611 0.044744 0.885 0.3760
regionWesMid 0.011040 0.038165 0.289 0.7724

Using the logit model, the probability that somebody from the London region gives a high score can be calculated as follows.

$$\log\left(\frac{p}{1-p}\right) = 1.046081 - 0.114166 = 0.931915$$
$$\frac{p}{1-p} = \exp(0.931915) = 2.539367413$$
$$p = (1-p)2.539367413$$
$$= \frac{2.539367413}{3.539367413}$$
$$= 0.717463635 = 0.717 \text{ (3 d.p.)}$$

Using the probit model, the probability that somebody from the London region gives a high score can be calculated as

$$Z^{-1}(p) = 0.643412 - 0.068089$$
$$= 0.575323 = 0.58 \text{ (2 d.p.)}$$

Keep this calculation to two decimal places because of the limited resolution of the tables and then use

$$p = Z(0.58) = 0.71904$$

Results thus give very small numerical differences between logit and probit models, which is what we would expect to find in practical examples.

Similarly, using the logit and probit models to calculate the probability that somebody gives a low score:

1 Compute the model
   low1.glm< −glm(ylow~region, family=binomial)
   low2.glm< −glm(ylow~region, family=binomial(link=probit))
2 Summarize the results
   summary(low1.glm)
   summary(low2.glm)

Again, these models should serve as a cross-check of each other in applications. You should expect to have similar models giving you similar interpretations and numerically similar estimates in reasonable practical datasets. Results for the logit model are shown below. The model presents no evidence ($p > 0.05$) for regional differences in the extent to which people award low scores.

```
Estimate Std error z-value Pr(>|z|)
(Intercept) -3.14340 0.09524 -33.005 <2e-16 ***
regionLonEsx 0.18064 0.12719 1.420 0.156
regionNEYor 0.02004 0.12919 0.155 0.877
regionNorWes -0.01845 0.12851 -0.144 0.886
regionScotlan -0.01334 0.14813 -0.090 0.928
regionSouth 0.02539 0.12796 0.198 0.843
regionSouWes 0.11757 0.14395 0.817 0.414
regionWales 0.16271 0.15733 1.034 0.301
regionWesMid -0.11741 0.14590 -0.805 0.421
```

Results for the probit model are shown below. The model presents no evidence ($p > 0.05$) for regional differences in the extent to which people award low scores.

```
Estimate Std error z-value Pr(>|z|)
(Intercept) -1.735207 0.042645 -40.689 <2e-16 ***
regionLonEsx 0.081926 0.057602 1.422 0.155
regionNEYor 0.008987 0.057924 0.155 0.877
regionNorWes -0.008251 0.057477 -0.144 0.886
regionScotlan -0.005966 0.066254 -0.090 0.928
regionSouth 0.011390 0.057387 0.198 0.843
regionSouWes 0.053084 0.065063 0.816 0.415
regionWales 0.073699 0.071491 1.031 0.303
regionWesMid -0.052143 0.064720 -0.806 0.420
```

Classical binomial models are constructed for the special case of two categories. Common examples might include yes/no, male/female, successful/unsuccessful etc. In the case of three categories here (high scores, low scores, medium scores), we have used two regression equations to separately estimate the probability of obtaining a high score and the probability of obtaining a low score. Alhough, mathematically, this should be a redundant step, it is instructive to check this and fit the third regression equation to explain the probability that somebody will award a medium score. Mathematically, if you have n categories, you would need $n-1$ probability calculations. Mathematically, the technically correct analysis would use multinomial regression models corresponding to multiple (> 2) categories (although this is something we do not discuss here).

Using the logit and probit models to calculate the probability that somebody gives a medium score:

1 Compute the model
mediuml.glm< −glm(ymedium~region, family=binomial)
medium2.glm< −glm(ymedium~region, family=binomial(link=probit))
2 Summarize the results
summary(mediuml.glm)
summary(medium2.glm)

Again, these models should serve as a cross-check of each other in applications. You should expect to have similar models giving you similar interpretations and numerically similar estimates in reasonable practical datasets. Results for the logit model are shown below. The model presents no evidence ($p > 0.05$) for regional differences in the extent to which people award low scores.

```
Estimate Std error z-value Pr(>|z|)
(Intercept) -1.655e+00 5.168e-02 -32.035 <2e-16 ***
regionLonEsx 3.642e-02 7.125e-02 0.511 0.609
regionNEYor -9.664e-03 7.050e-02 -0.137 0.891
regionNorWes -9.264e-02 7.048e-02 -1.314 0.189
regionScotlan 1.793e-02 7.980e-02 0.225 0.822
regionSouth -7.973e-02 7.068e-02 -1.128 0.259
regionSouWes -1.273e-01 8.272e-02 -1.539 0.124
regionWales -6.257e-02 9.089e-02 -0.688 0.491
regionWesMid -6.615e-05 7.680e-02 -0.001 0.999
```

Results for the probit model are shown below. The model presents no evidence ($p > 0.05$) for regional differences in the extent to which people award low scores. Note that once again the logit and probit models lead to the same interpretation.

```
Estimate Std error z-value Pr(>|z|)
(Intercept) -9.929e-01 2.856e-02 -34.772 <2e-16 ***
regionLonEsx 2.017e-02 3.946e-02 0.511 0.609
regionNEYor -5.337e-03 3.894e-02 -0.137 0.891
regionNorWes -5.088e-02 3.873e-02 -1.314 0.189
regionScotlan 9.917e-03 4.416e-02 0.225 0.822
regionSouth -4.383e-02 3.886e-02 -1.128 0.259
regionSouWes -6.978e-02 4.524e-02 -1.542 0.123
regionWales -3.443e-02 4.994e-02 -0.689 0.491
regionWesMid -3.655e-05 4.244e-02 -0.001 0.999
```

10.4   Generalized linear mixed models

With linear mixed and generalized linear mixed models the 'mixed' term indicates correlation problems caused by the sampling structure. In both cases, we retain the same basic interpretation of previous models but account for correlations caused by repeat observations and the nature of the data collection. This, in turn, should lead to more precise estimates of the regional effect. These, notwithstanding the interpretation of the model and calculations involving the fixed effects terms, are very similar to those contained in previous chapters.

By incorporating these so-called mixed models, Chapter 10.5 presents a professional-standard solution to Problem 1. Chapter 10.6 presents a professional-standard solution to Problem 2.

10.5   Proper solution of Problem 1 using linear mixed models

To fit a linear mixed effects model in R, you have to download the R package lme4, which stands for linear mixed effects. In R to upload this package, use
Packages→load packages→lme4→OK
The process of loading and installing R packages is discussed in Chapter 5. Analysis in R proceeds in four steps:

1   Download the lme4 package.
2   Fit a model with no regional effect but correlation caused by repeated measures.
     abl< −lmer(rating~l+(l|product), REML=F)
3   Fit a model with regional effect but correlation caused by repeated measures.
     ab2< −lmer(rating~region+(l|product), REML=F)

An explanation of the R code used is in order. The R command lmer stands for linear mixed effects regression. As before, rating is the y-variable we are trying to model. The model divides into a **fixed effect** (constant term or a term adjusting for different regional effects) and a separate **mixed effect** +(l|product). Finally, we need to suppress the REML estimation method in order to run a standard maximum likelihood ratio (χ^2) test.

Mixed effects problems are hard. The problem structures may be very intricate dependant upon the complexity of the dataset and how the data has been collected. In this simple example, we have a +(l|product) term. This means there is an average rating associated with each product (hotel) irrespective of who reviews it. This is a simple illustrative example (albeit one that does does stem from a practical industrial problem).

4 Use a chi-squared test to test for a regional effect by distinguishing between the models fitted in Steps 2–3. Somewhat confusingly, the R command to run a chi-squared test in R is anova:

anova(ab1, ab2)
Data: NULL
Models:
ab1: rating ~ 1 + (1 | product)
ab2: rating ~ region + (1 | product)
Df AIC BIC logLik deviance Chisq Chi Df Pr(>Chisq)
ab1 3 68975 69000 -34485 68969
ab2 11 68948 69036 -34463 68926 43.825 8 6.141e-07 ***

Thus, results give significant evidence ($p = 6.141 \times 10^{-7}$) of a regional effect. In R, we need the command summary to present the results. R is like a robot in that it will do exactly what you tell it to do. The basic procedure in R usually works as follows:

1 Run a computational calculation.
2 Show the results but only if explicitly directed by the user.

The following results can be obtained from R.

summary(ab2)
Fixed effects:
Estimate Std error t-value
(Intercept) 3.965336 0.048813 81.235
regionLonEsx -0.119061 0.027666 -4.304
regionNEYor -0.003653 0.027090 -0.135
regionNorWes 0.005216 0.026742 0.195
regionScotlan 0.057297 0.030884 1.855
regionSouth -0.014028 0.026868 -0.522
regionSouWes 0.008482 0.031007 0.274
regionWales 0.014557 0.034456 0.422
regionWesMid 0.016191 0.029519 0.548

The interpretation and calculations work the same way as before although, this time, the results should be more robust as we have made a better attempt at accounting for the correlations in the data set. There is evidence of a London effect.

$$t = |-4.304| = 4.304 > 2; \; p < 0.05$$

There is no evidence of an effect for other regions, e.g. for Scotland,

$$t = 1.855 < 2; \; p > 0.05$$

The London term is negative and statistically significant. This supports the previous suggestion that London companies may be at a disadvantage.

The average scores for each region can then be calculated as

$$
\begin{aligned}
\text{East Midlands} &= \text{Intercept} = 3.965336 \\
\text{London} &= \text{intercept} - 0.119061 \\
&= 3.965336 - 0.119061 = 3.846275 \\
\text{North East/Yorkshire} &= \text{intercept} - 0.003653 \\
&= 3.965336 - 0.003653 = 3.961683 \\
\text{North West} &= \text{intercept} + 0.005216 \\
&= 3.965336 + 0.005216 = 3.970552 \\
\text{Scotland} &= \text{intercept} + 0.057297 \\
&= 3.965336 + 0.057297 = 4.022633 \\
\text{South} &= \text{intercept} - 0.014028 \\
&= 3.965336 - 0.014028 = 3.951308 \\
\text{South West} &= \text{intercept} + 0.008482 \\
&= 3.965336 + 0.008482 = 3.973818 \\
\text{Wales} &= \text{intercept} + 0.14557 \\
&= 3.965336 + 0.14557 = 4.110906 \\
\text{West Midlands} &= \text{intercept} + 0.016191 \\
&= 3.965336 + 0.016191 = 3.981527
\end{aligned}
$$

10.6 Proper solution of Problem 2 using generalized linear mixed models

The basic R command needed is glmmPQL in the R package MASS. Essentially, what you end up with is a repetition of the logistic regression models of the previous chapter. There is a further adjustment to reflect the repeated measurements from individual hotels (exactly as we did in the previous section). Here, the command glmmPQL stands for generalized linear mixed models fitted via penalized quasi likelihood.

Consider the following three problems:

1 Is there a regional effect in the probability of giving a high score?
2 Is there a regional effect in the probability of giving a low score?
3 Is there a regional effect in the probability of giving a medium score?

Testing for regional effects in the probability of giving a high score can be conducted as follows:

1 Compute the model
    high2< −glmmPQL(high ~ region, random = ~ 1 |
    product,family=binomial)

2 Show the results using the command summary
summary(high2)

Generalized linear mixed models are the harder version of generalized linear models. As such, there are similarities in the statistical interpretation and R commands of the models. Again, the random = ~ I I product reflects the same correlation structure as the linear mixed models discussed previously. In R, the statement family=binomial is needed to specify the distributional family as was the case with logit and probit models. Numerical examples work in the same way as logistic regression (see below). The following output from R shows how the probability of obtaining a high score depends on the region.

Fixed effects: high ~ region
Value Std.Error DF t-value p-value
(Intercept) 1.0760804 0.09293285 23427 11.579118 0.0000
regionLonEsx -0.2214280 0.06144537 23427 -3.603656 0.0003
regionNEYor -0.0109988 0.06057182 23427 -0.181582 0.8559
regionNorWes 0.0102060 0.06014998 23427 0.169675 0.8653
regionScotlan 0.0811167 0.06892505 23427 1.176883 0.2393
regionSouth -0.0064580 0.06077871 23427 -0.106255 0.9154
regionSouWes 0.0426359 0.07024479 23427 0.606962 0.5439
regionWales 0.0589384 0.07794753 23427 0.756129 0.4496
regionWesMid 0.0020951 0.06645689 23427 0.031526 0.9749

We may interpret these results as follows. We retain previous evidence of a London effect ($p = 0.003 < 0.05$). The coefficient of London is negative and statistically significant. This suggests that London respondents are less likely to award high marks. There is no evidence for any other regional effects $t < 2$, $p > 0.05$). It is noteworthy that, in this example, both linear mixed and generalized linear mixed models point to the same London effect. These similar models serve as a cross-check of each other.

In this case, we can calculate the probability that a London respondent gives a high score by setting

$$\ln\left(\frac{p}{1-p}\right) = \text{regression equation}$$

$$= 1.0760804 - 0.2214280 = 0.8546524$$

$$\frac{p}{1-p} = \exp(0.8546524) = 2.350557185$$

$$p = \frac{2.350557185}{3.350557185} = 0.701542177 = 0.702 \text{ (3 d.p.)}$$

Similarly, we can calculate the probability that a Scotland respondent gives a high score by setting

$$\ln\left(\frac{p}{1-p}\right) = \text{regression equation}$$
$$= 1.0760804 + 0.0811167 = 1.1571971$$
$$\frac{p}{1-p} = \exp(1.1571971) = 3.181004731$$
$$p = \frac{3.181004731}{4.181004731} = 0.76082304 = 0.761 \text{ (3 d.p.)}$$

These results also provide a sanity check in that, consistent with the previously identified regional effect, this calculated probability is higher for Scotland than for London.

Testing for regional effects in the probability of awarding a low score can be conducted as follows:

1 Compute the model
   low2< −glmmPQL(low ~ region, random = ~ l l
   product,family=binomial)
2 Show the results using the command summary
   summary(low2)

The following results are obtained from R.

Fixed effects: low ~ region
Value Std.Error DF t-value p-value
(Intercept) -3.361186 0.1479072 23427 -22.724961 0.0000
regionLonEsx 0.278707 0.1263615 23427 2.205636 0.0274
regionNEYor -0.046161 0.1276307 23427 -0.361674 0.7176
regionNorWes -0.045858 0.1270027 23427 -0.361076 0.7180
regionScotlan -0.184987 0.1463020 23427 -1.264419 0.2061
regionSouth 0.145506 0.1264916 23427 1.150325 0.2500
regionSouWes 0.175125 0.1423506 23427 1.230239 0.2186
regionWales 0.196901 0.1554111 23427 1.266972 0.2052
regionWesMid -0.089078 0.1438397 23427 -0.619284 0.5357

Thus, we retain previous evidence of a London effect ($p = 0.0274$). The coefficient for London is positive and statistically significant. This suggests that London respondents are more likely to award low marks. There is no evidence for any other regional effects ($t < 2$, $p > 0.05$). Look for similar models serving as a cross-check of each other. Here, it is significant that linear mixed and generalized linear mixed models now all point to the same London effect.

Using this model, the probability that a London respondent gives a low score can be calculated by setting

$$\ln\left(\frac{p}{1-p}\right) = \text{regression equation}$$
$$= -3.361186 + 0.278707 = -3.082479$$
$$\frac{p}{1-p} = \exp(-3.082479) = 0.045845464$$
$$p = \frac{0.045845464}{1.045845464} = 0.043835792 = 0.044 \text{ (3 d.p.)}$$

Similarly, the probability that a Scotland respondent gives a low score can be calculated by setting

$$\ln\left(\frac{p}{1-p}\right) = \text{regression equation}$$
$$= -3.361186 - 0.184987 = -3.546173$$
$$\frac{p}{1-p} = \exp(-3.546173) = 0.028834779$$
$$p = \frac{0.028834779}{1.028834779} = 0.028026637 = 0.028 \text{ (3 d.p.)}$$

These results also provide another sanity check since the calculated probability is lower for Scotland than for London. This is consistent with the previously identified regional effect.

Recall that we have three categories so we only need two regression equations to describe the system. As a final cross-check, we fit a generalized linear mixed model to estimate the probability of awarding a medium score. Technically, this should be a redundant step so no new regional effects should be identified at this stage. This can be conducted in R as follows:

1 Compute the model
   medium2< −glmmPQL(medium ~ region, random = ~ 1 |
   product,family=binomial)
2 Show the results using the command summary
   summary(medium2)

The following results are obtained from R.

```
(Intercept) -1.6659027 0.07813808 23427 -21.319984 0.0000
regionLonEsx 0.1104438 0.07210366 23427 1.531737 0.1256
regionNEYor -0.0389842 0.07111155 23427 -0.548212 0.5836
regionNorWes -0.0954841 0.07111438 23427 -1.342684 0.1794
regionScotlan -0.0474800 0.08058379 23427 -0.589200 0.5557
regionSouth -0.0297179 0.07128690 23427 -0.416877 0.6768
regionSouWes -0.1083780 0.08335193 23427 -1.300246 0.1935
regionWales -0.0585106 0.09148767 23427 -0.639546 0.5225
regionWesMid 0.0069602 0.07736476 23427 0.089966 0.9283
```

Thus, there is no evidence ($t < 2$, $p > 0.05$) of a regional effect in this case. This is consistent with the above. Although technically a redundant step, this serves as a cross-check of our earlier results and suggests that we can be more confident that our earlier analysis is correct.

Using the above model, we can calculate the probability that a London respondent gives a medium score by setting

$$\ln\left(\frac{p}{1-p}\right) = \text{regression equation}$$

$$= -1.6659027 + 0.1104438 = -1.5554589$$

$$\frac{p}{1-p} = \exp(-1.5554589) = 0.21109249$$

$$p = \frac{0.21109249}{1.21109249} = 0.174299231 = 0.174 \text{ (3 d.p.)}$$

Similarly, we can calculate the probability that a Scotland respondent gives a medium score by setting

$$\ln\left(\frac{p}{1-p}\right) = \text{regression equation}$$

$$= -1.6659027 - 0.0474800 = -1.7133827$$

$$\frac{p}{1-p} = \exp(-1.7133827) = 0.180255011$$

$$p = \frac{0.180255011}{1.180255011} = 0.152725478 = 0.153 \text{ (3 d.p.)}$$

These calculations also serve as a sanity check. Both answers are similar, reflecting no statistically significant evidence for differences between London and Scotland for this category.

10.7 Tutorial exercises

The data for these exercises comes from past student dissertations. Question 1 outlines the kind of analysis that a student might apply using simple linear regression models before moving on to more complex linear mixed effects models. This reflects the fact that these are potentially highly complex models. However, this also means that good dissertations may ultimately be obtained if the analysis is competently rather than perfectly performed. Questions 2–5 below outline a more advanced approach that may be applied once one becomes more experienced in applied statistics.

1 The data in BankData.txt seeks to analyse the effect of balance, capital, expenses, inflation, the interest rate and GDP growth on performance. Two alternative measures of performance return on assets (ROA) and return on equity (ROE) are used.
   (a) Read this data into R using the following:
       BankData<-read.table("E:BankData.txt")

```
name<-BankData[,1]
year<-BankData[,2]
ROA<-BankData[,3]
ROE<-BankData[,4]
banksize<-BankData[,5]
capital<-BankData[,6]
expenses<-BankData[,7]
inflation<-BankData[,8]
interestrate<-BankData[,9]
gdpgrowth<-BankData[,10]
```

(b) Fit a regression model for ROA against bank size, capital, expenses, inflation, the interest rate and GDP growth. Is there any detectable effect on performance?

(c) Explain why the above analysis may be misleading? Can you suggest an alternative solution using linear mixed models?

(d) Repeat the analysis in part (c) but this time using ROE as the dependent variable. What conclusions can you draw in this case?

2 Using the data in **BankData.txt**, apply forward selection to find an appropriate linear mixed model for the ROA in terms of the year, book size, capital, expenses, inflation, interest rate and GDP growth.

3 Using the data in **BankData.txt**, apply forward selection to find an appropriate linear mixed model for the ROE in terms of the year, book size, capital, expenses, inflation, interest rate and GDP growth.

4 Using the data in **BankData.txt**, apply backward selection to find an appropriate linear mixed model for the ROA in terms of the year, book size, capital, expenses, inflation, interest rate and GDP growth.

5 Using the data in **BankData.txt**, apply backward selection to find an appropriate linear mixed model for the ROE in terms of the year, book size, capital, expenses, inflation, interest rate and GDP growth.

10.8 Solutions

1 (a) n/a

(b) a.lm<-lm(ROA~banksize+capital+expenses+inflation
+interestrate+gdpgrowth)summary(a.lm)
Coefficients:
Estimate Std error t-value Pr(>|t|)
(Intercept) 2.273e+00 1.498e+00 1.518 0.1314
banksize -1.243e-06 5.157e-06 -0.241 0.8099
capital -1.577e-02 8.032e-03 -1.964 0.0516 .
expenses 4.280e-01 3.635e-02 11.773 <2e-16 ***
inflation -4.202e-01 1.983e-01 -2.119 0.0359 *
interestrate -3.415e+00 2.109e+00 -1.619 0.1078
gdpgrowth -2.688e-01 3.547e-01 -0.758 0.4500

In the above regression model, the coefficient of expenses is positive and statistically significant ($p < 0.05$). This suggests that as the expenses increase, the ROA increases. The coefficient of inflation is negative and statistically significant ($p < 0.05$). This suggests as inflation increases the ROA decreases.

(c) The above regression analysis does not take into account correlations caused by repeat measurements from the same bank. After loading the lme4 package, we can conduct a more advanced linear mixed model analysis. This suggests that once we take into account correlation caused by repeat measurements, only capital affects performance.

```
a.lmer<-lmer(ROA~banksize+capital+expenses+inflation+
interestrate+gdpgrowth+(1|name))
summary(a.lmer)
Fixed effects:
Estimate Std error t-value
(Intercept) -1.384e-01 1.397e+00 -0.099
banksize 9.288e-07 1.146e-05 0.081
capital 9.830e-02 1.723e-02 5.705
expenses 4.599e-02 8.420e-02 0.546
inflation -2.293e-01 1.466e-01 -1.564
interestrate -9.092e-01 1.606e+00 -0.566
gdpgrowth -9.338e-02 2.592e-01 -0.360
```

(d) Note that if you have a different measure of performance, then different variables may be seen to have an effect. Here, the coefficient of expenses is positive and statistically significant ($|t| > 2$). This suggests that as expenses increase, the ROE increases. The coefficient of inflation is negative and statistically significant ($|t| > 2$). This suggests that as inflation increases, the ROE decreases.

```
b.lmer<-lmer(ROE banksize+capital+expenses+inflation
+interestrate+gdpgrowth+(1|name))
summary(b.lmer)
Fixed effects:
Estimate Std error t-value
(Intercept) 1.729e+01 6.957e+00 2.485
banksize -3.820e-05 3.393e-05 -1.126
capital -5.560e-02 5.263e-02 -1.056
expenses 1.339e+00 2.409e-01 5.559
inflation -2.611e+00 9.072e-01 -2.879
interestrate -1.762e+01 9.688e+00 -1.819
gdpgrowth -1.508e+00 1.621e+00 -0.931
```

2 In the first stage, a high t-value indicates that capital should enter the model:

```
onevar.lmer<-lmer(ROA~year+(1|name))
summary(onevar.lmer)
onevar.lmer<-lmer(ROA~balance+(1|name)) summary(onevar.lmer)
onevar.lmer<-lmer(ROA~capital+(1|name)) summary(onevar.lmer)
onevar.lmer<-lmer(ROA~expenses+(1|name)) summary(onevar.lmer)
onevar.lmer<-lmer(ROA~inflation+(1|name)) summary(onevar.lmer)
onevar.lmer<-lmer(ROA~interestrate+(1|name)) summary(onevar.lmer)
onevar.lmer<-lmer(ROA~gdpgrowth+(1|name)) summary(onevar.lmer)
```

In the second stage, none of the t-values are sufficiently large to suggest that another variable should enter the model. Thus, the ROA seems to primarily depend on bank capital and little else.

```
twovar.lmer<-lmer(ROA~capital+year+(llname)) summary(twovar.lmer)
twovar.lmer<-lmer(ROA~capital+banksize+(llname))
summary(twovar.lmer)
twovar.lmer<-lmer(ROA~capital+expenses+(llname))
summary(twovar.lmer)
twovar.lmer<-lmer(ROA~capital+inflation+(llname))
summary(twovar.lmer)
twovar.lmer<-lmer(ROA~capital+interestrate+(llname))
summary(twovar.lmer)
twovar.lmer<-lmer(ROA~capital+gdpgrowth+(llname))
summary(twovar.lmer)
```

3 In the first stage, high t-values indicate that expenses should enter the model:

```
onevar.lmer<-lmer(ROE~year+(llname))
summary(onevar.lmer)
onevar.lmer<-lmer(ROE~banksize+(llname))
summary(onevar.lmer)
onevar.lmer<-lmer(ROE~capital+(llname))
summary(onevar.lmer)
onevar.lmer<-lmer(ROE~expenses+(llname))
summary(onevar.lmer)
onevar.lmer<-lmer(ROE~inflation+(llname))
summary(onevar.lmer)
onevar.lmer<-lmer(ROE~interestrate+(llname))
summary(onevar.lmer)
onevar.lmer<-lmer(ROE~gdpgrowth+(llname))
summary(onevar.lmer)
```

In the second stage, high t-values indicate that year should enter the model:

```
twovar.lmer<-lmer(ROE~expenses+year+(llname))
summary(twovar.lmer)
twovar.lmer<-lmer(ROE~expenses+banksize+(llname))
summary(twovar.lmer)
twovar.lmer<-lmer(ROE~expenses+capital+(llname))
summary(twovar.lmer)
twovar.lmer<-lmer(ROE~expenses+inflation+(llname))
summary(twovar.lmer)
twovar.lmer<-lmer(ROE~expenses+interestrate+(llname))
summary(twovar.lmer)
twovar.lmer<-lmer(ROE~expenses+gdpgrowth+(llname))
summary(twovar.lmer)
```

In the third stage, high t-values indicate that inflation should enter the model:
```
threevar.lmer<-lmer(ROE~expenses+year+banksize+(llname))
summary(threevar.lmer)
threevar.lmer<-lmer(ROE~expenses+year+capital+(llname))
summary(threevar.lmer)
threevar.lmer<-lmer(ROE~expenses+year+inflation+(llname))
summary(threevar.lmer)
threevar.lmer<-lmer(ROE~expenses+year+interestrate+(llname))
summary(threevar.lmer)
threevar.lmer<-lmer(ROE~expenses+year+gdpgrowth+(llname))
summary(threevar.lmer)
```

In the fourth stage, low t-values indicate that no further variables should enter the model:
```
fourvar.lmer<-lmer(ROE~expenses+year+inflation+banksize
+(llname))summary(fourvar.lmer)
fourvar.lmer<-lmer(ROE~expenses+year+inflation+capital+(llname))
summary(fourvar.lmer)
fourvar.lmer<-lmer(ROE~expenses+year+inflation+interestrate+
(llname))summary(fourvar.lmer)
fourvar.lmer<-lmer(ROE~expenses+year+inflation+gdpgrowth+(llname))
summary(fourvar.lmer)
```

Thus, the conclusion is that a model with expenses, year and inflation is most appropriate. As expenses increase, ROE increases. The ROE also appears to be generally increasing over time. Finally, as inflation increases, ROE decreases. To fit this model in R, use the following:
```
threevar.lmer<-lmer(ROE expenses+year+inflation+(llname))
summary(threevar.lmer)
Fixed effects:
Estimate Std error t-value
(Intercept) -1890.3162 788.5847 -2.397
expenses 1.3708 0.2521 5.438
year 0.9393 0.3912 2.401
inflation -1.5339 0.7460 -2.056
```
4 Begin by fitting the full model:
```
full.lmer<-lmer(ROA~year+banksize+capital+expenses+inflation
+interestrate+gdpgrowth+(llname))
summary(full.lmer)
```

Low t-values indicate that bank size should be removed from the model:
```
minusone.lmer<-lmer(ROA~year+capital+expenses+
inflation+interestrate+gdpgrowth+(llname))
summary(minusone.lmer)
```

Low *t*-values indicate that year should be removed from the model:
```
minustwo.lmer<-lmer(ROA~capital+expenses+inflation+
interestrate+gdpgrowth+(Ilname))
summary(minustwo.lmer)
```

Low *t*-values indicate that gdp growth should be removed from the model:
```
minusthree.lmer<-lmer(ROA~capital+expenses+inflation+
interestrate+(Ilname))summary(minusthree.lmer)
```

Low *t*-values indicate that expenses should be removed from the model:
```
minusfour.lmer<-lmer(ROA~capital+inflation+interestrate+(Ilname))
summary(minusfour.lmer)
```

Low *t*-values indicate that the interest rate should be removed from the model:
```
minusfive.lmer<-lmer(ROA~capital+inflation+(Ilname))
summary(minusfive.lmer)
```

Low *t*-values suggest that inflation should be removed from the model and backward selection can be seen to give the same answers as forward selection for this data (see Question 2).

5 Start by fitting the full model for ROE:
```
full.lmer<-lmer(ROE~year+banksize+capital+expenses+inflation+
interestrate+gdpgrowth+(Ilname))
summary(full.lmer)
```

Low *t*-values indicate that the interest rate should be removed from the model:
```
minusone.lmer<-lmer(ROE~year+banksize+capital+expenses+
inflation+gdpgrowth+(Ilname))summary(minusone.lmer)
```

Low *t*-values indicate that gdp growth should be removed from the model:
```
minustwo.lmer<-lmer(ROE~year+banksize+capital+expenses+
inflation+(Ilname))summary(minustwo.lmer)
```

Low *t*-values indicate that bank size should be removed from the model:
```
minusthree.lmer<-lmer(ROE~year+capital+expenses+inflation+
(Ilname))summary(minusthree.lmer)
```

Low *t*-values indicate that capital should be removed from the model. All the remaining terms are statistically significant and backward selection gives the same results as forward selection for this data. See Question 3.
```
minusfour.lmer<-lmer(ROE year+expenses+inflation+(Ilname))
summary(minusfour.lmer)
```

11 Non-financial time series

11.1 Overview

Very generally, a time series refers to a set of observations that have been collected over time. Time-series models essentially solve two basic problems:

1 Accounting for correlations in related observations that have been collected close together in time.
2 Characterizing seasonal and cyclical behaviour that may often be found in datasets in, for example, business economics and in the natural sciences.

As discussed in Venables and Ripley (2003), there is a lot of mileage in simple graphical plots and qualitative analyses to characterize general time-series problems in layman's terms. For example, are seasonal patterns present? Is the series generally increasing or decreasing over time?

To account for correlations in related observations that have been collected close together in time, suitable methods include AR, MA, ARMA, ARIMA together with more specialized financial time-series models such as ARCH/-GARCH. Characterizing seasonal and cyclical behaviour may be achieved using SARIMA modelling.

A further complication is the issue of non-stationarity. There are two obvious ways in which non-stationary time series can occur in financial and economic contexts:

1 Seasonality, e.g. different seasons and time of the year affect customer behaviour and consumption.
2 Most financial and economic time series show (exponential?) growth trends over time.

It is prudent to take steps to try to account for these stylized empirical facts – albeit imperfectly! In this chapter, we therefore consider general ARIMA modelling of economic time series. There is an entire subject that considers financial time series models derived from prices on financial markets such stock and currency markets. Financial time-series models are thus an entirely different set of models in their own right but share foundational motivations, e.g.:

1 ARCH models are AR models for price volatility.
2 GARCH models are ARMA models for price volatility.

11.2 ARIMA modelling

ARIMA modelling allows you to systematically account for correlations caused by observations being collected close together in time, e.g. correlations in, say, Monday's and Tuesday's sales figures. The construction of ARIMA models has a modular structure. Model selection can therefore be performed rigorously using a graphical approach known as the Box–Jenkins method. Time series contain challenging mathematical and statistical aspects. However, in practical terms, much of the R commands and model interpretation shares commonalities with the standard statistical and regression approaches seen previously.

Conventional time-series models can be thought of as satisfying a hierarchical structure:

1 **Basic models** Autoregressive (AP(p)) and autoregressive moving average (MA(q))
2 **Hybrid I: ARMA(p, q) models** ARMA models = AR(p) combined with MA(q)
3 **Hybrid II: ARIMA(p, d, q) models** Use difference, d, times to get an approximately stationary series and then fit an ARMA model to the resultant series

As evidence of the underlying modular structure, we thus have that

$$ARMA(p, 0) = AR(p)$$
$$ARMA(0, q) = MA(q)$$
$$ARIMA(p, 0, q) = ARMA(p, q) \tag{11.1}$$

Equation (11.1) therefore has important implications both in terms of how these models are constructed and how they are ultimately fitted in R using the command *arima*.

A discussion of time-series models and differencing involves some maths and a polynomial in the differencing shift operator $(1 - B)^d$. The terminology used can make the subject sound more difficult than it really is. However, the terminology is probably justified as it leads to as systematic approach as possible which will be important for problems of a practical size. The main thing to remember is that, as the name suggests, the effect of the backward shift operator B is to shift the series backwards! The simplest possible case $d = 0$ gives the original series

$$(1 - B)^0 Z_t = Z_t$$

The case $d = 1$ gives the first differences

$$(I - B)^1 Z_t = (I - B)Z_t = Z_t - Z_{t-1}$$

The more complex $d = 2$ case gives

$$(1 - B)^2 Z_t = (I - 2B + B^2)Z_t = Z_t - 2Z_{t-1} + Z_{t-2}$$

Usually, low values of d ($d = 0$ or $d = 1$) are sufficient. Higher values of d begin to lose interpretability. In R, the basic function to perform differencing is **diff**:

$$\text{diff(series, number of lags)}$$

By default, **diff**(series) will return the first differences. This makes sense as first differences are the most commonly encountered scenario associated with practical modelling work. Consider the following example in R.

```
z<-seq(1, 10)
z2<-z^2
z2
[1] 1 4 9 16 25 36 49 64 81 100
diff(z2)
[1] 3 5 7 9 11 13 15 17 19
```

Note that the sequence above can be constructed as

$$4 - 1, 9 - 4, 16 - 9, 25 - 16, 36 - 25, 49 - 36, 64 - 49, 81 - 61, 100 - 81$$

As an alternative, consider

```
diff(z2, 2)
[1] 8 12 16 20 24 28 32 36
```

The sequence above is constructed from the first sequence by subtracting the values that are written two terms previously

$$9 - 1, 16 - 4, 25 - 9, 36 - 16, 49 - 25, 64 - 36, 81 - 49, 100 - 64$$

The ARMA(p, q) model is defined by the equation

$$\phi_\alpha(B)Z_t = \phi_\beta(B)\epsilon_t$$

where ϵ_t is an uncorrelated white noise sequence with $E[\epsilon_t] = 0$, $\text{Var}(\epsilon_t) = \sigma^2$.

Here, $\phi_\alpha(B)$ is an order p autoregressive (AR) polynomial in B

$$\phi(B) = 1 - \alpha_1 B^1 - \dots - \alpha_p B^p$$

Similarly, $\phi_\beta(B)$ is an order q moving average (MA) polynomial in B

$$\theta(B) = 1 - \beta_1 B^1 - \dots - \beta_p B^p$$

ARIMA models can be extended in modular fashion as follows. Let $\nabla = (1 - B)$. Then $W_t = \nabla^d Z_t = (1 - B)^d Z_t$ is an ARMA process satisfying the earlier definition with Z_t replaced by $\nabla^d Z_t$. The original series Z_t is then said to follow an ARIMA model. The underlying maths may actually be a whole lot simpler than it might first seem if you see the equations written out in full. In words:

1 Take the dth difference.
2 Once you do this, you should end up with an ARMA model.
3 If $d = 0$, you already have an ARMA model without having to do any additional differencing.

The ARIMA(p, d, q) model is thus defined by the equation

$$\phi_\alpha(B)\nabla^d Z_t = \phi_\beta(B)\epsilon_t$$

where ϵ_t is an uncorrelated white noise sequence with $E[\epsilon_t] = 0$ and $\text{Var}(\epsilon_t) = \sigma^2$. $\phi_\alpha(B)$ is an order p autoregressive (AR) polynomial in B

$$\phi(B) = 1 - \alpha_1 B^1 - \dots - \alpha_p B^p$$

Similarly, $\phi_\beta(B)$ is an order q moving average (MA) polynomial in B

$$\phi_\beta(B) = 1 - \beta_1 B^1 - \dots - \beta_p B^p$$

Thus, the basic idea is that, by taking differences, an ARIMA model reduces to a regular ARMA model. As a result, the name that is often used for this is an autoregressive integrated moving average model. By analogy with regular calculus, this is assumed to be an integrated model since you need to take differences ('differentiate') to get back to an ARMA model. Perhaps 'integrated ARMA model' would be a better term but, unfortunately, ARIMA is the term that is in widespread usage.

Some further comments about differencing are in order. It is important to recognize that differencing is not a panacea. Differencing a stationary time series will produce another stationary time series. However, it is important not to over-difference a series. Firstly, we want as faithful a statistical description of the data-generating process as possible. Moreover, inappropriate differencing can lead to numerical problems with computational software. Generally, standard statistical techniques work best for data that is only moderately correlated. Numerical examples exist whereby inappropriate differencing can be shown to actually increase correlations (see below). These examples can have particular relevance for theoretical financial modelling as conventional models typically assume that series of asset market returns should be uncorrelated as is, for example, the case with the classical random walk model.

As an example, let ϵ_t denote an uncorrelated white noise sequence with $E[\epsilon_t] = 0$ and $\mathrm{Var}(\epsilon_t) = \sigma^2$. Consider the first differences W_t of ϵ_t: $W_t = \epsilon_t - \epsilon_{t-1}$

$$\begin{aligned}
\mathrm{Var}(W_t) &= \mathrm{Var}(\epsilon_t - \epsilon_{t-1}) \\
&= \mathrm{Var}(\epsilon_t) + \mathrm{Var}(\epsilon_{t-1}) - 2\mathrm{Cov}(\epsilon_t, \epsilon_{t-1}) \\
&= \sigma^2 + \sigma^2 - 0 = 2\sigma^2
\end{aligned}$$

$$\begin{aligned}
\gamma_1 = \mathrm{Cov}(W_t, W_{t-1}) &= \mathrm{Cov}(\epsilon_t - \epsilon_{t-1}, \epsilon_{t-1} - \epsilon_{t-2}) \\
&= -\mathrm{Cov}(\epsilon_{t-1}, \epsilon_{t-1}) + 0 \\
&= -\mathrm{Var}(\epsilon_{t-1}) = -\sigma^2
\end{aligned}$$

$$\mathrm{Correlation}(W_t, W_{t-1}) = \frac{\mathrm{Cov}(W_t, W_{t-1})}{\sqrt{\mathrm{Var}(W_t)\mathrm{Var}(W_{t-1})}} = \frac{-\sigma^2}{\sqrt{2\sigma^2 . 2\sigma^2}} = -\frac{1}{2}$$

In this case, we can also calculate $\mathrm{Covariance}(W_t, W_{t-2})$ as

$$\begin{aligned}
\mathrm{Cov}(W_t, W_{t-2}) &= \mathrm{Cov}(\epsilon_t - \epsilon_{t-1}, \epsilon_{t-2} - \epsilon_{t-3}) \\
&= 0 \text{ since none of the subscripts match}
\end{aligned}$$

As an example of the construction of ARIMA models, consider an ARIMA(0, 1, 1) model. Firstly, note that $p = 0$ so there is no autoregressive component. Secondly, note that $d = 1$ so there is need to take first differences

$$Z_t - Z_{t-1}$$

Finally, note that $q = 1$ so there is one moving average term in addition to the observation error

$$\epsilon_t - \beta_1 \epsilon_{t-1}$$

In this case, note that the presence of random statistical error means that an ϵ_t term is always present and the full model becomes

$$Z_t - Z_{t-1} = \epsilon_t - \beta_1 \epsilon_{t-1} \tag{11.2}$$

As an introductory forecasting example, suppose the model in Eq. (11.2) is fitted to a time series of 197 observations. Suppose that we have estimates $\hat{\beta}_1 = 0.699$,

$\hat{\epsilon}_{197} = -0.15$ and the last observation is $z_{197} = 17.4$. The next three forecasts for this model are

$$Z_{198} - Z_{197} = \epsilon_{198} - \hat{\theta}a_{197}$$
$$E[Z_{198}] = Z_{197} + 0 - (0.699)(-0.15) = 17.505$$
$$E[Z_{199}] = E[Z_{198}] + E[\epsilon_{199}] - \hat{\theta}E[\epsilon_{198}] = E[Z_{198}]$$
$$E[Z_{200}] = E[Z_{199}] + E[\epsilon_{200}] - \hat{\theta}E[\epsilon_{199}] = E[Z_{199}]$$

11.3 SARIMA modelling

A second problem that time-series models typically focus upon is the modelling of seasonal effects. This can be achieved using SARIMA models. This combines:

1 An ARIMA-type modelling approach discussed earlier.
2 An explicit link to the underlying human calendar to quantify the impact upon financial and social systems.

The original motivation behind SARIMA models was modelling passenger demand for airlines (Venables and Ripley 2003). However, SARIMA models are thought to have a particularly broad range of application. See, e.g., Fry et al. (2021b) for an application to business-cycle effects in corporate bank accounts.

Seasonal effects are very important in forecasting. Examples might include monthly ice-cream sales (dependent on the weather) and intraday stock price data (dependent on the time of day and the opening of US markets). For example, if you have monthly data, as there are 12 months in a year, it would make sense to model

$$B^{12}Z_t = Z_{t-12}; \quad \nabla_{12}Z_t = Z_t - Z_{t-12}$$

rather than looking at

$$BZ_t = Z_{t-1}; \quad \nabla Z_t = Z_t - Z_{t-1}$$

When you consider models of this form, look for two key ingredients:

1 A clear link to the human calendar
2 A realistic underlying physical mechanism, e.g. the seasonal effects of temperature and climate will obviously affect ice-cream sales, heating gas consumption etc.

A SARIMA model can be constructed from first principles as follows. Start with a general ARIMA model defined in terms of seasonal effects

$$\Phi_{SAR}(B^S)(1 - B^S)^D Z_t = \Phi_{SMA}(B^S)\epsilon_t \tag{11.3}$$

where the S in Eq. (11.3) refers to a seasonal term and D reflects the order of differencing (usually $D = 0$ or $D = 1$). Next, apply a regular ARIMA model to the de-seasonalized series. Firstly, apply the differencing operator $(I - B)^d$ to the left-hand side of Eq. (11.3)

$$(I - B)^d \Phi_{SAR}(B^S)(1 - B^S)^D Z_t = \Phi_{SMA}(B^S)\epsilon_t \qquad (11.4)$$

Since polynomials in the backward shift operator B commute, rewrite Eq. (11.4) as

$$\Phi_{SAR}(B^S)(I - B)^d(1 - B^S)^D Z_t = \Phi_{SMA}(B^S)\epsilon_t \qquad (11.5)$$

Now apply an autoregressive term to the left-hand side and a moving average term to the right-hand side

$$\Phi_{AR}(B)\Phi_{SAR}(B^S)(I - B)^d(1 - B^S)^D Z_t = \Phi_{MA}(B)Phi_{SMA}(B^S)\epsilon_t \qquad (11.6)$$

Thus, Eq. (11.6) defines a SARIMA $(p, d, q) \times (P, D, Q)_S$ model. Note that S denotes the length of the seasonal difference and the capital letters refer to the components of the seasonal term.

We now give a concrete example of how to construct an SARIMA model. Venables and Ripley (2003) give the example of a SARIMA $(0, 1, 1) \times (0, 1, 1)_{12}$ model fitted to monthly series of aircraft passenger numbers. This has the interpretation of two moving average models: one moving average model associated with the time of the year; one moving average model to account for effects that remain once seasonality is adjusted for. Using Eq. (11.6), the model can be constructed as follows. In the absence of any autoregressive components, the left-hand side of Eq. (11.6) reduces to

$$\begin{aligned}(I - B)(I - B^{12})Z_t &= Z_t - BZ_t - B^{12}Z_t + B^{13}Z_t \\ &= Z_t - Z_{t-1} - Z_{t-12} + Z_{t-13} \qquad (11.7)\end{aligned}$$

Similarly, the right-hand side of Eq. (11.6) reduces to

$$\begin{aligned}(I - \beta_1 B)(I - \beta_{12}B^{12})\epsilon_t &= (I - \beta_1 B - \beta_{12}B^{12} + \beta_1\beta_{12}B^{13})\epsilon_t \\ &= \epsilon_t - \beta_1\epsilon_{t-1} - \beta_{12}\epsilon_{t-12} + \beta_1\beta_{12}\epsilon_{t-13} \qquad (11.8)\end{aligned}$$

Finally, combining Eqs (11.7–11.8) gives

$$Z_t = Z_{t-1} + Z_{t-12} - Z_{t-13} + \epsilon_t - \beta_1\epsilon_{t-1} - \beta_{12}\epsilon_{t-12} + \beta_1\beta_{12}\epsilon_{t-13}$$

11.4   Examples

11.4.1   ARIMA modelling

Data in the file Airlines.txt gives information about monthly airline passenger figures. Simple summary plots give clear evidence of a monthly seasonal effect (see Fig. 11.1). As discussed in Venables and Ripley (2003), a simple descriptive analysis can nonetheless be very useful. In this case, the suggestion is that passenger numbers are generally increasing over time subject to significant seasonal variations. In R, use the command ts.plot to produce a simple time-series plot.

Airlines<-read.table("E:Airlines.txt")
passengers<-Airlines[,1]
ts.plot(passengers)

In this section, we will fit simple ARIMA models to this data. Our approach reduces to fitting ARMA models to the first-differenced series. Here, first-differencing is an artificial way of generating an approximately stationary time series without a clear underlying trend. We will see later, at the end of this section, that, in this case, a more specialized SARIMA model is ultimately needed to capture underlying seasonal effects in this data.

We apply ARMA models applied to the first differences constructed in R using firstdifferences<-diff(passengers).
We consider three simple models:

1   AR(1) model
2   MA(1) model
3   ARMA(1, 1) model

Lots of similar models should ultimately give similar interpretations. It is often easiest to just assume (as here) that AR and MA effects may be present and just fit the lowest possible first-order model. The Box–Jenkins approach shown in the next subsection gives a principled way of selecting the order of the models.

1   AR(1)/ARIMA(1, 0, 0) model. The model fitted in this case is

$$Z_t = \mu + \alpha_1(Z_{t-1} - \mu) + \epsilon_t$$

In R, use
arima(firstdifferences, order = c(I, 0, 0))
Coefficients:
arl intercept
0.3037 2.3700
s.e. 0.0797 3.8369
Conduct a t-test using
length(firstdifferences)
[1] 143

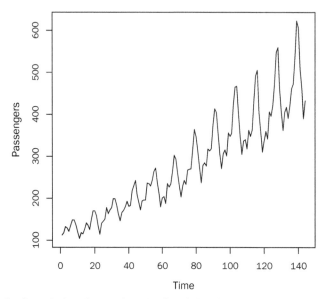

Figure 11.1   Descriptive time-series plot for airline data

The residual degrees of freedom can thus be calculated as $143 - 2$ estimated parameters. A t-test of the significance of the AR(1) term can thus be conducted using
```
1-pt(0.3037/0.0797, 141)
[1] 0.0001032107
```
Results, therefore, present significant evidence of an autoregressive effect.
2   MA(1)/ARIMA(0, 0, 1) model. The model fitted in this case is

$$Z_t = \mu + \beta_1 \epsilon_{t-1} + \epsilon_t$$

In R, use
```
arima(firstdifferences, order = c(0, 0, 1))
Coefficients:
mal intercept
0.4012 2.4213
s.e. 0.0893 3.6858
```
Conduct a t-test using
```
length(firstdifferences)
[1] 143
```
The residual degrees of freedom can thus be calculated as $143 - 2$ estimated parameters. A t-test of the significance of the MA(1) term can thus be conducted using
```
1-pt(0.4012/0.0893, 141)
[1] 7.264574e-06
```
Results, therefore, present significant evidence of a moving average effect.

3 ARMA(1, 1)/ARIMA(1, 0, 1) model. The model fitted in this case is

$$Z_t = \mu + \alpha_1 (Z_{t-1} - \mu)\beta_1 \epsilon_{t-1} + \epsilon_t$$

In R, use
arima(firstdifferences, order = c(l, 0, l))
Coefficients:
arl mal intercept
-0.4767 0.8645 2.4509
s.e. 0.1153 0.0714 3.2660
Conduct a *t*-test using
length(firstdifferences)
[1] 143
The residual d.f. $= 143 - 3$ estimated parameters. In this case, the *t*-statistics can be constructed using
c(2*(l-pt(0.4767/0.1153, 140)), 2*(l-pt(0.8645/0.0714, 140)))
[1] 6.101428e-05 0.000000e+00
Results, therefore, give significant evidence of an autoregressive effect and a moving average effect.

11.4.2 Box–Jenkins method

Model selection for time series is difficult. The previous example serves to demonstrate that various models will perform approximately as well as each other. The basic idea behind the Box–Jenkins method (see Table 11.1) is that you can choose a model in a principled fashion based upon the autocorrelation function (ACF) and the partial autocorrelation function (PACF). However, since this is a graphical method, this will contain some artistic rather than purely scientific elements, which may be open to some interpretation and may work imperfectly with real datasets.

Table 11.1 Graphical ACF and PACF model selection procedure

Model	Typical ACF	Typical PACF
AR(p)	Exponential decay or damped sine wave pattern	Significant spikes through lag p
MA(q)	Significant spikes through lag q	Exponential decay or damped sine wave pattern
ARMA(p, q)	Exponential decay or damped sine sine wave pattern	Exponential decay or damped sine wave pattern

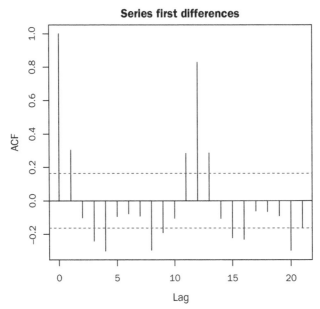

Figure 11.2 ACF plot for the first-differenced series

The autocorrelation function measures the correlation of Z_t with itself τ time periods later

$$\rho_t = \mathrm{Corr}(X_t, X_{t+\tau}) \qquad (11.9)$$

The partial autocorrelation function essentially repeats Eq. (11.8) but makes a further adjustment for correlations in intervening lags. In R, the relevant functions are acf and pacf. For our example in R, use
acf(firstdifferences)
pacf(firstdifferences)
ACF and PACF plots for our data are shown in Figs 11.2 and 11.3 and should be interpreted as follows. The ACF plot shows a damped sine wave pattern with a spike at lag 1. The PACF plot shows a damped sine wave pattern with a spike at lag 1. Combining both observations, the suggestion would then be to fit an ARMA(1, 1) to the first-differenced series. This graphical interpretation would then tally with the significant t-statistics found for the ARMA(1, 1) model in the previous subsection. (In practical data examples, look for a combination of numerical and graphical information telling you the same thing.)

11.4.3 SARIMA modelling

Plotting the first differences of the data suggests that some residual seasonality may be present (see Fig. 11.4). The suggestion, in this case, is that more specialized SARIMA models may ultimately be needed. In R, use

Series first differences

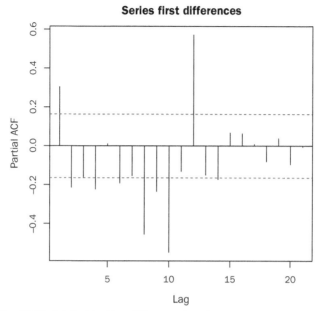

Figure 11.3 PACF plot for the first-differenced series

firstdifferences<-diff(passengers)
ts.plot(firstdifferences)

Venables and Ripley (2003) describe a SARIMA $(0, 1, 1) \times (0, 1, 1)_{12}$ as being a classical model for airline passenger data. Looking at Fig. 11.1, the suggestion is that you need a differencing procedure to get rid of the underlying time trend. The interpretation of this airline model is that, once you have done this initial differencing, it is simplest to just include a single moving average term both for the seasonal component and for the de-seasonalized series.

SARIMA models can be fitted using the function arima. In this case, you need to specify separate ARIMA components for the seasonal component and for the de-seasonalized series. You also need to specify the period – here 12 months, making up one year. In R, a SARIMA model can be fitted using
arima(passengers, order=c(0, 1, 1), seasonal=list(order=c(0, 1, 1), period=12))
Coefficients:
mal smal
-0.3087 -0.1074
s.e. 0.0890 0.0828

In order to run t-tests, use
length(passengers)
[1] 144

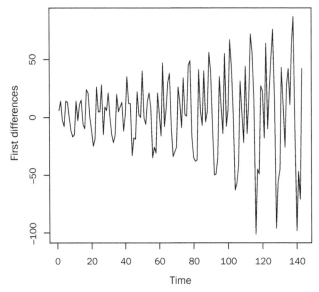

Figure 11.4   Residual seasonality remaining in first-differenced series

The residual degrees of freedom can then be calculated as 144 observations −
2 differencing parameters − 2 estimated parameters. In this case, t-tests can be
conducted using
c(2*(1-pt(3087/0.0890, 140)), 2*(1-pt(0.1074/0.0828, 140)))
[1] 0.0000000 0.1967298
Results, therefore, give significant evidence of a moving average effect
($p = 0.000$) but no formal evidence of a monthly effect in this case ($p = 0.197$).

11.5   Tutorial exercises

1 ARIMA models are often thought to be unsuitable for financial time
   series. Consider the logarithm of the stock price data in the file
   ShanghaiComposite.txt.
   (a) Show, graphically, that the first differences of the logarithm of the
        stock price is approximately stationary but that the logarithm of the
        stock price is not.
   (b) Test for the significance of an AR(1) model applied to the first differ-
        ences of the log-price.
   (c) Test for the significance of a MA(1) model applied to the first differ-
        ences of the log-price.
   (d) Consider an AR(1) model for the log-price X_t

$$X_t = \mu + \alpha X_{t-1} + \epsilon_t \qquad (11.10)$$

Show that if $\alpha \neq 1$ in Eq. (11.10), then successive returns are correlated.

(e) Show that if $\alpha = 1$ in Eq. (11.10), then successive returns are uncorrelated.

(f) Fit the model shown in Eq. (11.10) and test the null hypothesis that $\alpha = 1$.

2 The data in the file **BrexitBookies.txt** contains implied probabilities for the probability of a remain win and the probability of a leave win in the EU referendum from May 11th 2015 to June 22nd 2016. An analysis of this data can be found in Fry and Brint (2017).

(a) Explain why there is a redundancy in this data.

(b) Read the data into R using the following:

betodds<-read.table("E:BrexitBookies.txt")
remain<-betodds[,1]
firstdifferences<-diff(remain, 1)

(c) Assess the graphical evidence for stationarity in the first differences of the remain probability and in the series itself.

(d) Plot the ACF and PACF of the first differences of the remain probability.

(e) Fit an ARIMA(1, 1, 1) model to the remain probability. Using this model as the starting point, use forward selection to chose an appropriate ARIMA model for this data.

(f) Using the best model from part (d) and the R function **predict**, forecast the probability of a remain victory in the next-day's referendum.

(g) Comment on your findings in part (f).

3 The data in **HousePrices.txt** records quarterly UK house prices, alongside an adjustment for inflation, together with a projected trend which assumes 2.5% growth per year from 1971 values.

(a) Read this data into R using the following:

house<-read.table("E:HousePrices.txt")
realprice<-house[,4]
realprice<-rev(realprice)
firstdifferences<-diff(realprice, 1)

(b) Using the Box–Jenkins methodology applied to the first-differenced series, suggest a possible ARMA model for this data.

(c) Using the model suggested in part (b), forecast house prices for the 3rd and 4th quarters of 2021.

4 (a) Using the data in Question 3, use the **arima** command to find an ARMA model for the first differences that has the lowest value of the AIC.

(b) Explain why this approach may be preferable to a purely graphical approach such as Box–Jenkins.

(c) Using the best model in part (a), forecast prices for Q3 and Q4 of 2021.

(d) Comment on your results.

5 The data in the file **UKCovidDeaths.txt** records daily Covid deaths for the UK over time.

(a) Read in the data using the following:

covid<-read.table("E:UKCovidDeaths.txt")
date<-covid[,1]

```
date<-rev(date)
deaths<-covid[,2]
deaths<-rev(deaths)
firstdifferences<-diff(deaths, 1)
```

(b) Use the AIC statistic to suggest a low-order ARMA model for the first-differenced series.

(c) Use the best model found in part (b) to forecast Covid deaths for the next seven days.

(d) Comment on your results.

11.6 Solutions

1 (a) The code to produce Fig. 11.5 is shown below.
```
Shanghai<-read.table("E:ShanghaiComposite.txt")
logprice<-log(Shanghai[,2])
firstdifferences<-diff(logprice, 1)
par(mfrow=c(1, 2))
ts.plot(firstdifferences)
ts.plot(logprice)
```

(b) ```arima(firstdifferences, order=c(1, 0, 0))```
Coefficients:
arl intercept
0.0200 2e-04
s.e. 0.0131 2e-04

The t-ratio can then be constructed as follows. Since this is less than 2, it shows that the AR(1) term is non-significant:
0.0200/0.0131
[1] 1.526718

(c) ```arima(firstdifferences, order=c(0, 0, 1))```
Coefficients:
mal intercept
0.0210 2e-04
s.e. 0.0135 2e-04

The t-ratio can then be constructed as follows. Since this is less than 2, it shows that the MA(1) term is non-significant:
0.0210/0.0135
[1] 1.555556

(d) $$\text{Cov}(X_t - X_{t-1}, X_{t-1} - X_t) = \text{Cov}(X_t, X_{t-1}) - \text{Cov}(X_t, X_{t-2})$$
$$-\text{Cov}(X_{t-1}, X_{t-1}) + \text{Cov}(X_{t-1}, X_{t-2})$$
$$\text{Cov}(X_t - X_{t-1}, X_{t-1} - X_t) = \alpha\text{Cov}(X_{t-1}, X_{t-1}) - \alpha^2\text{Cov}(X_{t-2}, X_{t-2})$$
$$-\text{Cov}(X_{t-1}, X_{t-1}) + \alpha\text{Cov}(X_{t-2}, X_{t-2})$$
$$\text{Cov}(X_t - X_{t-1}, X_{t-1} - X_t) = (\alpha - 1)\text{Var}(X_{t-1}) + (\alpha - \alpha^2)\text{Var}(X_{t-2})$$

(e) Plugging $\alpha = 1$ into the above leads to a covariance of zero.

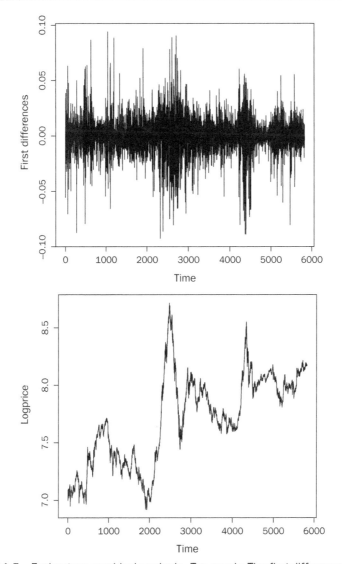

Figure 11.5 Exploratory graphical analysis. Top graph: The first-differenced series is approximately stationary. Bottom graph: The raw series is clearly non-stationary

(f) arima(logprice, order=c(1, 0, 0))
Coefficients:
ar1 intercept
0.9993 7.7049
s.e. 0.0005 0.2505

A t-statistic can then be constructed as follows. Since this is less than 2, we can retain the null hypothesis that $\alpha = 1$.

```
1-0.9993
[1] 7e-04
0.0007/0.0005
[1] 1.4
```

2 (a) Given the structure of the data, the probability of a remain win plus the probability of a leave win has to add up to 100%.

(b) n/a

(c) The R code to produce Fig. 11.6 is shown below. The interpretation, in this case, is perhaps a little unclear. However, it is perhaps more realistic to assume that the first-differenced series is approximately stationary.

```
par(mfrow=c(1, 2))
ts.plot(firstdifferences)
ts.plot(remain)
```

(d) The R code to produce Fig. 11.7 is shown below. If we interpret both the ACF and PACF as showing a damped sine wave pattern, then the implication from the Box–Jenkins methodology is that an ARMA model may be appropriate for the first-differenced series.

```
par(mfrow=c(1, 2))
acf(firstdifferences)
pacf(firstdifferences)
```

(e) Running the analysis in R, a t-statistics greater than 2 indicates that both terms in the ARIMA(1, 1, 1) model are significant.

```
arima(remain, order=c(1, 1, 1))
Coefficients:
ar1 ma1
0.6050 -0.3909
s.e. 0.1026 0.1129
0.6050/0.1026
[1] 5.896686
0.3909/0.1129
[1] 3.462356
```

Next, when fitting an ARIMA(2, 1, 1) model, the AR(1) term becomes non-significant suggesting that there is a redundancy within this model:

```
arima(remain, order=c(2, 1, 1))
Coefficients:
ar1 ar2 ma1
0.2901 0.1387 -0.1108
s.e. 0.2489 0.0788 0.2466
0.2901/0.2489
[1] 1.165528
```

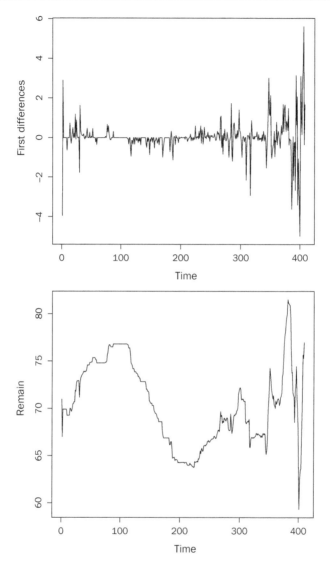

Figure 11.6 Exploratory graphical analysis. Top graph: First-differenced series. Bottom graph: Raw series

Next, when fitting an ARIMA(1, 1, 2) model, all the terms seem to be needed within this model:
arima(remain, order=c(l, l, 2))
Coefficients:
arl mal ma2
0.4986 -0.3304 0.1199
s.e. 0.1264 0.1307 0.0584

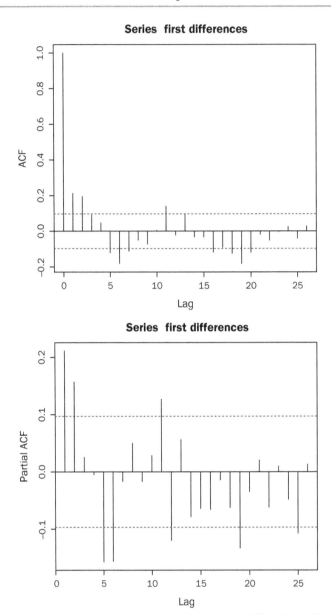

Figure 11.7   Exploratory graphical analysis. Top graph: ACF of first-differenced series showing damped sine wave pattern. Bottom graph: PACF of first-differenced series showing damped sine wave pattern

0.4986 /0.1264
[1] 3.94462
0.3304/0.1307
[1] 2.527927
0.1199/0.0584
[1] 2.053082

Next, trying an ARIMA(2, 1, 2) model, all these terms seem to be needed in the model:
arima(remain, order=c(2, 1, 2))
Coefficients:
ar1 ar2 ma1 ma2
1.6971 -0.9861 -1.5827 0.9194
s.e. 0.0160 0.0148 0.0367 0.0422
1.6971/0.0160
[1] 106.0687
0.9861/0.0148
[1] 66.62838
1.5827/0.0367
[1] 43.12534
0.9194/0.0422
[1] 21.78673

Now, trying an ARIMA(2, 1, 3) model, the t statistics indicate that there seems to be some redundancy in this model:
arima(remain, order=c(2, 1, 3))
Coefficients:
ar1 ar2 ma1 ma2 ma3
1.6980 -0.9850 -1.5953 0.9430 -0.0199
s.e. 0.0173 0.0168 0.0548 0.0855 0.0623
0.0199/0.0623
[1] 0.3194222

Similarly, fitting an ARIMA(3, 1, 2) model leads to broadly the same conclusion:
arima(remain, order=c(3, 1, 2))
Coefficients:
ar1 ar2 ar3 ma1 ma2
1.6742 -0.9444 -0.0235 -1.5727 0.9077
s.e. 0.0712 0.1260 0.0699 0.0505 0.0568
0.0235/0.0699
[1] 0.3361946

(f) Using the ARIMA(2, 1, 2) from part (d) and performing the prediction using the following R code leads to an estimated probability of 76.43345%.

```
al.arima<-arima(remain, order=c(2, I, 2))
predict(al.arima, I)
```

(g) High estimated probabilities of a remain win indicate a certain level of over-confidence on the part of bookmakers.

3 (a) n/a

(b) The R code to produce Fig. 11.8 is shown below. If we interpret this as showing spikes up to and including lag 4 in the ACF and a damped sine wave in the PACF, it suggests that an MA(4) model may be most suitable for this data.

(c) To fit this model and run the predictions use

```
bj.arima<-arima(firstdifferences, order=c(0, 0, 4))
predict(bj.arima, 2)
[I] I0188.246 368I.00I
```

Price forecasts can then be obtained using

$$\text{Price Q3} - \text{Price Q2} = 10188.246$$
$$\text{Price Q3} = 242709 + 10188.246 = 252897.2$$
$$\text{Price Q4} - \text{Price Q3} = 3681.001$$
$$\text{Price Q4} = \text{Price Q3} + 3681.001 = 256578.2$$

4 (a) Collect AIC values according to the following. The suggestion is that an ARMA(3, 2) model is best.

Order 1: AR(1) 3484.55, MA(1) 3507.09
Order 2: AR(2) 3485.46, MA(2) 3491.08, ARMA(1, 1) 3484.96
Order 3: AR(3) 3479.35, MA(3) 3492.07, ARMA(1, 2) 3481.95, ARMA(2, 1) 3484.33
Order 4: AR(4) 3480.36, MA(4) 3473.47, ARMA(1, 3) 3483.79, ARMA(2, 2) 3483.92, ARMA(3, 1) 3481.02
Order 5: AR(5) 3475.16, MA(5) 3472.31, ARMA(1, 4) 3473.4, ARMA(2, 3) 3484.24, **ARMA(3, 2) 3456.92**, ARMA(4, 1) 3482
Order 6: AR(6) 3476.74, MA(6) 3473.65, ARMA(1, 5) 3473.99, ARMA(2, 4) 3473.1, ARMA(3, 3) 3457.75, ARMA(4, 2) 3457.53, ARMA(5, 1) 3477

(b) Use of score statistics in this way may take out some of the imprecision and subjective judgements associated with graphical methods.

(c) Conduct the forecasts using

```
aic.arima<-arima(firstdifferences, order=c(3, 0, 2))
predict(aic.arima, 2)
8264.767 4500.426
```

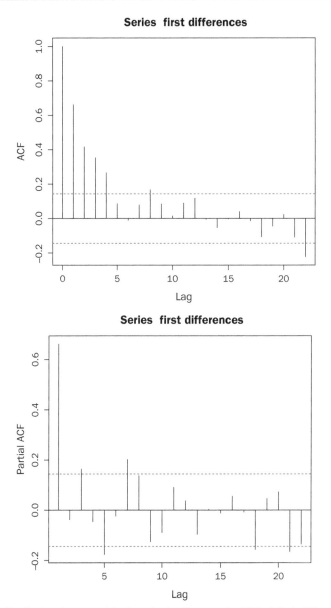

Figure 11.8 Exploratory graphical analysis. Top graph: ACF of first-differenced series. Bottom graph: PACF of first-differenced series

Forecast prices are therefore

$$\text{Price Q3} - \text{Price Q2} = 8264.767$$
$$\text{Price Q3} = 242709 + 8264.767 = 250173.8$$
$$\text{Price Q4} - \text{Price Q3} = 4500.426$$
$$\text{Price Q4} = \text{Price Q3} + 4500.426 = 255474.2.$$

(d) It is to be expected that similar time-series models should lead to similar forecast values.

5 (a) n/a

(b) From an examination of the AIC statistic, it seems that a low-order ARMA(1, 3) model will suffice. The AIC statistics are as follows:
Order 1: AR(1) 4856.91, MA(1) 4857.89
Order 2: AR(2) 4849.73, MA(2) 4856.22, ARMA(1, 1) 4789.83
Order 3: AR(3) 4800.53, MA(3) 4821.8, ARMA(1, 2) 4737.26, ARMA(2, 1) 4770.58
Order 4: AR(4) 4766.95, MA(4) 4802.85, **ARMA(1, 3) 4691.98**, ARMA(2, 2) 4694.72, ARMA(3, 1) 4735.61
Order 5: AR(5) 4735.13, MA(5) 4773.79, ARMA(1, 4) 4693.22, ARMA(2, 3) 4692.79, ARMA(3, 2) 4694.29, ARMA(4, 1) 4729.53

(c) In R, use
```
arima.aic<-arima(firstdifferences, c(1, 0, 3))
length(deaths)
[1] 513
prediction<-deaths[513]+cumsum(predict(arima.aic, 7)$pred)
prediction
[1] 22.75072 18.82859 8.10493 -1.83484 -11.04887 -19.59099
-27.51105
```

Thus, predicted values for the next week would be 23, 19, 8, 0, 0, 0, 0.

(d) The model is really too simplistic to draw any meaningful conclusions. However, it does give an early example of a complex problem where reasonable-looking statistical forecasts may only be possible a few days ahead – in this case, three days.

12 Modelling financial price data

The subject is inherently quantitative but is a core part of finance. The list of potential applications includes econometric studies, options pricing, risk management etc. The subject is often a core part of dissertations. However, the subject can look a bit strange to somebody studying it for the first time. Here are some basic ground rules:

1 You need to model percentage price changes.
2 This is usually simplified, in practice, to modelling the log-returns.
3 The log-returns are the first differences of the log-price.

We illustrate these general methods with an application to cryptocurrency data, although modelling stock market data will work just as well. The modelling of price data from cryptocurrencies is a live topic of academic research (see, e.g., Katsiampa 2017). We have also supervised BSc and MSc dissertations on related topics in recent years. This topic extends from the classical study of statistical models for stock price data. As far as cryptocurrency applications are concerned, this is not an ideological judgement, in itself, that cryptocurrencies are more of a speculative asset than a genuine currency.

Which data do we model? We almost never model the price index directly. It is usually more informative to look at the percentage change in price. The returns, R_t, can be characterized as

$$R_t = \frac{P_{t+1} - P_t}{P_t}$$

In practice, it is usually easier to look at the log-returns. Define $X_t = \ln P_t$ and analyse the log-returns, ΔX_t, defined as

$$\Delta X_t = X_{t+1} - X_t = \ln\left(\frac{P_{t+1}}{P_t}\right)$$

Percentage price changes are usually more informative. Some simple examples include the following:

1 'The price today is £100'. Now, this piece of information does not make sense in isolation. Was the price yesterday £5 or £300?
2 'The difference between today's price and yesterday's price, $P_t - P_{t-1}$, is £0.1'. This piece of information does not make sense in isolation. Was the price yesterday £5.50 or £0.5?

Percentage price changes, therefore, give an added sense of scale and direction. For example, $R_t = 0.0003$ means that the price has increased by 0.03% compared with yesterday's value. Similarly, $R_t = -0.0002$ means that the price has decreased by 0.02% compared with yesterday's value. In particular, when they are calculated over short time horizons such as days and weeks, stock market returns tend to show quite low values unless the market is extremely volatile. As an illustration, Black Monday, 19 October 1987 would have resulted in a value of $R_t = -0.2261$ as the Dow Jones Industrial Average index lost 22.61% of its value.

It clearly makes sense to look at returns but the usual convention is to instead look at the series of log-returns. There are several reasons for this:

1 Tractability and consistency with standard mathematical finance models.
2 The log-returns series are typically approximately stationary and so easier to model statistically.
3 The log-returns series are typically approximately uncorrelated and so easier to model statistically.

Note that there is usually not much difference between looking at the returns and the log-returns (see below). Note too that being uncorrelated is not the same as being independent.

Looking at the log-returns is consistent with standard mathematical finance models such as the Black–Scholes model (Black and Scholes 1973). Under this model

$$dP_t = \mu P_t dt + \sigma P_t dW_t$$

$$dX_t = \left(\mu - \frac{\sigma^2}{2}\right) dt + \sigma dW_t$$

The log-returns $\Delta X_t = X_{t+1} - X_t$ are then independent and normally distributed with mean

$$\int_t^{t+1} \left(\mu - \frac{\sigma^2}{2}\right) du = \mu - \frac{\sigma^2}{2}$$

and variance

$$\int_t^{t+1} \sigma^2 du = \sigma^2$$

Moreover the differences between the returns and the log-returns are likely to be very small. Compare the exact return $r_t = \dfrac{P_{t+1} - P_t}{P_t}$ with the log-return $\Delta X_t = \ln\left(\dfrac{P_{t+1}}{P_t}\right)$ that is used to approximate it

$$\ln\left(\frac{P_{t+1}}{P_t}\right) = \ln\left(\left(\frac{P_{t+1} - P_t}{P_t}\right) + 1\right)$$
$$= \left(\frac{P_{t+1} - P_t}{P_t}\right) + O(r_t^2)$$
$$= r_t + O(r_t^2)$$

12.1 Computational work with price data

It is possible to obtain a wealth of cryptocurrency data from **coinmarket-cap.com**. We usually focus on the log-returns calculated from each day's closing price – so we may only need a small subset of the available data. An example using Bitcoin prices is discussed below. We recommend that you read the data in from .**txt** format using the command **read.table**. You need to get rid of any commas in the .**txt** file using the **Edit**→**Replace** function. If, instead, you directly copy the log-returns from, e.g., MS Excel into R, this can be a hidden source of rounding error.

Read in the data using the read.table command:

`BitcoinData<-read.table("E:BitcoinData.txt")`

Clarify how many columns are in the downloaded dataset. In this case, the computer tells you that there are four columns:

`ncol(BitcoinData)`

`[1] 4`

The price then has to be identified as the last (fourth) column:

`price<-BitcoinData[,4]`

Now you need the data to be in chronological order from oldest to newest. You may have to reverse the data if it is not already in this format. In R, the command to do this is **rev**:

`price<-rev(price)`

R's command-line structure offers various time and efficiency savings compared with alternatives such as MS Excel. In R, calculate the log-returns as the first difference of the log-prices. This can be a bit hard to see at first but can be achieved by creating two series:

1 Series one with the first observation deleted
2 Series two with the last observation deleted

The log-return can then be calculated as

$$\text{Log-return} = \text{Series one} - \text{Series two}$$

In R, use
length(price)
[1] 2482
logreturn<-log(price[-1])-log(price[-2482])
In R, the command length tells you how long the series is and the number corresponding to the last observation. The minus sign indicates that you thus delete the 1st and 2482nd observations.

In financial econometric work in R, we have personally found the following function helpful for calculating log-returns based on a price series x listed in chronological order from oldest to newest
gradrel<-function(x){
n<-length(x)
logreturns<-log(x[-1])-log(x[-n])
logreturns}
In R, you would need to copy the above code into the command window so that R then recognizes this function. Once this is done, you could then, equivalently, calculate the log-returns using
logreturn<-gradrel(price)
Note that the more times you have to calculate the log-returns, the more efficient this command becomes.

12.2 The random walk model

The random walk model is the simplest possible financial model that can give you 'reasonable answers'. The random walk model has links with both the efficient markets hypothesis and with corporate finance, although it is not always presented in this way. The random walk model is useful for illustrating that finance is inherently quantitative and also for being the lens through which we can see how stock market prices really behave – essentially, by helping us to identify ways in which stock prices differ from the random walk model.

Mathematically, a random walk is defined as

$$S_n = \sum_{i=1}^{n} X_i$$

where the X_i are independent and identically distributed (not necessarily normally distributed!) Under the Black–Scholes model, the log-price X_t can be constructed as

$$X_t = \sum_{i=1}^{t} \Delta X_i$$

where the X_i are normally distributed with mean $\tilde{\mu} = \mu - \dfrac{\sigma^2}{2}$ and variance σ^2.

The random walk model has a rich history and hints at close links between physics and finance (Weatherall 2013). It was originally used as an options-pricing model by Bachelier in 1900. This predates Einstein's work on Brownian motion by 5 years. For various reasons, there was a growth in mathematical finance in the 1950s–1960s. As with a lot of things, this was primarily computer driven. Osborne then improved upon Bachelier's original model. Other important contributions were made by Mandelbrot and Thorp. The first tests of the random walk model and the efficient markets hypothesis were made by Fama.

In 1973, seminal options-pricing papers were published by Black–Scholes and by Merton. The Chicago Board Options Exchange was also established. In the early 1970s, physics research funding was dramatically cut in the aftermath of the space race. This period coincided with increased use of quantitative computer-driven models in financial industries. As a subject, finance has become increasingly quantitative – and will probably continue to do so! From the 1980s onwards, there have been developments in time-series econometrics such as ARCH/GARCH in response to empirical failings of the random walk model (see Chapter 13). From the 1990s onwards, increases in computer power and data availability occurred alongside developments in computational modelling. This has led to further growth in the subject of quantitative finance and is likely to fuel future developments.

Under the Black–Scholes model, the log-returns are normally distributed and are independent. Under a Markowitz interpretation, the mean of the log-returns provides a measure of the rate of return on investment. Similarly, the variance of the log-returns provides a measure of the rate of risk associated with an investment. For the daily Bitcoin log-returns discussed earlier, the mean log-returns is 0.001716242 and the variance of the log-returns is 0.001801658. In R, use **mean(logreturn)** and **var(logreturn)** to calculate these.

The key advantage of the random walk model is that it is conceptually interesting and tractable – especially in regard to devising numerical options-pricing models. However, it is important not to view the random walk model as a purely theoretical device. The random walk model lays the foundation for more advanced and accurate study of financial time series via widely documented *stylized empirical facts*. The random walk model is also not restricted to having a normal distribution. Heavy-tailed multivariate random walk models can lead to fruitful risk management applications including analysing contagion (Malevergne and Sornette 2006).

12.3   Stylized empirical facts

The random walk model is not just theoretically interesting. The Black–Scholes model is used as a baseline from which stylized empirical facts are defined. Financial time series are widely studied, are obviously important, and the results of these studies are widely documented. Stylized empirical facts use historical data to describe how real stock market prices truly behave – these are not theoretical models. The key stylized empirical facts as identified in Cont (2001) and Cont and Tankov (2003) are:

1 Heavy tails – higher probabilities of extreme events than under the normal distribution.
2 Log-returns are approximately uncorrelated.
3 Log-returns are not independent.
4 Volatility clustering.
5 Central limit theorem – returns calculated over a longer time horizon (e.g. days, weeks, months) are closer to a normal distribution.
6 Leverage effect – volatility is negatively correlated with asset returns.
7 Volume is positively correlated with volatility.

Stylized empirical facts are general rules rather than mathematical laws of nature. There may also be exceptions to every rule. Stylized empirical facts are typically formulated for large efficient and liquid stock markets. Thus, one may observe differences for thinly traded, less efficient and less liquid developing and emerging markets. As such, it is interesting to look at the stylized empirical facts of cryptocurrency markets. We would naturally expect cryptocurrency price data to share much in common with these generic stylized empirical facts. However, if we compare cryptocurrencies to, for example, a developing stock market index, we might expect to find some autocorrelation in asset returns (see, e.g., empirical work in Katsiampa (2017)). We might also expect to find very heavy tails as a reflection of extreme price risks. This stylized empirical fact may thus be especially true for cryptocurrencies.

12.4   Some tests of stylized empirical facts

In this section, we discuss graphical and numerical tests for stylized empirical facts 1–5. Stylized empirical facts 6–7 require separate estimates of volatility. Whilst this is possible, e.g. from recently established derivative markets for Bitcoin, this is more involved so we omit it here.

12.4.1   Heavy tails

In R, you can test for the normality of a series using the command shapiro.test. The null hypothesis is that the data is normally distributed. In finance, rejection of the null hypothesis will usually mean that the data has heavy tails (a higher probability of extreme events than under the normal distribution). This is the conclusion from our Bitcoin example since shapiro.test(logreturn) gives
data: logreturn
W = 0.88778, p-value < 2.2e-l6

However, we want to see how the normal approximation breaks down, not just that it is an inaccurate model. The easiest way to do this is to use a kernel density estimate which is a special kind of histogram expressed as a smooth curve rather than as a bar chart. The kernel density plot gives us the best estimate of the probability density function of the log-returns. We can then see how the fitted normal distribution compares with this kernel density. estimate.

In R, a kernel density estimate can be constructed using the function density applied to the log-returns series:

dens<-density(logreturn)

This produces a grid of x values over which a corresponding y value (kernel density estimate or histogram value is calculated). It is easiest to compare this with the y-values that would correspond to the normal distribution. In order to do the comparison, the R function for the normal probability density is dnorm. You also need:

1 The mean of the log-returns series
   mean(logreturn)
   [1] 0.001716242
2 The standard deviation of the log-returns series
   sd(logreturn)
   [1] 0.04244594
3 To plot the kernel density estimate using the x and y co-ordinates of the kernel density estimate
   plot(dens$x, dens$y, type="l")
4 To overlay a line showing the fit of the corresponding normal distribution
   lines(dens$x, dnorm(dens$x, 0.001716242, 0.04244594), lty=2)

Note

1 This should show much heavier tails in empirical financial data compared with the normal distribution
2 Sometimes the effect is better shown using a plot of the log density. In this case, replace the above with
   plot(dens$x, log(dens$y), type="l")
   lines(dens$x, log(dnorm(dens$x, 0.001716242, 0.04244594), lty=2))
   The plots obtained are shown below in Figs 12.1–12.2.

12.4.2 Log-returns approximately uncorrelated

If this stylized empirical fact is true, then the ACF plot constructed should have all the points within the 'tramlines'. In R, use acf(logreturn). Results shown in Fig. 12.3 suggest that this stylized empirical fact is approximately true for the Bitcoin price data.

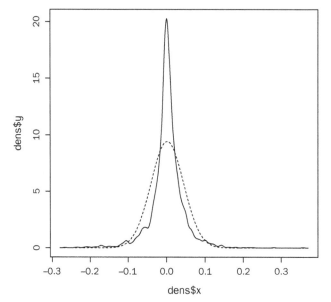

Figure 12.1 Probability density plot of the log-returns

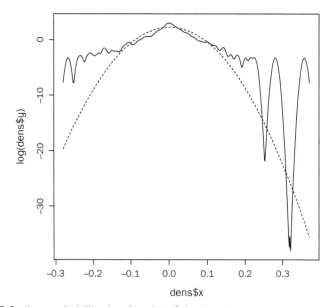

Figure 12.2 Log probability density plot of the log-returns

Series log-return

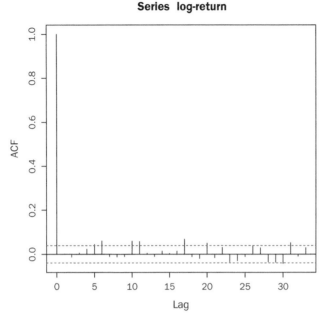

Figure 12.3 Autocorrelation function plot of the log-returns

12.4.3 Log-returns are not independent

The log-returns may be approximately uncorrelated but are not independent. This feature is also sometimes described as long-range dependence in volatility. To see this, the ACF of the absolute value or modulus of the log-returns should suggest autocorrelation. In R, use acf(abs(logreturn)). Results shown in Fig. 12.4 suggest that this stylized empirical fact is approximately true for our Bitcoin data.

12.4.4 Volatility clustering

We will discuss ARCH/GARCH modelling to account for volatility clustering in the next chapter. Whilst ARCH and GARCH models give a formal statistical test for volatility clustering, some important points to bear in mind are as follows. Firstly, purely graphical measures of volatility clustering are still useful. Secondly, the behaviour of price volatility will be richer (and inevitably more dangerous) than any mathematical or statistical model can describe (see also related discussion in Taleb (2007)).

In contrast to the way in which simulated data from the normally distributed random walk model prices clump together around groups of large spikes, simulated data from a normal random walk model looks too smooth compared with real price series. The other thing to look at here would be the scale on the y-axis chosen by R (see Figs 12.5–12.6). These plots can be produced as follows.

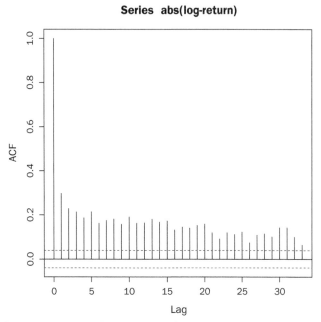

Figure 12.4 Autocorrelation function plot of the absolute value of the log-returns

In R, the time-series plot in Fig. 12.5 is produced using ts.plot(logreturn). In R, to produce the simulated data plot in Fig. 2.6, you need to know:

1 The length of the series
  length(logreturn)
  [1] 2481
2 The mean of the series
  mean(logreturn)
  [1] 0.001716242
3 The standard deviation of the series
  sd(logreturn)
  [1] 0.04244594

A plot of the simulated data can then be constructed using ts.plot(rnorm(2481, 0.001716242, 0.04244594), ylab="simulated log return")

12.4.5 Central limit effect

A typical finding is that as the return horizon increases, prices should become closer to a normal distribution. There is thus a smoothing process whereby the returns smooth out as the time horizon over which they are calculated increases.

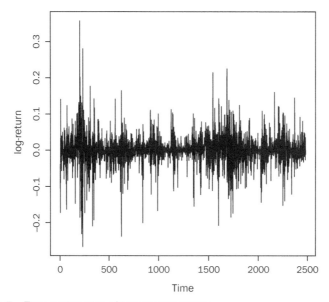

Figure 12.5 Time-series plot of Bitcoin log-returns

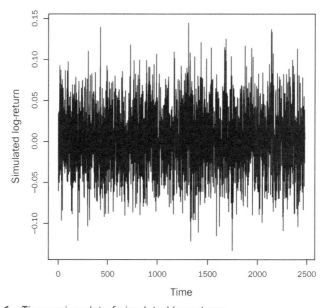

Figure 12.6 Time-series plot of simulated log-returns

Simple examples about how the effect should manifest itself include the following:

1 Returns calculated over a day should be closer to a normal distribution than returns calculated every 15 minutes.
2 Returns calculated over a week should be closer to a normal distribution than returns calculated over a day.
3 Returns calculated over a month should be closer to a normal distribution than returns calculated over a week.
4 Returns calculated over a year should be closer to a normal distribution than returns calculated over a month.

Note that stock price data recorded over different intervals can be readily and freely downloaded from, e.g., Yahoo Finance or Google Finance. Thus, we were keen to include material on the stylized empirical facts of financial time series in this chapter as we feel it is potentially a good subject to set for dissertation students. It also combines challenging theoretical components with a wealth of freely available data.

12.5 Tutorial exercises

The purpose of this set of exercises is to provide examples where relatively simple techniques – nothing harder than regression or autocorrelation – can be used to provide meaningful analyses of financial project data.

1 The data in the four files FTSE100after.txt, FTSE100before.txt, FTSE250after.txt and FTSE250before.txt details UK stock price data one year before and after the Covid pandemic – with the date of the outbreak of the pandemic taken to be 16 March 2020.
   (a) Explain the choice of indices in this study.
   (b) Read the data into R using the following commands:
      largeafter<-read.table("F:FTSE100after.txt")
      largebefore<-read.table("F:FTSE100before.txt")
      smallafter<-read.table("F:FTSE250after.txt")
      smallbefore<-read.table("F:FTSE250before.txt")
   (c) Calculate the log-returns, ΔX_t, for each stock price series.
   (d) Construct the empirical volatility proxy, $\sigma_t = |\Delta X_t - \mu|$, for each of the four series, where μ denotes the average of the log returns series.
   (e) Use the function t.test to test for a difference in the empirical volatility both before and after Covid.
   (f) Use a t-test with unequal variances to test for a difference in the average rate of return both before and after Covid.
   (g) Interpret the results in parts (e–f)
2 The data in the file ShanghaiComposite.txt lists daily stock prices from 2/7/1997–20/7/2021.

(a) Enter this data into R and calculate the log-returns using the following code (note that you will need to make sure that you define the function gradrel first, as per the previous examples):

```
chinastock<-read.table("F:shanghaiComposite.txt")
price<-chinastock[,2]
logreturn<-gradrel(price)
```

To what extent does this data conform to the following stylized empirical facts of financial time series?
(a) Heavy tails
(b) Log-returns approximately uncorrelated
(c) Log-returns are not independent
(d) Volatility clustering

3 The data in the file **TetherData.txt** lists daily closing prices for the cryptocurrency Tether.
(a) Read this data into R and calculate the log-returns.
(b) Give examples how this data violates the stylized empirical facts of financial time series.
(c) Comment on your findings.

4 *The relationship between pay and performance.* Does pay in one year affect performance in the next? Does performance in one year affect pay in the next? This exercise lays out an approximate Granger causality test devised by a past dissertation student to try to answer this question.

The data in **payperformance.txt** lays out directors' pay in years 2017 and 2018 in relation to three separate measures of accounting and finance performance: the log-return of the stock market price, the ROA and the ROE.
(a) How many years of stock market data is needed to construct this data set?
(b) Explain why different sets of performance are used?
(c) Read the data into R using the following commands:

```
payperformance<-read.table("E:Payperformancedata.txt")"
pay2018<-payperformance[,1]
pay2017<-payperformance[,2]
logreturn2018<-payperformance[,3]
logreturn2017<-payperformance[,4]
roe2017<-payperformance[,5]
roe2018<-payperformance[,6]
roa2017<-payperformance[,7]
roa2018<-payperformance[,8]
```

(d) A regression model to test whether pay affects performance is constructed as

$$\text{Performance}_t = \alpha + \beta \text{performance}_{t-1} + \gamma \text{pay}_{t-1} \qquad (12.1)$$

Use the model in Eq. (12.1) to see whether pay affects performance.

(e) A regression model to test whether performance affects pay is constructed as

$$\text{Pay}_t = \alpha + \beta \text{pay}_{t-1} + \gamma \text{performance}_{t-1} \qquad (12.2)$$

Use the model in Eq. (12.2) to see whether performance affects pay.

(f) Comment on your findings in parts (d–e).

5 *Event study.* Following an analysis by Alam et al. (2020) using Australian data, we examine the impact of the Covid 19 outbreak upon the transportation and pharmaceutical sectors.

(a) Read in the data using the following:
```
marketdata<-read.table("E:CovidMarketData.txt")
marketindex<-marketdata[,4]
transportation<-marketdata[,5]
pharmaceutical<-marketdata[,6]
```

(b) Split the data up into two segments: one segment before 23 March 2020 and one segment from 23 March 2020 onwards.

(c) Calculate the log-returns for this data.

(d) Fit the regression model

$$\text{Returns}_t = \alpha + \beta \text{market index return}_t \qquad (12.3)$$

(e) Calculate the out-of-sample prediction errors corresponding to the regression in (12.3).

(f) Conduct a t-test of the out-of-sample prediction errors in part (e). Is there any evidence of an abnormal return?

(g) Comment on your findings.

12.6 Solutions

1 (a) Setting up the study in this way gives us a chance to compare the effects upon larger companies in the FTSE 100 against smaller companies in the FTSE 250.

(b) n/a

(c) To calculate the log-returns use
```
gradrel<-function(x){
n<-length(x)
gradrel<-log(x[-1])-log(x[-n])
gradrel}
logret1<-gradrel(as.numeric(largeafter[,2]))
logret2<-gradrel(largebefore[,2])
logret3<-gradrel(smallafter[,2])
logret4<-gradrel(smallbefore[,2])
```

(d) To construct the volatility proxies use
```
vol1<-abs(logret1-mean(logret1))
vol2<-abs(logret2-mean(logret2))
vol3<-abs(logret3-mean(logret3))
vol4<-abs(logret4-mean(logret4))
```

(e) The t-tests present evidence of an increase in volatility brought upon by the pandemic.
```
t.test(vol1, vol2)
t = 11.021, df = 251.7, p-value < 2.2e-16
alternative hypothesis: true difference in means is not equal to 0
mean of x mean of y
0.19711233 0.00714784
t.test(vol3, vol4)
t = 4.8745, df = 473.05, p-value = 1.492e-06
alternative hypothesis: true difference in means is not equal to 0
mean of x mean of y
0.011415501 0.006803963
```

(f) The t-tests present evidence of a change in the rate of return for small companies only.
```
t.test(logret1, logret2, var.equal=FALSE)
t = 0.87624, df = 251.69, p-value = 0.3817
alternative hypothesis: true difference in means is not equal to 0
t.test(logret3, logret4, var.equal=FALSE)
t = 1.9804, df = 447.99, p-value = 0.04827
alternative hypothesis: true difference in means is not equal to 0
mean of x mean of y
0.0016085646 -0.0008960163
```

(g) There is clear evidence that the pandemic has increased stock market volatility for both large and small companies. However, there is a suggestion that the returns for smaller domestic companies have also increased over the same period.

2 (a) n/a

(b) A log-density plot gives clear evidence of heavy tails in this price data.
```
a1<-density(logreturn)
plot(a1$x, log(dnorm(a1$x, mean(logreturn), sd(logreturn))),
type="l",
lty=2, xlab="x", ylab="Log(Density)")
lines(a1$x, log(a1$y))
```

(c) Using acf(logreturn) suggests only weak evidence for autocorrelation.

(d) Using acf(abs(logreturn)) gives clear evidence of long-range dependence in volatility.

(e) Using ts.plot(logreturn) gives clear graphical evidence of volatility clustering.

3 (a)
```
Tether<-read.table("F:TetherData.txt")
price<-Tether[,4]
price<-rev(price)
logreturn<-gradrel(price)
```

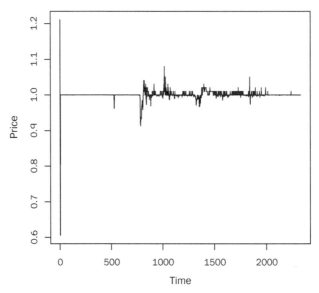

Figure 12.7 Time-series plot of Tether price data

(b) In answer to this question, there is no substitute for common sense. Looking at a plot of the price data in Fig. 12.7 suggests that Tether is fundamentally different from other assets. Accordingly, a plot of the absolute log-returns in Fig. 12.8 indicates that there is less evidence of long-range dependence in volatility for Tether data compared with other assets.

(c) Generally, most asset prices should conform to the stylized empirical facts of financial markets. If they do not, then a separate underlying economic mechanism may be at play. By its construction, Tether is designed to be a stablecoin with a value set to be approximately equal to $1. This means that Tether prices may differ considerably compared with other assets.

4 (a) Three years of data is needed in order to construct two yearly log-returns.

(b) It is interesting to see whether the conclusions change if the definition of performance changes. It is also interesting to compare stock market performance with different accounting measures of performance.

(c) n/a

(d) To fit the regression models use
```
perf1.lm<-lm(roe2018~roe2017+pay2017)
summary(perf1.lm)
perf2.lm<-lm(roa2018~roa2017+pay2017)
summary(perf2.lm)
perf3.lm<-lm(logreturn2018~logreturn2017+pay2017)
summary(perf3.lm)
```

Series abs(log-return)

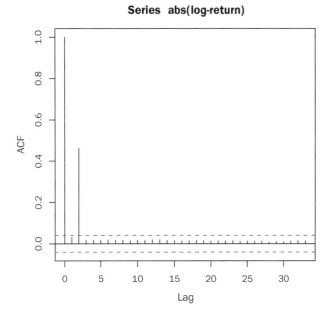

Figure 12.8 ACF plot of absolute log-returns for Tether showing limited evidence of long-range dependence in volatility

There is no evidence from the t-statistics produced that the level of pay affects performance.

(e) The code to fit the regressions is

```
payl.lm<-lm(pay2018~pay2017+roe2017)
summary(payl.lm)
pay2.lm<-lm(pay2018~pay2017+roa2017)
summary(pay2.lm)
pay3.lm<-lm(pay2018~pay2017+logreturn2017)
summary(pay3.lm)
Coefficients:
Estimate Std error t-value Pr(>|t|)
(Intercept) -1.147e+06 8.110e+05 -1.414 0.16066
pay2017 1.018e+00 2.552e-02 39.894 < 2e-16 ***
logreturn2017 6.308e+06 2.117e+06 2.980 0.00366 **
```

The only significant relationship is between the log-return. In the above, the coefficient of log-return is positive and statistically significant ($p = 0.00366$). This suggests that as stock market performance increases, pay increases.

(f) Results suggest that the relationship between pay and performance is complex. We found no evidence that pay increases performance, but we found some evidence that stock market performance increases pay.

214 Quantitative Methods in Finance Using R

However, this may still represent a troubling finding depending on the level of purely speculative behaviour that may be driving prices.

5 (a) n/a

(b) Since the second segment corresponds to the first 11 lines of the data set use

```
length(marketindex)
[1] 131
indexsector2<-marketindex[1:11]
indexsector1<-marketindex[12:131]
transportation2<-transportation[1:11]
transportation1<-transportation[12:131]
pharmaceutical2<-pharmaceutical[1:11]
pharmaceutical1<-pharmaceutical[12:131]
```

(c) To calculate the log-returns use

```
gradrel<-function(x){
n<-length(x)
gradrel<-log(x[-1])-log(x[-n]) gradrel}
logret1<-gradrel(indexsector1)
logret2<-gradrel(transportation1)
logret3<-gradrel(pharmaceutical1)
logret1b<-gradrel(indexsector2)
logret2b<-gradrel(transportation2)
logret3b<-gradrel(pharmaceutical2)
```

(d) To fit the regression models use

```
transport.lm<-lm(logret2~logret1)
pharma.lm<-lm(logret3~logret1)
```

(e) The calculation can be performed using

```
abnormalreturn1<-logret2b-transport.lm$coeff[1]
+transport.lm$coeff[2]*logret1babnormalreturn2<-logret3b
-pharma.lm$coeff[1]+pharma.lm$coeff[2]*logret1b
```

(f) Run the event study using

```
t.test(abnormalreturn1)
t = -0.5832, df = 9, p-value = 0.5741
t.test(abnormalreturn2)
t = -1.0309, df = 9, p-value = 0.3295
```

(g) There is no evidence of an impact using the event study methodology for UK data. The suggestion is that it might be harder than anticipated to disentangle the true economic effects of Covid.

13 ARCH/GARCH models

This subject is a key part of research in finance and accounting. There is a cottage industry on time-series models in financial econometrics. Deeper analyses are possible using key concepts from mathematical finance and from statistical physics. However, ARCH/GARCH and related financial time-series models are a natural place to start. ARCH/GARCH models mark the starting point of the professional analysis of financial time series. Lots of generalizations are possible – almost a cottage industry it its own right (see, e.g., E-GARCH, M-GARCH, T-GARCH models). The econometric analysis of, for example, cryptocurrency data is also a live topic of academic research (see, e.g., Katsiampa (2017)).

In the last chapter and in Figs 12.5–12.6, we saw that, typically in financial time series, the volatility is not constant. Market returns tend to cluster into periods of extreme volatility and more tranquil periods. Market returns also show marked differences compared with simulated returns from mathematical models. All markets, especially cryptocurrency markets, can show very volatile behaviour. This volatility will ultimately be more extreme than any mathematical/statistical model used to describe it.

ARCH/GARCH models solve the following problem. Mathematical models such as Black–Scholes often assume that volatility is constant. However, in reality, volatility is not constant and market returns can typically be clustered into periods of high volatility and more tranquil periods of low-volatility. This basic problem has various different names, e.g. volatility clustering or long-range dependence in volatility.

13.1 Mathematical formulation of the model – what ARCH and GARCH do

Under the Black–Scholes model, the first differences of the log-price ΔX_t satisfy

$$\Delta X_t \sim N\left(\mu, \sigma_t^2\right) \tag{13.1}$$

$$\sigma_t^2 = \sigma^2 = \text{constant} \tag{13.2}$$

However, this model is at odds with real stock market data. To partially fix this problem, the ARCH(1) model is formulated as

$$\Delta X_t \sim N\left(\mu, \sigma_t^2\right)$$
$$\sigma_t^2 = \alpha_0 + \alpha_1 u_{t-1}^2$$
$$u_t = (\Delta X_t - \mu) \text{ the residual}$$

This model thus solves the problem of σ^2 being constant in Eq. (13.2) by allowing for high values of volatility to follow other high values. Similarly, the model also allows for low values of volatility to follow other low values. This partially reconstructs observed volatility clustering patterns. This basic intuition can be expanded further using a more general ARCH(p) model

$$\Delta X_t \sim N\left(\mu, \sigma_t^2\right)$$
$$\sigma_t^2 = \alpha_0 + \alpha_1 u_{t-1}^2 + \dots + \alpha_p u_{t-p}^2$$
$$u_t = (\Delta X_t - \mu) \text{ the residual}$$

ARCH and GARCH models spawned a cottage industry in financial econometrics, e.g. E-GARCH, M-GARCH and S-GARCH. ARCH stands for autoregressive conditional heteroskedasticity. Similarly, GARCH stands for generalized autoregressive conditional heteroskedasticity. As the name suggests, GARCH is a generalization of ARCH that allows for slightly richer behaviour in volatility.

There is a whole statistical subject considering time series that is inherently specialist. Financial time series are a little less specialist but are a subject in their own right and are very different from the regular ARMA time-series models commonly studied in mainstream statistics. We cannot hope to be able to do justice to either subject in the space available. However, in brief:

ARCH = autoregressive conditional heteroskedasticity
GARCH = generalized autoregressive conditional heteroskedasticity
AR = autoregressive model for volatility
ARMA = autoregressive moving average model for volatility

In view of the above, the GARCH(1, 1) model presents a slightly more advanced partial fix to the problem identified in Eq. (13.2).

$$\Delta X_t \sim N\left(\mu, \sigma_t^2\right)$$
$$\sigma_t^2 = \alpha_0 + \alpha_1 u_{t-1}^2 + \beta_1 \sigma_{t-1}^2$$

The GARCH model is more complicated as it involves an unobserved volatility component, but the basic idea remains the same. The model allows for high values of volatility to follow other high values. The model also allows for low values of volatility to follow other low values. This basic intuition can be expanded further using a more general GARCH(p, q) model.

$$\Delta X_t \sim N\left(\mu, \sigma_t^2\right)$$

$$\sigma_t^2 = \alpha_0 + \alpha_1 u_{t-1}^2 + \ldots + \alpha_p u_{t-p}^2 + \beta_1 \sigma_{t-1}^2 + \ldots + \beta_q \sigma_{t-q}^2$$

$$u_t = (\Delta X_t - \mu) \text{ the residual}$$

$$\sigma_t^2 = \text{unobserved volatility component}$$

Choosing the order of an ARCH/GARCH model is difficult and there are several different approaches:

1 ARCH(1)/GARCH(1, 1) It is often easier to assume that both ARCH and GARCH effects are present and just use a first-order model.
2 Choose the order to coincide with certain time periods (see below).
3 Use t-tests to determine the order. This works in a similar way to t-tests in regression (see the worked examples in the remainder of this chapter).
4 Choose the model with the lowest Schwarz criterion or BIC value. This is similar, in spirit, to advanced approaches in computer science/Bayesian statistics. Therefore, this seeks to choose the model with the highest posterior probability of being correct.

It is often easier to choose the order of the ARCH/GARCH model to coincide with certain time intervals. A non-exhaustive list of how this can be achieved is shown below.

1 Daily data
   – Order 1: volatility from yesterday affects today
   – Order 5: volatility from last week affects today
   – Order 10: volatility from the last 2 weeks affects today
2 Weekly data
   – Order 1: Volatility from last week affects this week
   – Order 4: volatility from last month affects this week
3 Monthly data
   – Order 3: volatility from last quarter affects this month
   – Order 12: volatility from last year affects this quarter
4 Quarterly data
   – Order 4: volatility from last year affects this quarter

Example 13.12

Suppose, in common with the rest of the this chapter, that you are interested in selecting an ARCH/GARCH model for daily cyrptocurrency price data. Choosing the order of the ARCH/GARCH model to coincide with the time interval over which the data has been collected leads to the following two main possibilities.

1 *GARCH(1, 1). The assumption here is that a low-order model (and, indeed, the lowest possible order model) may be sufficient to give a good (albeit imperfect) description of volatility correlations on real markets.*
2 *GARCH(7, 7). Since currency and cryptocurrency markets trade seven days a week, the interpretation of this model would be that volatility from the previous week feeds forward and affects today.*

13.2   ARCH and GARCH in R

The easiest way to fit ARCH/GARCH models in R is using the **tseries** package. This fits a conditionally normally distributed model to the mean-corrected log-returns series. More advanced ARCH/GARCH models may be possible using other packages, e.g. **fGARCH** and **RUgarch**. Fancier ARCH/GARCH models may be required for cryptocurrency data, on occasion, to account for:

1 Autocorrelation in the returns series (see, e.g., Katsiampa 2017).
2 Heavier tails than the conditional normal distributions in the GARCH model (e.g. fit the model with student t-distributed rather than normally distributed errors).

When undertaking ARCH/GARCH modelling in R, the basic command is **garch** even if you fit a purely ARCH model without any GARCH terms. The basic command is
garch(x, order=(q, p**)**

There are two quirky features of this set of R commands:

1 x is a demeaned log-returns series.
2 Mathematically, we tend to write GARCH models as GARCH(p, q), where p is the ARCH bit and q is the GARCH bit. In R, in the **tseries** package, this ordering is reversed. In contrast, a lot of the R commands for regression modelling are more logically and carefully constructed.

Other aspects of the R coding are more familiar. When fitting ARCH and GARCH models the basic way of working shows some similarities with how R works in relation to regression and extended regression models. The basic procedure is as follows:

1 Fit the model using the command **garch** and save this as something.
2 Then, use the command **summary** to display the required results, e.g. t-statistics.

As with regression, we can formally test for the presence of an ARCH and GARCH effect by using individual t-statistics. These, in turn, can be best interpreted as follows:

1 If any of a_1, a_2, ..., a_p are significant, then we have evidence of the ARCH effect.
2 If any of b_1, b_2, ..., b_q are significant, then we have evidence of the GARCH effect.

These t-statistics for the ARCH and GARCH effect follow on from other topics discussed in earlier chapters. However, there is a notable difference in that the ubiquity of ARCH/GARCH effects in financial time series means that these ARCH and GARCH terms are more likely to show significant effects provided that the order of the model is chosen appropriately. Some additional worked examples can be found below in the remainder of this chapter.

13.3   Example 1: Ethereum data

We have price data on Ethereum from 7 August 2015 to 13 February 2020. The data is in the file **EthereumData.txt**, available online. We want to do the following tasks in R:

1 Read in the data.
2 Load the package **tseries** if you have not done this already.
3 Fit low-order ARCH(1) and GARCH(1, 1) models.
4 Experiment with the fitting of a higher-order GARCH(7, 7) model that has the interpretation of volatility from the previous week feeding forward and affecting today.

The solution works as follows:

1 Following previous examples
```
EthereumData<-read.table("E:EthereumData.txt")
ncol(EthereumData)
[1] 4
price<-EthereumData[,4]
price<-rev(price)
length(price)
[1] 1652
logreturn<-log(price[-1])-log(price[-1652])
```
2 Load the package **tseries** if you have not already done this.
3 Apply ARCH and GARCH models to the mean-corrected log-returns
```
resid<-logreturn-mean(logreturn)
```
ARCH(1) and GARCH(1, 1) models can then be fitted to this data, remembering that the R syntax works the other way round to standard econometric

notation.
```
archl<-garch(resid, order=c(0, 1))
garchll<-garch(resid, order=c(1, 1))
summary(archl)
summary(garchll)
```
Using the command summary in R then gives conclusive evidence of the ARCH effect.
```
Estimate Std error t-value Pr(>|t|)
a0 2.759e-03 5.856e-05 47.11 <2e-16 ***
a1 3.487e-01 2.960e-02 11.78 <2e-16 ***
```
The equivalent by-hand calculation for an exam-type question would be

$$t = |\text{estimate}|/\text{e.s.e.} = 3.487 \times 10^{-1}/2.960 \times 10^{-2}$$
$$t = 11.78041 > 2, \ p < 0.05$$

Similarly, the command summary in R also gives conclusive evidence of both the ARCH effect and the GARCH effects.
```
Estimate Std error t-value Pr(>|t|)
a0 0.0003819 0.0000383 9.971 <2e-16 ***
a1 0.1949723 0.0181241 10.758 <2e-16 ***
b1 0.7070688 0.0216811 32.612 <2e-16 ***
```

The by-hand calculation for the ARCH effect would be

$$t = |\text{estimate}|/\text{e.s.e.} = 0.1949723/0.0181241$$

using

$$t = 10.75763 > 2, \ p < 0.05$$

The by-hand calculation for the GARCH effect would be

$$t = |\text{estimate}|/\text{e.s.e.} = 0.7070688/0.0216811$$
$$t = 32.61222 > 2, \ p < 0.05$$

4 Fit a GARCH(7, 7) model using
```
garch77<-garch(resid, order=c(7, 7))
summary(garch77)
```

The following results give some evidence of an ARCH effect but not of the GARCH effect. However, non-significant terms suggest that there is some redundancy in this model and really that a lower-order model is more appropriate.

Estimate Std error t-value Pr(>|t|)
a0 9.852e-04 9.396e-04 1.049 0.294
a1 1.324e-01 1.928e-02 6.867 6.57e-12 ***
a2 8.610e-02 1.489e-01 0.578 0.563
a3 5.899e-02 1.133e-01 0.521 0.602
a4 3.406e-02 7.287e-02 0.467 0.640
a5 4.179e-02 6.539e-02 0.639 0.523
a6 4.043e-02 5.282e-02 0.765 0.444
a7 1.596e-15 3.082e-02 0.000 1.000
b1 4.686e-02 1.125e+00 0.042 0.967
b2 4.258e-02 6.122e-01 0.070 0.945
b3 3.804e-02 4.072e-01 0.093 0.926
b4 3.961e-02 4.325e-01 0.092 0.927
b5 4.095e-02 4.196e-01 0.098 0.922
b6 4.109e-02 4.377e-01 0.094 0.925
b7 4.560e-02 2.418e-01 0.189 0.850

13.4   Example 2: Ripple data

We have price data on Ripple from 4 August 2013 to 13 February 2020. The data is available online in the file **RippleData.txt**. We want to do the following tasks in R:

1   Read in the data.
2   Load the package **tseries** if you have not done this already.
3   Fit low-order ARCH(1) and GARCH(1, 1) models.
4   Experiment with the fitting of a higher-order GARCH(7, 7) model that has the interpretation of volatility from the previous week feeding forward and affecting today.

The solution works as follows:

1   RippleData<-read.table("E:RippleData.txt")
   ncol(RippleData)
   [1] 4
   price<-RippleData[,4]
   price<-rev(price)
   length(price)
   [1] 2385
   logreturn<-log(price[-1])-log(price[-2385])
2   Load the package **tseries** if you have not already done this.
3   Apply models to the mean-corrected log-returns
   resid<-logreturn-mean(logreturn)

You then need to fit ARCH(1) and GARCH(1, 1) models to this data, remembering that the R syntax works the other way round to standard econometric notation.

```
arch1<-garch(resid, order=c(0, 1))
garch11<-garch(resid, order=c(1, 1))
summary(arch1)
summary(garch11)
```

Using the command **summary** in R then gives conclusive evidence of the ARCH effect.

```
Estimate Std error t-value Pr(>|t|)
a0 2.486e-03 2.726e-05 91.17 <2e-16 ***
a1 9.300e-01 2.188e-02 42.51 <2e-16 ***
```

The by-hand calculation for the ARCH effect would be

$$t = |\text{estimate}|/\text{e.s.e.} = 9.300\times10^{-1}/2.188\times10^{-2}$$
$$t = 42.50457 > 2,\ p < 0.05$$

Similarly, using the command **summary** in R gives conclusive evidence of the both the ARCH and the GARCH effects.

```
Estimate Std error t-value Pr(>|t|)
a0 3.634e-04 1.453e-05 25.01 <2e-16 ***
a1 3.363e-01 1.652e-02 20.36 <2e-16 ***
b1 6.413e-01 1.261e-02 50.84 <2e-16 ***
```

The by-hand calculation for the ARCH effect would be

$$t = |\text{estimate}|/\text{e.s.e.} = 3.363\times10^{-1}/1.652\times10^{-2}$$
$$t = 20.35714 > 2,\ p < 0.05$$

The by-hand calculation for the GARCH effect would be

$$t = |\text{estimate}|/\text{e.s.e.} = 6.413\times10^{-1}/1.261\times10^{-2}$$
$$t = 50.85646 > 2,\ p < 0.05$$

4   In this case, a higher-order model can be fitted using
```
garch77<-garch(resid, order=c(7, 7))
summary(garch(77)
```

R reports problems with numerical instabilities here, suggesting that the higher-order model does not work properly and contains some redundancies. The suggestion would be that, for this data, a simpler lower-order model would be more appropriate.

13.5   Example 3: Bitcoin data

We use price data on Bitcoin from 29 April 2013 to 13 February 2020. The data is in the file **BitcoinData.txt**, available online. We want to do the following tasks in R:

1 Read in the data.
2 Load the package **tseries** if you have not already done this.
3 Fit low-order ARCH(1) and GARCH(1, 1) models.
4 Experiment with the fitting of a higher-order GARCH(7, 7) model that has the interpretation of volatility from the previous week feeding forward and affecting today.

The example can be solved as follows:

1 As previously,
```
BitcoinData<-read.table("E:BitcoinData.txt")
ncol(BitcoinData)
[1] 4
price<-BitcoinData[,4]
price<-rev(price)
length(price)
[1] 2482
logreturn<-log(price[-1])-log(price[-2482])
```
2 Load the package **tseries** if you have not already done this.
3 You need to apply models to the mean-corrected log-returns
```
resid<-logreturn-mean(logreturn)
```

You then need to fit ARCH(1) and GARCH(1, 1) models to this data, remembering that the R syntax works the other way round to standard econometric notation.:
```
arch1<-garch(resid, order=c(0, 1))
garch11<-garch(resid, order=c(1, 1))
summary(arch1)
summary(garch11)
```
Using the command **summary** in R gives conclusive evidence of the ARCH effect.
```
Estimate Std error t-value Pr(>|t|)
a0 1.286e-03 2.132e-05 60.34 <2e-16 ***
a1 2.893e-01 2.023e-02 14.29 <2e-16 ***
```

The by-hand calculation for the ARCH effect would be

$$t = |\text{estimate}|/\text{e.s.e.} = 2.893 \times 10^{-1}/2.023 \times 10^{-2}$$
$$t = 14.30054 > 2, \; p < 0.05$$

Similarly, using the command summary in R gives conclusive evidence of the both the ARCH and the GARCH effects.

```
Estimate Std error t-value Pr(>|t|)
a0 7.265e-05 5.197e-06 13.98 <2e-16 ***
a1 1.411e-01 9.449e-03 14.93 <2e-16 ***
b1 8.256e-01 9.227e-03 89.48 <2e-16 ***
```

The by-hand calculation for the ARCH effect would be

$$t = |\text{estimate}|/\text{e.s.e.} = 1.411 \times 10^{-1}/9.449 \times 10^{-3}$$
$$t = 14.9328 > 2,\ p < 0.05$$

The by-hand calculation for the GARCH effect would be

$$t = |\text{estimate}|/\text{e.s.e.} = 8.256 \times 10^{-1}/9.229 \times 10^{-3}$$
$$t = 89.47654 > 2,\ p < 0.05$$

4   A GARCH(7, 7) model can be fitted using
```
garch77<-garch(resid, order=c(7, 7))
summary(garch77)
```

The results shown below give some evidence of an ARCH effect. However, non-significant terms suggest that there is some redundancy in this model and that a lower-order model is more appropriate.

```
Estimate Std error t-value Pr(>|t|)
a0 3.138e-04 3.925e-04 0.799 0.4240
a1 1.494e-01 1.556e-02 9.604 <2e-16 ***
a2 7.778e-02 2.610e-01 0.298 0.7657
a3 4.519e-02 1.309e-01 0.345 0.7299
a4 2.248e-05 4.625e-02 0.000 0.9996
a5 8.639e-02 4.722e-02 1.829 0.0673 .
a6 2.898e-02 1.517e-01 0.191 0.8485
a7 1.267e-02 6.592e-02 0.192 0.8475
b1 5.031e-02 1.744e+00 0.029 0.9770
b2 4.727e-02 1.009e+00 0.047 0.9627
b3 5.221e-02 3.924e-01 0.133 0.8942
b4 5.608e-02 2.004e-01 0.280 0.7796
b5 5.591e-02 1.291e-01 0.433 0.6650
b6 5.588e-02 1.370e-01 0.408 0.6834
b7 6.721e-02 1.397e-01 0.481 0.6305
```

13.6 Tutorial exercises

Question 1 below derives from a genuine dissertation project. Question 2 discusses using GARCH models to codify aspects of the stylized empirical facts of financial time series discussed in Chapter 12. Questions 3–5 use forward selection to choose an appropriate GARCH model for the cryptocurrency data introduced in Chapter 13.5.

1 Given uncertainty as to the precise economic definition of Bitcoin, it is interesting to see whether Bitcoin price data is closer to being a speculative asset (stock index) or a genuine currency. To investigate this, we compare price data from Bitcoin with three national currencies (the dollar price of pounds sterling, the yen and the euro) and three stock indices (Nasdaq, Dow Jones and S&P 500).

(a) In large problems, it is sometimes easier to read in data one column at a time. Read the data into R using the following code:

```
bitcoin<-read.table("E:StudentBTC.txt")
bitcoin<-bitcoin[,1]
gbp<-read.table("E:StudentSterling.txt")
gbp<-gbp[,1]
yen<-read.table("E:StudentYen.txt")
yen<-yen[,1]
euro<-read.table("E:StudentEuro.txt")
euro<-euro[,1]
nasdaq<-read.table("E:StudentNasdaq.txt")
nasdaq<-nasdaq[,1]
dowjones<-read.table("E:StudentDowJones.txt")
dowjones<-dowjones[,1]
sap500<-read.table("E:StudentSAP500.txt")
sap500<-sap500[,1]
```

(b) Calculate the log-returns for this data.

(c) Using the function **ks.test**, use the Kolomogorov–Smirnov distance to measure the distance between the Bitcoin returns and the returns distribution for the other assets. Which asset does Bitcoin seem closest to?

(d) If we fit a GARCH(1, 1) model to two asset-returns series, an alternative measure of distance can be defined as

$$\text{Distance} = \sqrt{(\alpha_{0,1} - \alpha_{0,2})^2 + (\alpha_{1,1} - \alpha_{1,2})^2 + (\beta_{0,1} - \beta_{0,2})^2} \quad (13.3)$$

where $\alpha_{0,1}, \alpha_{1,1}, \beta_{0,1}$ and $\alpha_{0,2}, \alpha_{1,2}, \beta_{0,2}$ denote the two sets of GARCH(1, 1) parameters. Now, using the distance as defined in Eq. (13.3), which asset does Bitcoin seem closest to?

(e) Comment on the results in parts (c–d).

2 (a) Using the data in **TetherData.txt**, test for the presence of the ARCH effect and the GARCH effect.

(b) Comment on your findings.

3 Use forward selection to choose an appropriate GARCH model for the Bitcoin data in Chapter 13.5.

4 Use forward selection to choose an appropriate GARCH model for the Ethereum data in Chapter 13.5.

5 Use forward selection to choose an appropriate GARCH model for the Ripple data in Chapter 13.5.

13.7 Solutions

1 (a) n/a

   (b) To calculate the log-returns, define the function gradrel (as defined earlier) and then use
```
bitcoinreturns<-gradrel(bitcoin)
gbpreturns<-gradrel(gbp)
yenreturns<-gradrel(yen)
euroreturns<-gradrel(euro)
nasdaqreturns<-gradrel(nasdaq)
dowjonesreturns<-gradrel(dowjones)
sapreturns<-gradrel(sap500)
```

   (c) Using, e.g., ks.test(bitcoinreturns, gbpreturns), the sequence of Kolmogorov–Smirnov distances is 0.36146, 0.39225, 0.39909, 0.24971, 0.27024, 0.5268. The lowest value suggests that Bitcoin is closest to the Nasdaq.

   (d) An R function to calculate the required distance is
```
distance<-function(x, y){ distance<-sum(x-y)^2
sqrt(distance)}
```
You need to load the **tseries** package and then apply the command garch to the sequence of mean-corrected log-returns, as above. Since you just need the vector of estimated parameters, the following code offers a neat solution whilst suppressing the superfluous output that would otherwise be generated by R.
```
bitcoinobs<-bitcoinreturns-mean(bitcoinreturns)
btcgarch<-garch(bitcoinobs, order=c(I, I))
bitcoingarch<-btcgarch$coef
gbpobs<-gbpreturns-mean(gbpreturns)
gbpgarch<-garch(gbpobs, order=c(I, I))
gbpgarch<-gbpgarch$coef
yenobs<-yenreturns-mean(yenreturns)
yengarch<-garch(yenobs, order=c(I, I))
yengarch<-yengarch$coef
euroobs<-euroreturns-mean(euroreturns)
eurogarch<-garch(euroobs, order=c(I, I))
eurogarch<-eurogarch$coef
nasobs<-nasdaqreturns-mean(nasdaqreturns)
nasgarch<-garch(nasobs, order=c(I, I))
```

```
nasdaqgarch<-nasgarch$coef
dowobs<-dowjonesreturns-mean(dowjonesreturns)
dowgarch<-garch(dowobs, order=c(I, I))
dowjonesgarch<-dowgarch$coef
sapobs<-sapreturns-mean(sapreturns)
sapgarch<-garch(sapobs, order=c(I, I))
sapgarch<-sapgarch$coef
```

The distance values can then be computed in R using
```
distance(bitcoingarch, gbpgarch)
[I] 0.09146637
distance(bitcoingarch, yengarch)
[I] 0.03683269
distance(bitcoingarch, eurogarch)
[I] 0.8334247
distance(bitcoingarch, nasdaqgarch)
[I] 0.05245798
distance(bitcoingarch, dowjonesgarch)
[I] 0.06364534
distance(bitcoingarch, sapgarch)
[I] 0.8969132
```

The lowest value indicates that Bitcoin is most similar to the yen.

(e) Results depend on whether a distributional or a time-series notion of distance is used. From a distributional perspective, Bitcoin appears closer to a speculative asset or stock (as signified by the Nasdaq). From a time-series perspective, Bitcoin seems closest to a currency (yen).

2 (a) To enter this data into R and test for the GARCH effect use
```
TetherData<-read.table("E:TetherData.txt")
price<-TetherData[,4]
price<-rev(price)
logreturn<-gradrel(price)
resid<-logreturn-mean(logreturn)
garchII<-garch(resid, order=c(I, I))
summary(garchII)
Coefficient(s):
Estimate Std error t-value Pr(>|t|)
a0 2.086e-04 8.383e-06 24.888 <2e-16 ***
al 5.000e-02 2.555e-02 1.957 0.0504 .
bl 5.000e-02 2.568e-02 1.947 0.0515 .
```

Results thus give no evidence of an ARCH or GARCH effect at the 5% level, since, in both cases, $p > 0.05$.

(b) Lack of evidence for an ARCH or GARCH effect reflects the fact that the economic role that Tether plays is different. It is designed to be a stablecoin. The above results quantify marked qualitative differences between Tether and other assets, as discussed in the exercises in Chapter 12.

3 Working through the problem and loading the **tseries** package, we can see that terms up to and including a GARCH(1, 1) model are needed in the model.

```
BitcoinData<-read.table("E:BitcoinData.txt")
price<-BitcoinData[,4]
price<-rev(price)
logreturn<-gradrel(price)
resid<-logreturn-mean(logreturn)
arch1<-garch(resid, order=c(0, 1))
summary(arch1)
garch11<-garch(resid, order=c(1, 1))
summary(garch11)
```

Next, we find that a GARCH(2, 1) model is not a significant improvement but that a GARCH(1, 2) model is.

```
garch21<-garch(resid, order=c(1, 2))
summary(garch21)
garch12<-garch(resid, order=c(2, 1))
summary(garch12)
```

Starting from a GARCH(1, 2) model, neither a GARCH (2, 2) nor a GARCH(1, 3) model offers a significant improvement. The final model chosen is therefore a GARCH(1, 2) model.

```
garch22<-garch(resid, order=c(2, 2))
summary(garch22)
garch13<-garch(resid, order=c(3, 1))
summary(garch13)
summary(garch12)
Coefficient(s):
Estimate Std error t-value Pr(>ItI)
a0 9.078e-05 7.131e-06 12.730 < 2e-16 ***
a1 1.873e-01 1.357e-02 13.806 < 2e-16 ***
b1 3.104e-01 5.560e-02 5.581 2.39e-08 ***
b2 4.606e-01 4.770e-02 9.655 < 2e-16 ***
```

4 Working through the problem and loading the **tseries** package, we can see that terms up to and including a GARCH(2, 1) model are needed in the model.

```
EthereumData<-read.table("E:EthereumData.txt")
price<-EthereumData[,4]
price<-rev(price)
logreturn<-gradrel(price)
resid<-logreturn-mean(logreturn)
arch1<-garch(resid, order=c(0, 1))
summary(arch1)
```

```
garchll<-garch(resid, order=c(l, l))
summary(garchll)
garch2l<-garch(resid, order=c(l, 2))
summary(garch2l)
```

From this point, a GARCH(2, 2) is non-significant and a GARCH(3, 1) model contains non-significant terms. The final conclusion is that a GARCH(2, 1) model is the appropriate choice.

```
garch22<-garch(resid, order=c(2, 2))
summary(garch22)
garch3l<-garch(resid, order=c(l, 3))
summary(garch3l)
summary(garch2l)
Coefficient(s):
Estimate Std error t-value Pr(>ltl)
a0 3.752e-04 3.959e-05 9.479 <2e-16 ***
al 1.752e-0l 1.843e-02 9.507 <2e-16 ***
a2 2.462e-02 1.196e-02 2.059 0.0395 *
bl 7.070e-0l 2.280e-02 31.013 <2e-16 ***
```

5 Working through the problem and loading the **tseries** package, we can see that terms up to and including a GARCH(1, 1) model are needed in the model.

```
RippleData<-read.table("E:RippleData.txt")
price<-RippleData[,4]
price<-rev(price)
logreturn<-gradrel(price)
resid<-logreturn-mean(logreturn)
archl<-garch(resid, order=c(0, l))
summary(archl)
garchll<-garch(resid, order=c(l, l))
summary(garchll)
```

At this point, a GARCH(2, 1) model is non-significant and a GARCH(1, 2) model contains non-significant terms. The final conclusion is that a GARCH(1, 1) is most appropriate.

```
garch2l<-garch(resid, order=c(l, 2))
summary(garch2l)
garch22<-garch(resid, order=c(2, 2))
summary(garch22)
summary(garchll)
Coefficient(s):
Estimate Std error t-value Pr(>ltl)
a0 3.634e-04 1.453e-05 25.01 <2e-16 ***
al 3.363e-0l 1.652e-02 20.36 <2e-16 ***
bl 6.413e-0l 1.261e-02 50.84 <2e-16 ***
```

Appendix: Statistics tables

Table A.1 One-sided critical values of the student t distribution

DF	0.100	0.050	0.025	0.010	0.005
1	3.078	6.314	12.706	31.821	63.657
2	1.886	2.920	4.303	6.965	9.925
3	1.638	2.353	3.182	4.541	5.841
4	1.533	2.132	2.776	3.747	4.604
5	1.476	2.015	2.571	3.365	4.032
6	1.440	1.943	2.447	3.143	3.707
7	1.415	1.895	2.365	2.998	3.499
8	1.397	1.860	2.306	2.896	3.355
9	1.383	1.833	2.262	2.821	3.250
10	1.372	1.812	2.228	2.764	2.169
11	1.363	1.796	2.201	2.718	2.106
12	1.356	1.782	2.179	2.681	2.055
13	1.350	1.771	2.160	2.650	2.012
14	1.345	1.761	2.145	2.624	2.977
15	1.341	1.753	2.131	2.602	2.947
16	1.337	1.746	2.120	2.583	2.921
17	1.333	1.740	2.110	2.567	2.898
18	1.330	1.734	2.101	2.552	2.878
19	1.328	1.729	2.093	2.539	2.861
20	1.325	1.725	2.086	2.528	2.845
21	1.323	1.721	2.080	2.518	2.831
22	1.321	1.717	2.074	2.508	2.819
23	1.319	1.714	2.069	2.500	2.807
24	1.318	1.711	2.064	2.492	2.797

Continued

Table A.1 Continued

DF	0.100	0.050	0.025	0.010	0.005
25	1.316	1.708	2.060	2.485	2.787
26	1.315	1.706	2.056	2.479	2.779
27	1.314	1.703	2.052	2.473	2.771
28	1.313	1.701	2.048	2.467	2.763
29	1.311	1.699	2.045	2.462	2.756
30	1.310	1.697	2.042	2.457	2.750
31	1.309	1.696	2.040	2.453	2.744
32	1.309	1.694	2.037	2.449	2.738
33	1.308	1.692	2.035	2.445	2.733
34	1.307	1.691	2.032	2.441	2.728
35	1.306	1.690	2.030	2.438	2.724
36	1.306	1.688	2.028	2.434	2.719
37	1.305	1.687	2.026	2.431	2.715
38	1.304	1.686	2.024	2.429	2.712
39	1.304	1.685	2.023	2.426	2.708
40	1.303	1.684	2.021	2.423	2.704
50	1.299	1.676	2.009	2.403	2.678
60	1.296	1.671	2.000	2.390	2.660
70	1.294	1.667	1.994	2.381	2.648
80	1.292	1.664	1.990	2.374	2.639
90	1.291	1.662	1.987	2.368	2.632
100	1.290	1.660	1.984	2.364	2.626
110	1.289	1.659	1.982	2.361	2.621
120	1.289	1.658	1.980	2.358	2.617
∞	1.282	1.645	1.960	2.326	2.576

Table A.2 Tables of the one-sided 5% critical values for the F distribution with ν_1 and ν_2 degrees of freedom

ν_2	ν_1									
	1	**2**	**3**	**4**	**5**	**6**	**7**	**8**	**9**	**10**
1	161.45	199.50	215.71	224.58	230.16	233.99	236.77	238.88	240.54	241.88
2	18.51	19.00	19.16	19.25	19.30	19.33	19.35	19.37	19.38	19.40
3	10.13	9.55	9.28	9.12	9.01	8.94	8.89	8.85	8.81	8.79
4	7.71	6.94	6.59	6.39	6.26	6.16	6.09	6.04	6.00	5.96
5	6.61	5.79	5.41	5.19	5.05	4.95	4.88	4.82	4.77	4.74
6	5.99	5.14	4.76	4.53	4.39	4.28	4.21	4.15	4.10	4.06
7	5.59	4.74	4.35	4.12	3.97	3.87	3.79	3.73	3.68	3.64
8	5.32	4.46	4.07	3.84	3.69	3.58	3.50	3.44	3.39	3.35
9	5.12	4.26	3.86	3.63	3.48	3.37	3.29	3.23	3.18	3.14
10	4.96	4.10	3.71	3.48	3.33	3.22	3.14	3.07	3.02	2.98
11	4.84	3.98	3.59	3.36	3.20	3.09	3.01	2.95	2.90	2.85
12	4.75	3.89	3.49	3.26	3.11	3.00	2.91	2.85	2.80	2.75
13	4.67	3.81	3.41	3.18	3.03	2.92	2.83	2.77	2.71	2.67
14	4.60	3.74	3.34	3.11	2.96	2.85	2.76	2.70	2.65	2.60
15	4.54	3.68	3.29	3.06	2.90	2.79	2.71	2.64	2.59	2.54
16	4.49	3.63	3.24	3.01	2.85	2.74	2.66	2.59	2.54	2.49
17	4.45	3.59	3.20	2.96	2.81	2.70	2.61	2.55	2.49	2.45
18	4.41	3.55	3.16	2.93	2.77	2.66	2.58	2.51	2.46	2.41
19	4.38	3.52	3.13	2.90	2.74	2.63	2.54	2.48	2.42	2.38
20	4.35	3.49	3.10	2.87	2.71	2.60	2.51	2.45	2.39	2.35
21	4.32	3.47	3.07	2.84	2.68	2.57	2.49	2.42	2.37	2.32
22	4.30	3.44	3.05	2.82	2.66	2.55	2.46	2.40	2.34	2.30
23	4.28	3.42	3.03	2.80	2.64	2.53	2.44	2.37	2.32	2.27
24	4.26	3.40	3.01	2.78	2.62	2.51	2.42	2.36	2.30	2.25
25	4.24	3.39	2.99	2.76	2.60	2.49	2.40	2.34	2.28	2.24

Continued

Table A.2 Continued

ν_2	ν_1									
	1	**2**	**3**	**4**	**5**	**6**	**7**	**8**	**9**	**10**
26	4.23	3.37	2.98	2.74	2.59	2.47	2.39	2.32	2.27	2.22
27	4.21	3.35	2.96	2.73	2.57	2.46	2.37	2.31	2.25	2.20
28	4.20	3.34	2.95	2.71	2.56	2.45	2.36	2.29	2.24	2.19
29	4.18	3.33	2.93	2.70	2.55	2.43	2.35	2.28	2.22	2.18
30	4.17	3.32	2.92	2.69	2.53	2.42	2.33	2.27	2.21	2.16
40	4.08	3.23	2.84	2.61	2.45	2.34	2.25	2.18	2.12	2.08
60	4.00	3.15	2.76	2.53	2.37	2.25	2.17	2.10	2.04	1.99
∞	3.84	3.00	2.60	2.37	2.21	2.10	2.01	1.94	1.88	1.83

Table A.3 Tables of the one-sided 5% critical values for the F distribution with ν_1 and ν_2 degrees of freedom

ν_2					ν_1					
	11	**12**	**15**	**20**	**24**	**30**	**40**	**60**	**120**	∞
1	242.98	243.91	245.95	248.01	249.05	250.10	251.14	252.20	253.25	254.31
2	19.40	19.41	19.43	19.45	19.45	19.46	19.47	19.48	19.49	19.50
3	8.76	8.74	8.70	8.66	8.64	8.62	8.59	8.57	8.55	8.53
4	5.94	5.91	5.86	5.80	5.77	5.75	5.72	5.69	5.66	5.63
5	4.70	4.68	4.62	4.56	4.53	4.50	4.46	4.43	4.40	4.36
6	4.03	4.00	3.94	3.87	3.84	3.81	3.77	3.74	3.70	3.67
7	3.60	3.57	3.51	3.44	3.41	3.38	3.34	3.30	3.27	3.23
8	3.31	3.28	3.22	3.15	3.12	3.08	3.04	3.01	2.97	2.93
9	3.10	3.07	3.01	2.94	2.90	2.86	2.83	2.79	2.75	2.71
10	2.94	2.91	2.85	2.77	2.74	2.70	2.66	2.62	2.58	2.54
11	2.82	2.79	2.72	2.65	2.61	2.57	2.53	2.49	2.45	2.40
12	2.72	2.69	2.62	2.54	2.51	2.47	2.43	2.38	2.34	2.30
13	2.63	2.60	2.53	2.46	2.42	2.38	2.34	2.30	2.25	2.21
14	2.57	2.53	2.46	2.39	2.35	2.31	2.27	2.22	2.18	2.13
15	2.51	2.48	2.40	2.33	2.29	2.25	2.20	2.16	2.11	2.07
16	2.46	2.42	2.35	2.28	2.24	2.19	2.15	2.11	2.06	2.01
17	2.41	2.38	2.31	2.23	2.19	2.15	2.10	2.06	2.01	1.96
18	2.37	2.34	2.27	2.19	2.15	2.11	2.06	2.02	1.97	1.92
19	2.34	2.31	2.23	2.16	2.11	2.07	2.03	1.98	1.93	1.88
20	2.31	2.28	2.20	2.12	2.08	2.04	1.99	1.95	1.90	1.84
21	2.28	2.25	2.18	2.10	2.05	2.01	1.96	1.92	1.87	1.81
22	2.26	2.23	2.15	2.07	2.03	1.98	1.94	1.89	1.84	1.78
23	2.24	2.20	2.13	2.05	2.01	1.96	1.91	1.86	1.81	1.76
24	2.22	2.18	2.11	2.03	1.98	1.94	1.89	1.84	1.79	1.73

Continued

Table A.3 Continued

ν_2					ν_1					
	11	**12**	**15**	**20**	**24**	**30**	**40**	**60**	**120**	**∞**
25	2.20	2.16	2.09	2.01	1.96	1.92	1.87	1.82	1.77	1.71
26	2.18	2.15	2.07	1.99	1.95	1.90	1.85	1.80	1.75	1.69
27	2.17	2.13	2.06	1.97	1.93	1.88	1.84	1.79	1.73	1.67
28	2.15	2.12	2.04	1.96	1.91	1.87	1.82	1.77	1.71	1.65
29	2.14	2.10	2.03	1.94	1.90	1.85	1.81	1.75	1.70	1.64
30	2.13	2.09	2.01	1.93	1.89	1.84	1.79	1.74	1.68	1.62
40	2.04	2.00	1.92	1.84	1.79	1.74	1.69	1.64	1.58	1.51
60	1.95	1.92	1.84	1.75	1.70	1.65	1.59	1.53	1.47	1.39
∞	1.79	1.75	1.67	1.57	1.52	1.46	1.39	1.32	1.22	1.00

Table A.4 Tables of the normal distribution CDF $Z(x)$ for $x \geq 0$

	0.00	0.01	0.02	0.03	0.04	0.05	0.06	0.07	0.08	0.09
0.0	0.50000	0.50399	0.50798	0.51197	0.51595	0.51994	0.52392	0.52790	0.53188	0.53586
0.1	0.53983	0.54380	0.54776	0.55172	0.55567	0.55962	0.56356	0.56749	0.57142	0.57535
0.2	0.57926	0.58317	0.58706	0.59095	0.59483	0.59871	0.60257	0.60642	0.61026	0.61409
0.3	0.61791	0.62172	0.62552	0.62930	0.63307	0.63683	0.64058	0.64431	0.64803	0.65173
0.4	0.65542	0.65910	0.66276	0.66640	0.67003	0.67364	0.67724	0.68082	0.68439	0.68793
0.5	0.69146	0.69497	0.69847	0.70194	0.70540	0.70884	0.71226	0.71566	0.71904	0.72240
0.6	0.72575	0.72907	0.73237	0.73565	0.73891	0.74215	0.74537	0.74857	0.75175	0.75490
0.7	0.75804	0.76115	0.76424	0.76730	0.77035	0.77337	0.77637	0.77935	0.78230	0.78524
0.8	0.78814	0.79103	0.79389	0.79673	0.79955	0.80234	0.80511	0.80785	0.81057	0.81327
0.9	0.81594	0.81859	0.82121	0.82381	0.82639	0.82894	0.83147	0.83398	0.83646	0.83891
1.0	0.84134	0.84375	0.84614	0.84849	0.85083	0.85314	0.85543	0.85769	0.85993	0.86214
1.1	0.86433	0.86650	0.86864	0.87076	0.87286	0.87493	0.87698	0.87900	0.88100	0.88298
1.2	0.88493	0.88686	0.88877	0.89065	0.89251	0.89435	0.89617	0.89796	0.89973	0.90147
1.3	0.90320	0.90490	0.90658	0.90824	0.90988	0.91149	0.91309	0.91466	0.91621	0.91774
1.4	0.91924	0.92073	0.92220	0.92364	0.92507	0.92647	0.92785	0.92922	0.93056	0.93189
1.5	0.93319	0.93448	0.93574	0.93699	0.93822	0.93943	0.94062	0.94179	0.94295	0.94408
1.6	0.94520	0.94630	0.94738	0.94845	0.94950	0.95053	0.95154	0.95254	0.95352	0.95449
1.7	0.95543	0.95637	0.95728	0.95818	0.95907	0.95994	0.96080	0.96164	0.96246	0.96327
1.8	0.96407	0.96485	0.96562	0.96638	0.96712	0.96784	0.96856	0.96926	0.96995	0.97062
1.9	0.97128	0.97193	0.97257	0.97320	0.97381	0.97441	0.97500	0.97558	0.97615	0.97670
2.0	0.97725	0.97778	0.97831	0.97882	0.97932	0.97982	0.98030	0.98077	0.98124	0.98169
2.1	0.98214	0.98257	0.98300	0.98341	0.98382	0.98422	0.98461	0.98500	0.98537	0.98574
2.2	0.98610	0.98645	0.98679	0.98713	0.98745	0.98778	0.98809	0.98840	0.98870	0.98899
2.3	0.98928	0.98956	0.98983	0.99010	0.99036	0.99061	0.99086	0.99111	0.99134	0.99158
2.4	0.99180	0.99202	0.99224	0.99245	0.99266	0.99286	0.99305	0.99324	0.99343	0.99361
2.5	0.99379	0.99396	0.99413	0.99430	0.99446	0.99461	0.99477	0.99492	0.99506	0.99520
2.6	0.99534	0.99547	0.99560	0.99573	0.99585	0.99598	0.99609	0.99621	0.99632	0.99643
2.7	0.99653	0.99664	0.99674	0.99683	0.99693	0.99702	0.99711	0.99720	0.99728	0.99736
2.8	0.99744	0.99752	0.99760	0.99767	0.99774	0.99781	0.99788	0.99795	0.99801	0.99807
2.9	0.99813	0.99819	0.99825	0.99831	0.99836	0.99841	0.99846	0.99851	0.99856	0.99861
3.0	0.99865	0.99869	0.99874	0.99878	0.99882	0.99886	0.99889	0.99893	0.99896	0.99900

Continued

Table A.4 Continued

	0.00	0.01	0.02	0.03	0.04	0.05	0.06	0.07	0.08	0.09
3.1	0.99903	0.99906	0.99910	0.99913	0.99916	0.99918	0.99921	0.99924	0.99926	0.99929
3.2	0.99931	0.99934	0.99936	0.99938	0.99940	0.99942	0.99944	0.99946	0.99948	0.99950
3.3	0.99952	0.99953	0.99955	0.99957	0.99958	0.99960	0.99961	0.99962	0.99964	0.99965
3.4	0.99966	0.99968	0.99969	0.99970	0.99971	0.99972	0.99973	0.99974	0.99975	0.99976
3.5	0.99977	0.99978	0.99978	0.99979	0.99980	0.99981	0.99981	0.99982	0.99983	0.99983
3.6	0.99984	0.99985	0.99985	0.99986	0.99986	0.99987	0.99987	0.99988	0.99988	0.99989
3.7	0.99989	0.99990	0.99990	0.99990	0.99991	0.99991	0.99992	0.99992	0.99992	0.99992
3.8	0.99993	0.99993	0.99993	0.99994	0.99994	0.99994	0.99994	0.99995	0.99995	0.99995
3.9	0.99995	0.99995	0.99996	0.99996	0.99996	0.99996	0.99996	0.99996	0.99997	0.99997
4.0	0.99997	0.99997	0.99997	0.99997	0.99997	0.99997	0.99998	0.99998	0.99998	0.99998

Table A.5   One-sided critical values for the χ^2 distribution

Degrees of freedom	$\alpha = 0.1$	$\alpha = 0.05$	$\alpha = 0.01$
1	2.71	3.84	6.63
2	4.61	5.99	9.21
3	6.25	7.81	11.34
4	7.78	9.49	13.28
5	9.24	11.07	15.09
6	10.64	12.59	16.81
7	12.02	14.07	18.48
8	13.36	15.51	20.09
9	14.68	16.92	21.67
10	15.99	18.31	23.21
11	17.28	19.68	24.72
12	18.55	21.03	26.22
13	19.81	22.36	27.69
14	21.06	23.68	29.14
15	22.31	25.00	30.58
16	23.54	26.30	32.00
17	24.77	27.59	33.41
18	25.99	28.87	34.81
19	27.20	30.14	36.19
20	28.41	31.41	37.57
21	29.62	32.67	38.93
22	30.81	33.92	40.29
23	32.01	35.17	41.64
24	33.20	36.42	42.98
25	34.38	37.65	44.31
26	35.56	38.89	45.64
27	36.74	40.11	46.96
28	37.92	41.34	48.28
29	39.09	42.56	49.59
30	40.26	43.77	50.89

Bibliography

[1] Alam, M. M., Wei, H. and Wahid, A. N. M. (2020) Covid-19 outbreak and sectoral performance of the Australian stock market: An event study analysis, *Australian Economic Papers*, e12215

[2] Bachelier, L. (1900). Théorie de la spéculation. *Annales scientifiques de l'École normale supérieure*, 17: 21–86.

[3] Bingham, N, H, and Fry, J. M. (2010). *Regression: Linear Models in Statistics*. Springer Undergraduate Mathematics Series, London; Dordtrecht; Heidelberg; New York: Springer.

[4] Black, F. and Scholes, M. (1973) The pricing of options and corporate liabilities, *Journal of Political Economy*, 81: 637–654.

[5] Brint, A. and Fry, J. M. (2021). Regional bias when benchmarking services using customer satisfaction scores, *Total Quality Management and Business Excellence*, 32: 344–358.

[6] Brockwell, P. J. and Davis, R. A. (2016). *An Introduction to Time Series and Forecasting*. London; Dordtrecht; Heidelberg; New York: Springer.

[7] Burke, M. and Fry, J. M. (2019) How easy is it to understand consumer finance? *Economics Letters*, 177: 1–4.

[8] Cont, R. (2001). Empirical properties of asset returns: stylized facts and statistical issues, *Quantitative Finance*, 1: 223–236.

[9] Cont, R. and Tankov, P. (2004). *Financial Modelling with Jump Processes*. Boca Raton; London; New York; Washington D.C: Chapman and Hall/CRC.

[10] Cortinhas, C. and Black, K. (2012). *Statistics for Business and Economics*. Wiley.

[11] Draper, N. R. and Smith, H. (1998) *Applied Regression Analysis*. 3rd edn. Wiley.

[12] Fry, J. and Brint, A. (2017) Bubbles, blind-spots and Brexit, *Risks*, 5: 37.

[13] Fry, J. and Burke, M. (2020). An options pricing approach to election prediction, *Quantitative Finance*, 20: 1583–1589.

[14] Fry, J., Smart, O., Serbera, J-P. and Klar, B. (2021a) A variance gamma model for rugby union matches, *Journal of Quantitative Analysis in Sports*, 17: 67–75.

[15] Fry, J., Griguta, V-M., Gerber, L., Petty-Slater, H. and Crockett, K. (2021b). Modelling corporate bank accounts, *Economics Letters*, 205: 109924.

[16] Gamerman, D. and Lopes, H. F. (2006) *Markov Chain Monte Carlo: Stochastic Simulation for Bayesian Inference*, 2nd edn. Chapman and Hall/CRC.

[17] Gujarati, D. N. and Porter, D. C. (2009). *Basic Econometrics*, 5th edn. New York: McGraw Hill.

[18] Katsiampa, P. (2017). Volatility estimation for Bitcoin; A comparison of GARCH models, *Economics Letters*, 158: 3–6.

[19] Malevergne, Y. and Sornette, D. (2006) *Extreme Financial Risks: From Dependence to Risk Management*. Springer.

[20] Petersen, M. A. (2009) Estimating standard errors in finance panel data sets: comparing approaches, *Review of Financial Studies*, 22: 435–480.

[21] Pidd, M. and Broadbent, J. (2015). Business and management studies in the 2014 Research Excellence Framework, *British Journal of Management*, 15: 569–581.

[22] Taleb, N. N. (2007) *The Black Swan: The Impact of the Highly Improbable.* Allen Lane.

[23] Venables, W. N. and Ripley, B. D. (2003). *Modern Applied Statistics with S-Plus*, 4th edn. Springer.

[24] Weatherall, J. O. (2013). *The Physics of Finance. Predicting the Unpredictable. Can Science Beat the Market?* London: Short Books.

Index